MAD® ABOUT THE MOB

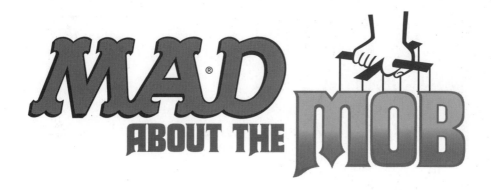

ALSO AVAILABLE
FROM MAD BOOKS

MAD About Super Heroes

MAD: Neumanisms

The *MAD* Bathroom Companion Number Two

The *MAD* Gross Book

The *MAD* Bathroom Companion

MAD About TV

MAD About the Movies—Special Warner Bros. Edition

"Sure. And Max Schmeling would've beat Joe Louis, too, if the Brown Bomber hadn't landed three or four hundred lucky punches."

MAD taught my generation how to laugh at ourselves. *MAD* taught us to examine every square centimeter of the comic strip and to hold the page up to the light looking for punchlines.

The whole human rights revolution—civil rights, women's rights, gay rights—that illuminated America in the last half of the twentieth century was fought by people who grew up reading *MAD*. And it's no coincidence. The truth is you can't be cowed by something once you make fun of it. You can't be held hostage by an idea once you've laughed at it. Groucho Marx is more dangerous than Karl Marx. And a lot funnier, too.

Of course when I was a kid I wasn't aware of any of that. Except that Groucho was funnier than Karl.

When I was a kid I dreamt of two things: to sleep with the prettiest girl in my class and to write for *MAD* Magazine.

About fifteen years ago I had an idea. I'd been on network television, I was making a lot of money, I figured I had a chance with the prettiest girl in my class. I asked a friend about her. A few years before she'd had an operation, changed her name to "Jim," and now her mustache was thicker than mine.

That means *MAD* was my only hope.

And then one day, out of the blue, my phone rang.

"Siegel? *MAD* Magazine here. We're putting together a little book called *MAD About the Mob* and we want you to write the introduction." Hang up.

Why me? I guess DeNiro turned them down. Or perhaps they had seen a recent piece I had done on the air about *MAD*'s fiftieth anniversary and the reissue of their first paperbacks. Either way, I couldn't say no. It was an offer I couldn't refuse.

I did some research: "The Oddfather." "Scarred Face." "The Sopranos Family Circus" (a personal favorite). Did I like these stories? I *loved* these stories. Some of 'em were better than the movies. All of 'em were shorter than the movies. And, besides, you can read *MAD* in places where you can't watch a movie. Multitasking, they call that today.

I started reading, I started writing.

Three days ago the phone rang again.

"Siegel? *MAD* here."

This time I snuck a word in. I asked about money.

"A thousand bucks. Take it or leave it."

"I'll take it," I said.

I could scrape up only $800 to include in the envelope with this manuscript. But I promised the guys at *MAD* that I'd round up the other $200 by the end of the week!

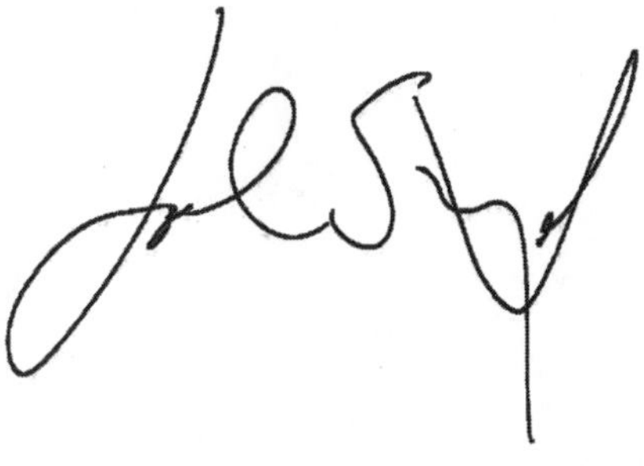

—**Joel Siegel**

Hey, Gang! Tired of all the garbage they're showing on motion picture screens lately? Well, here's a "Family" film for a change! And now, meet the "Family":

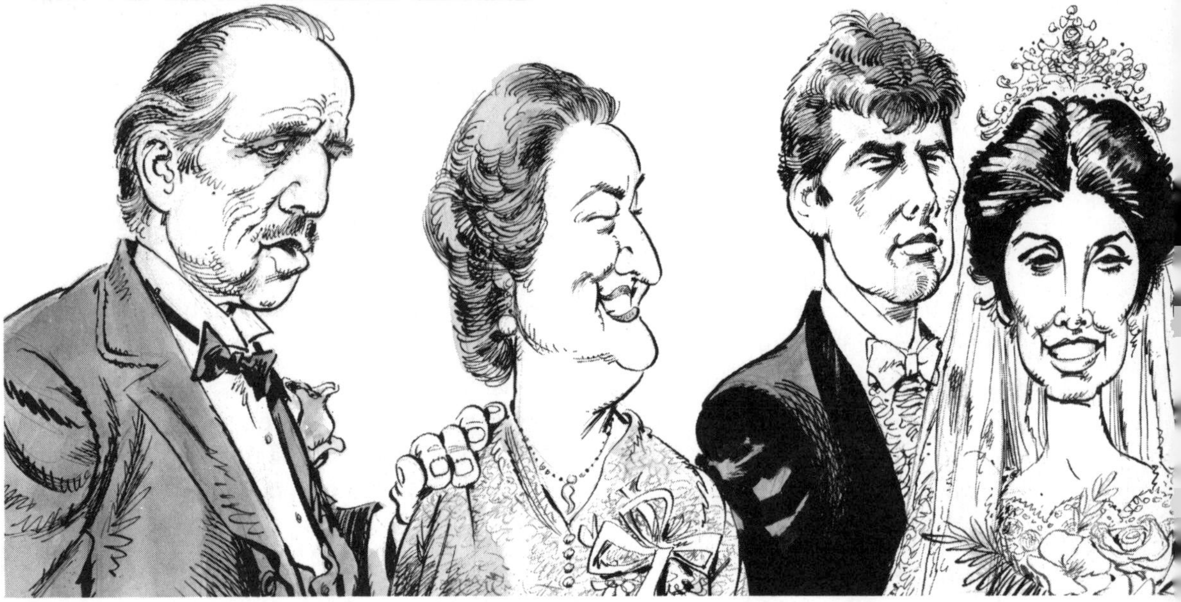

This is Don Vino Minestrone. Not too long ago, he was just a poor immigrant from Sicily. Now he's a leading racketeer, extortionist and killer. How did Don Vino get where he is today? By putting his faith in The American Way of Life.

Here's Mama Minestrone, a typical lovable Sicilian housewife. It seems like only yesterday at another wedding that Mama herself said, "I do!" Come to think of it, that was the last time she opened her mouth.

This is Don Vino's daughter Canny, and her bridegroom Carly. Such a nice couple Everyone is saying that Do Vino is not really losing daughter. No, actually, i this kind of Family, he' probably lose a Son-in-law

And so, with such a strange family and such weird childre

THE ODD

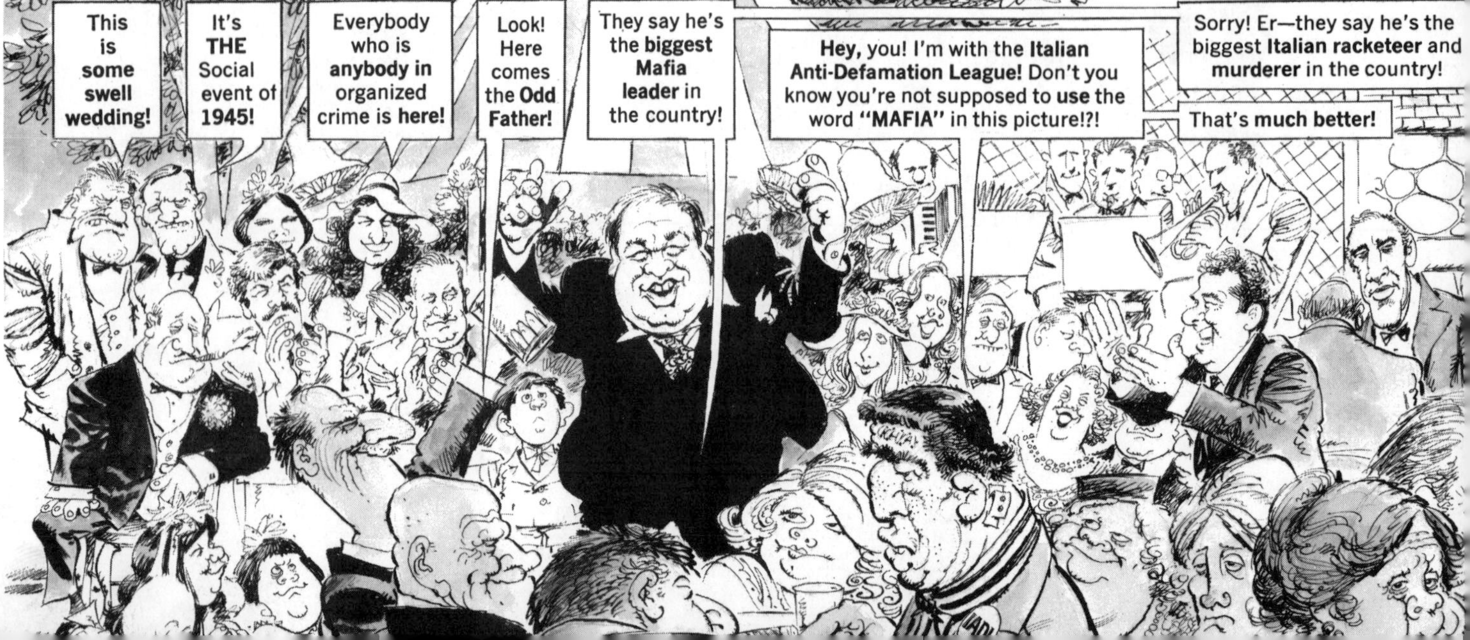
This is some swell wedding!
It's THE Social event of 1945!
Everybody who is anybody in organized crime is here!
Look! Here comes the Odd Father!
They say he's the biggest Mafia leader in the country!
Hey, you! I'm with the Italian Anti-Defamation League! Don't you know you're not supposed to use the word "MAFIA" in this picture!?!
Sorry! Er—they say he's the biggest Italian racketeer and murderer in the country!
That's much better!

MAD ABOUT THE MOB

BY "THE USUAL GANG OF IDIOTS"

EDITED BY NICK MEGLIN & JOHN FICARRA

INTRODUCTION BY JOEL SIEGEL

MAD
New York
BOOKS™

MAD BOOKS

William Gaines Founder

Jenette Kahn President & Editor-in-Chief
Paul Levitz Executive Vice President & Publisher
Nick Meglin & John Ficarra Editors
Charles Kochman Editor—Licensed Publishing
Jaye Gardner Associate Editor—Licensed Publishing

Editorial:
Charlie Kadau & Joe Raiola Senior Editors
Amy Vozeolas Associate Editor
Dick DeBartolo Creative Consultant

Art Department:
Sam Viviano Art Director
Nadina Simon Associate Art Director
Patricia Dwyer Assistant Art Director
Ryan Flanders Production Artist
Leonard Brenner Graphics Consultant

Administration:
Patrick Caldon Senior VP—Finance & Operations
Joel Ehrlich Senior VP—Advertising & Promotions
Alison Gill VP—Manufacturing
Lillian Laserson VP & General Counsel
John Nee VP—Business Development

Contributors:
The Usual Gang of Idiots

Published by MAD Books. An imprint of E.C. Publications, Inc., 1700 Broadway, New York, NY 10019.
A division of Warner Bros. — An AOL Time Warner Company.

ISBN 1-56389-883-7

Printed in Canada

First edition
10 9 8 7 6 5 4 3 2 1

Visit *MAD* online at www.madmag.com

Though Alfred E. Neuman wasn't the first to say "A fool and his money are soon parted," here's your chance to prove the old adage right—subscribe to *MAD*! Simply call 1-800-4-MADMAG and mention code 9MAM4. Operators are standing by (the water cooler).

CONTENTS

INTRODUCTION

I still remember the first *MAD* comic I ever saw. It was *MAD* #11 (May 1954) with Basil Wolverton's "Lena the Hyena" on the cover. Humor in a Jugular Vein. 10 cents. Tales Calculated to Drive You ... *MAD*.

It was a parody of a *Life* magazine cover, but I didn't know that at the time. Wolverton's Lena, I'd later learn, was the winner of a national *L'il Abner*, too-ugly-for-Sadie-Hawkins-Day contest. Wolverton parlayed the success into a kind of comic-book career, creating—I'm searching my memory now—"Powerhouse Pepper," as I'd learn much later when I started taking comic books seriously.

I remember, really remember, the first story in that comic book: "Flesh Garden!"

And there was Flash Gordon in torn tights, his arm around a very sexy Dale, staring at Dr. Zark on a silver platter, held in the tentacles of a drooling three-eyed monster. Next to Dr. Zark were salt and pepper shakers, a bottle of ketchup, a box of Wheaties, and a can of Spam. "Let us not leap to conclusions. What makes you think this alien creature is going to eat Dr. Zark?" Flesh asks Dale.

And when Dale tells Flesh she'll stay at his side while he fights the drooling, three-eyed alien with his silver sword, what does Flesh do?

He hands *Dale* the sword, runs out of the frame in a patented Wally Wood prance, and says, "Okay, you take the sword! No sense in both of us getting killed!"

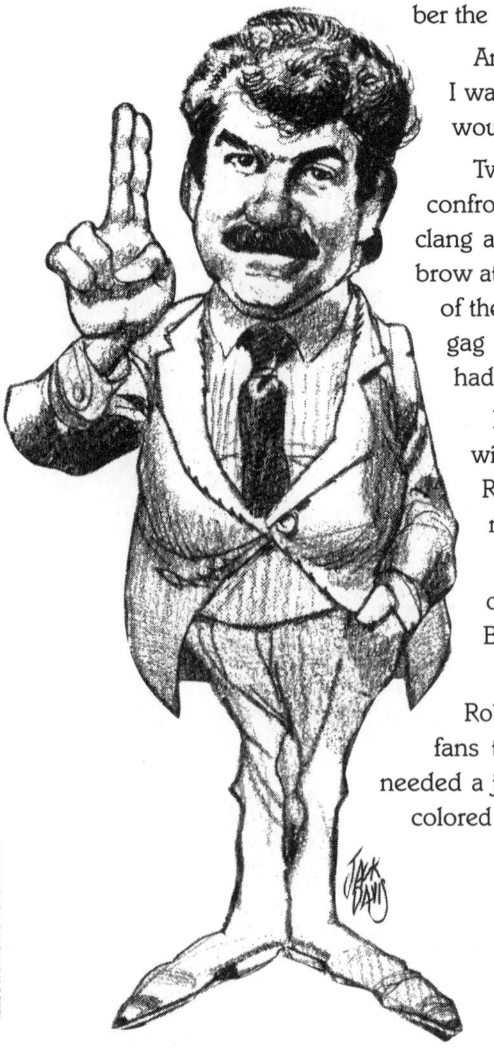

ILLUSTRATION BY JACK DAVIS

Yes, I remember that (although I may have mixed up a word or two). But I also remember the star on Flesh's chest changing labels from YMCA to UCLA to 100% Pure.

And I'll never forget the almost religious feeling of liberation and joy. Look, I wanted to shout from the rooftops, here was a hero who did exactly what I would do: chicken out and run!

Twenty-five years later I had that same epiphany when Indiana Jones confronts an immense Arab villain armed with twin scimitars. And as the swords clang and flash, signaling a huge fight to the finish, Harrison Ford furrows his brow at the camera, pulls his pistol out of its holster, and shoots the guy. It is one of the great moments in motion picture history. Did Steven Spielberg steal that gag from *MAD*? I'd bet on it. I'd bet my copy of *MAD* #11 if my mother hadn't thrown it away.

I remember the "Dragged Net!" parody in the same issue, singing along with the "Domm-Da-Dom-Domms!" I remember "Starchie," "Mickey Rodent!," and "Howdy Dooit!," sponsored by something called Bupgoo that made milk look just like beer.

I remember the gags that used to (and still do) hide out in the corners of the pages. "Max Schmeling would've beat Joe Louis if the Brown Bomber hadn't snuck in 3- or 400 lucky punches," one "marginal" read.

A confession: in 1982 I wrote a Broadway musical about Jackie Robinson. I was nominated for a Tony. I created a group of Brooklyn Dodger fans to mirror the way Americans felt about Jackie. In the second act we needed a joke to show how silly and stupid racism was. The racist fan says, "Ah, colored guys can't handle pressure. They cut and run." And another fan says,

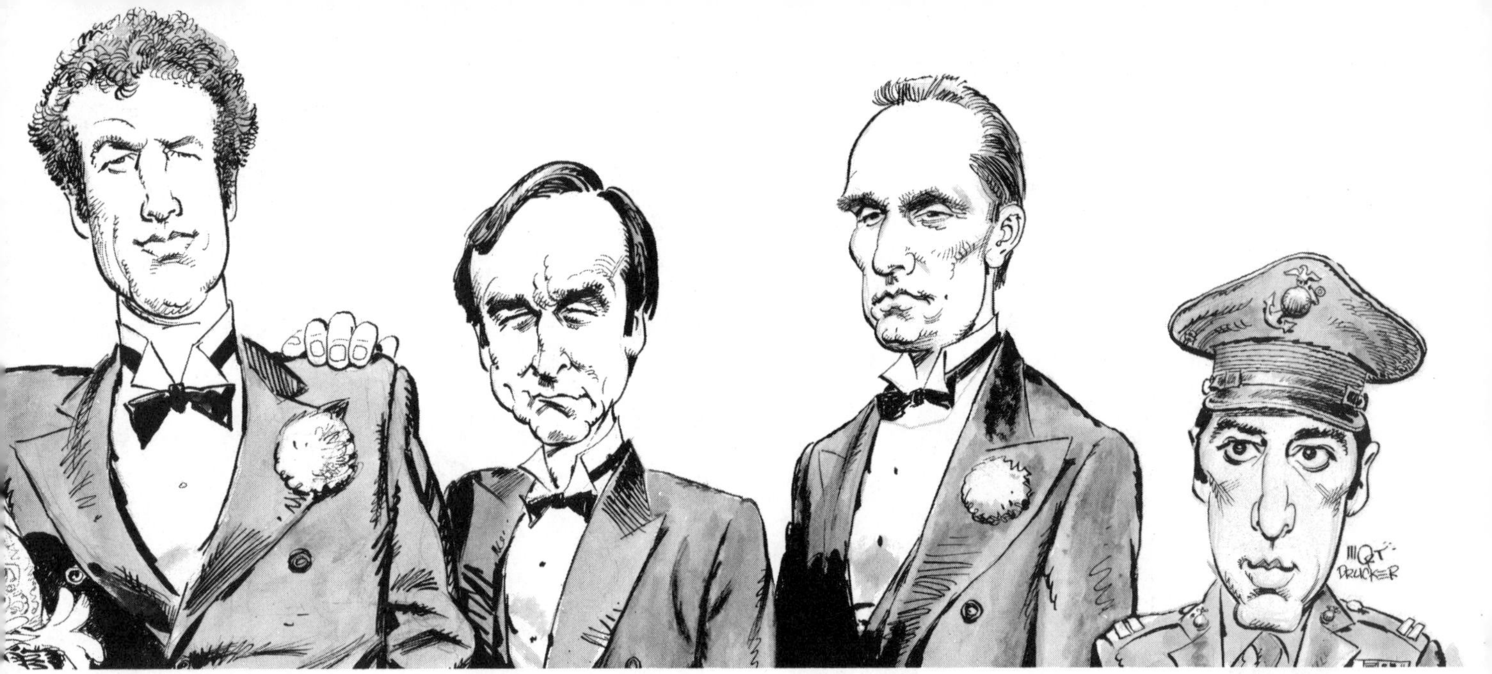

This is Sinny Minestrone, the Don's eldest son. He's next in line, and it's only a matter of time before he gets the Family business. That is, of course, unless a rival Family decides to give him the business first.

This is the Don's second son, Freako. He's a sad, gentle soul. He cries at weddings and all kinds of Family crises. But he can also be a barrel of laughs. Just catch him at a funeral some time.

This is Tim Haven, the Don's adopted son. He's shrewd and smart. All his life, he dreamed of being a criminal lawyer. But he only finished half of his education —the "criminal" part.

And this is Micrin, the Don's youngest son. He's a college graduate, a veteran war hero, an honest law-abiding citizen —and a disgrace to the entire Family.

's easy to see why Don Vino Minestrone is known as...

FATHER

ARTIST: MORT DRUCKER

WRITER: LARRY SIEGEL

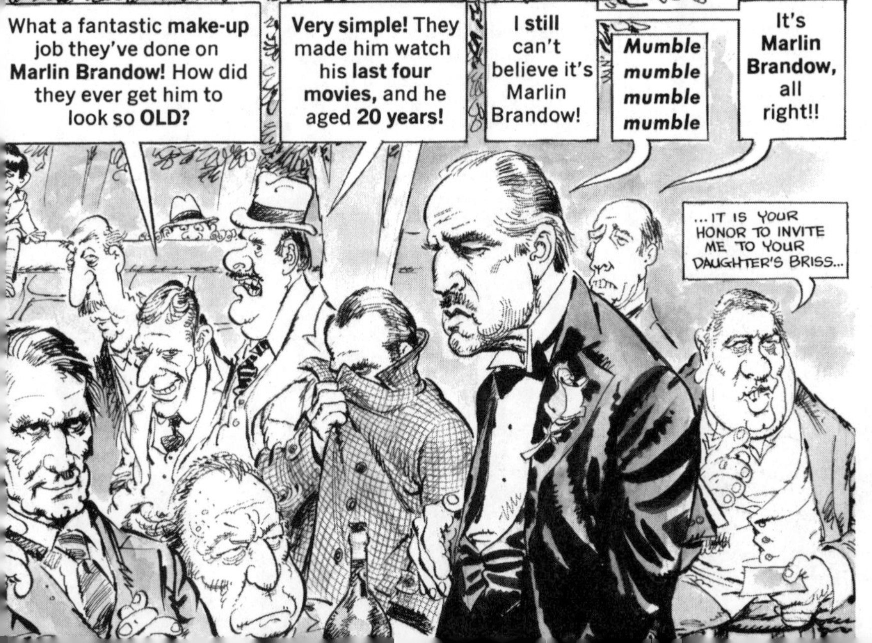

What a fantastic make-up job they've done on Marlin Brandow! How did they ever get him to look so OLD?
Very simple! They made him watch his last four movies, and he aged 20 years!
I still can't believe it's Marlin Brandow!
Mumble mumble mumble mumble
It's Marlin Brandow, all right!!
...IT IS YOUR HONOR TO INVITE ME TO YOUR DAUGHTER'S BRISS...

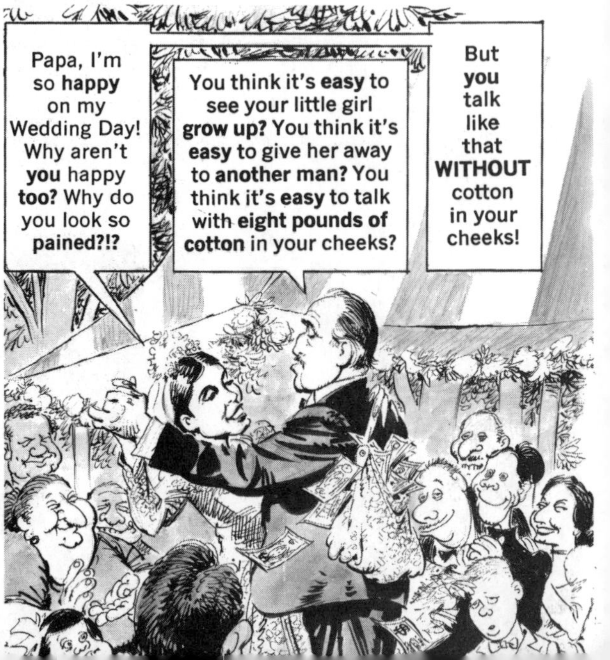

Papa, I'm so happy on my Wedding Day! Why aren't you happy too? Why do you look so pained?!?
You think it's easy to see your little girl grow up? You think it's easy to give her away to another man? You think it's easy to talk with eight pounds of cotton in your cheeks?
But you talk like that WITHOUT cotton in your cheeks!

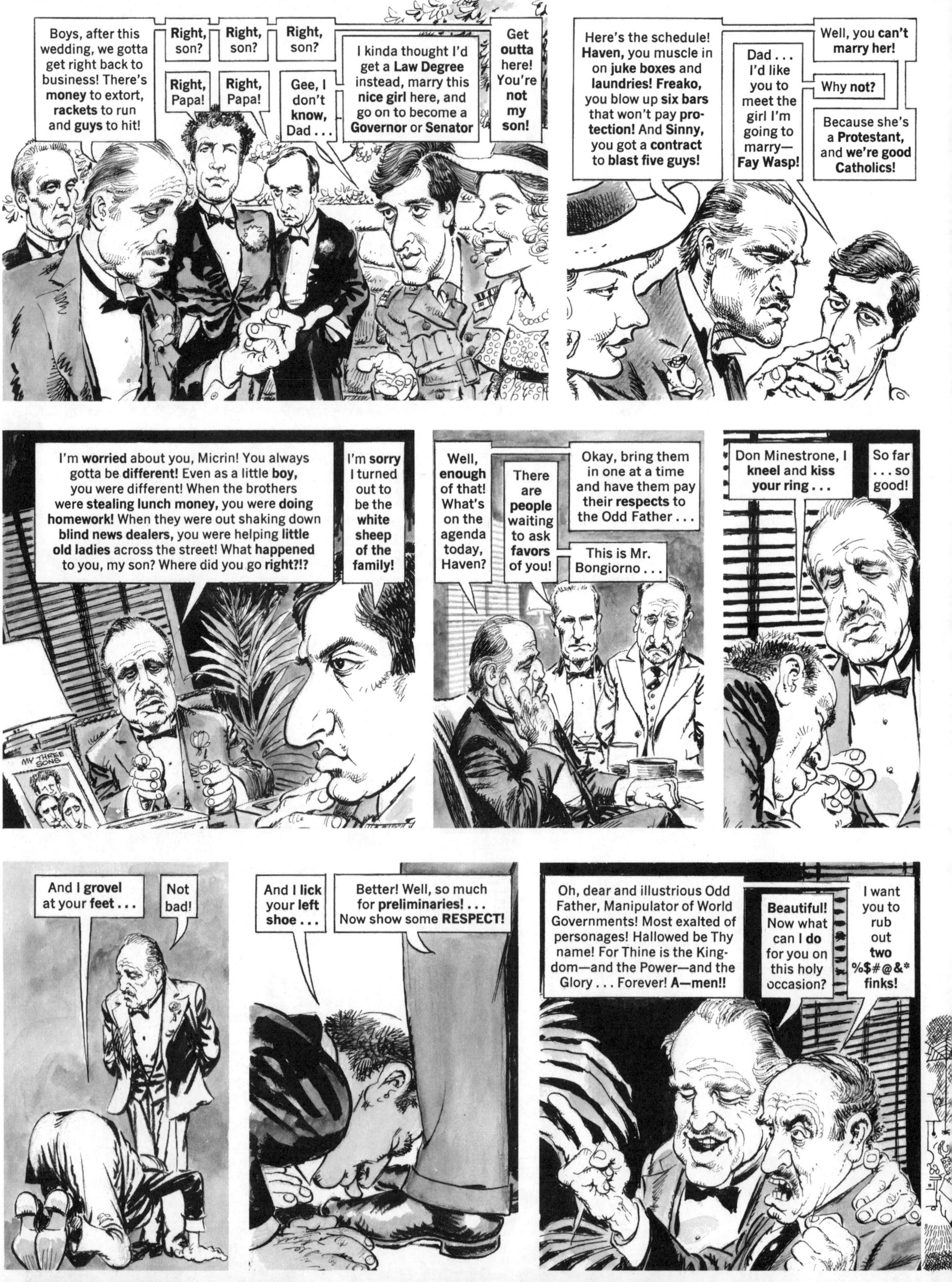
Boys, after this wedding, we gotta get right back to business! There's money to extort, rackets to run and guys to hit!
Right, son?
Right, Papa!
Right, son?
Right, Papa!
Right, son?
Gee, I don't know, Dad . . .
I kinda thought I'd get a Law Degree instead, marry this nice girl here, and go on to become a Governor or Senator
Get outta here! You're not my son!
Here's the schedule! Haven, you muscle in on juke boxes and laundries! Freako, you blow up six bars that won't pay protection! And Sinny, you got a contract to blast five guys!
Dad . . . I'd like you to meet the girl I'm going to marry— Fay Wasp!
Well, you can't marry her!
Why not?
Because she's a Protestant, and we're good Catholics!
I'm worried about you, Micrin! You always gotta be different! Even as a little boy, you were different! When the brothers were stealing lunch money, you were doing homework! When they were out shaking down blind news dealers, you were helping little old ladies across the street! What happened to you, my son? Where did you go right?!?
I'm sorry I turned out to be the white sheep of the family!
MY THREE SONS
Well, enough of that! What's on the agenda today, Haven?
There are people waiting to ask favors of you!
Okay, bring them in one at a time and have them pay their respects to the Odd Father . . .
This is Mr. Bongiorno . . .
Don Minestrone, I kneel and kiss your ring . . .
So far . . . so good!
And I grovel at your feet . . .
Not bad!
And I lick your left shoe . . .
Better! Well, so much for preliminaries! . . . Now show some RESPECT!
Oh, dear and illustrious Odd Father, Manipulator of World Governments! Most exalted of personages! Hallowed be Thy name! For Thine is the Kingdom—and the Power—and the Glory . . . Forever! A—men!!
Beautiful! Now what can I do for you on this holy occasion?
I want you to rub out two %$#@&* finks!

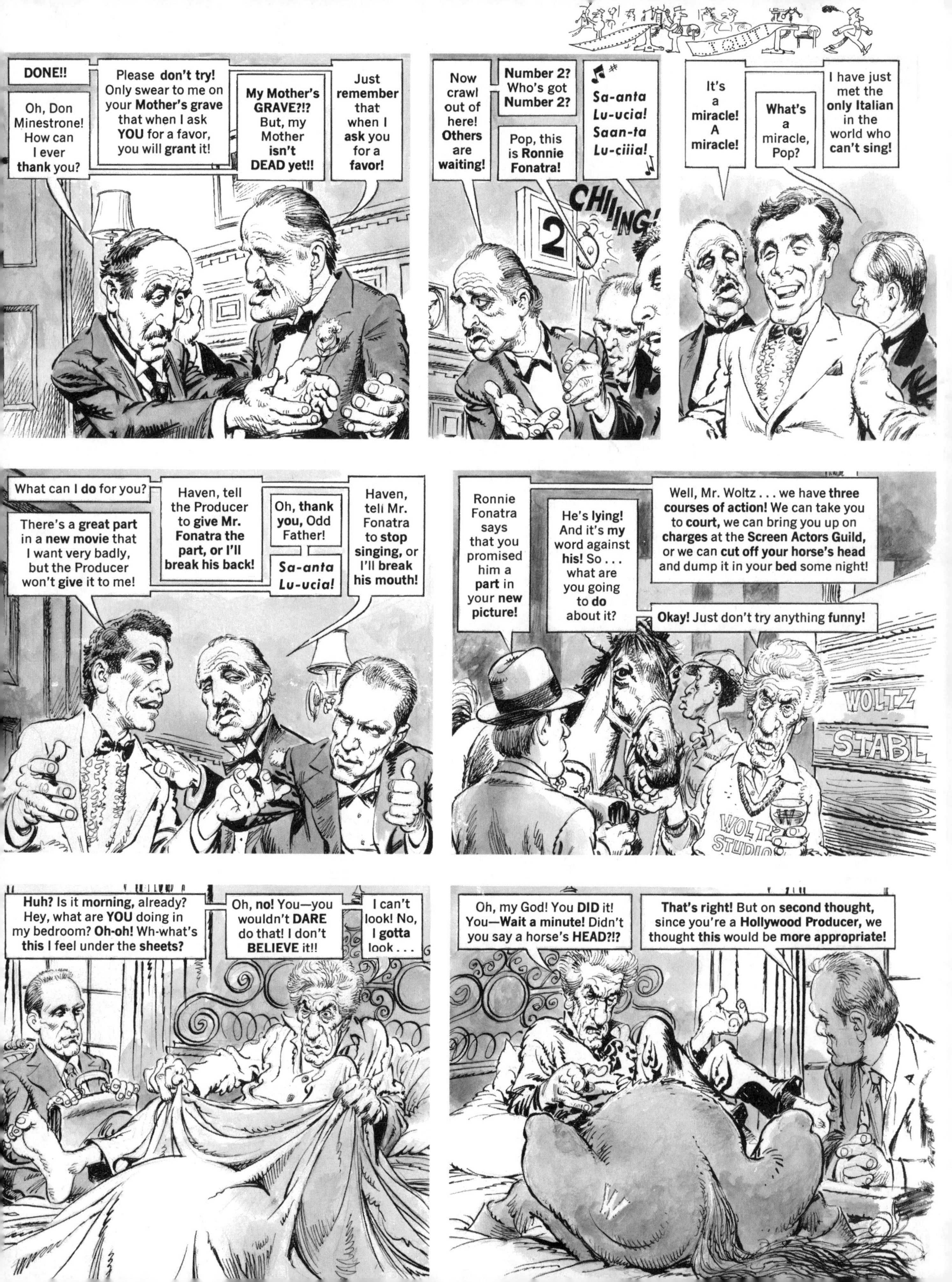
DONE!!
Oh, Don Minestrone! How can I ever thank you?
Please don't try! Only swear to me on your Mother's grave that when I ask YOU for a favor, you will grant it!
My Mother's GRAVE?!? But, my Mother isn't DEAD yet!!
Just remember that when I ask you for a favor!
Now crawl out of here! Others are waiting!
Number 2? Who's got Number 2?
Pop, this is Ronnie Fonatra!
Sa-anta Lu-ucia! Saan-ta Lu-ciiia!
2
CHIIING!
It's a miracle! A miracle!
What's a miracle, Pop?
I have just met the only Italian in the world who can't sing!
What can I do for you?
There's a great part in a new movie that I want very badly, but the Producer won't give it to me!
Haven, tell the Producer to give Mr. Fonatra the part, or I'll break his back!
Oh, thank you, Odd Father!
Sa-anta Lu-ucia!
Haven, tell Mr. Fonatra to stop singing, or I'll break his mouth!
Ronnie Fonatra says that you promised him a part in your new picture!
He's lying! And it's my word against his! So . . . what are you going to do about it?
Well, Mr. Woltz . . . we have three courses of action! We can take you to court, we can bring you up on charges at the Screen Actors Guild, or we can cut off your horse's head and dump it in your bed some night!
Okay! Just don't try anything funny!
WOLTZ
STABL
Huh? Is it morning, already? Hey, what are YOU doing in my bedroom? Oh-oh! Wh-what's this I feel under the sheets?
Oh, no! You—you wouldn't DARE do that! I don't BELIEVE it!!
I can't look! No, I gotta look . . .
Oh, my God! You DID it! You—Wait a minute! Didn't you say a horse's HEAD?!?
That's right! But on second thought, since you're a Hollywood Producer, we thought this would be more appropriate!

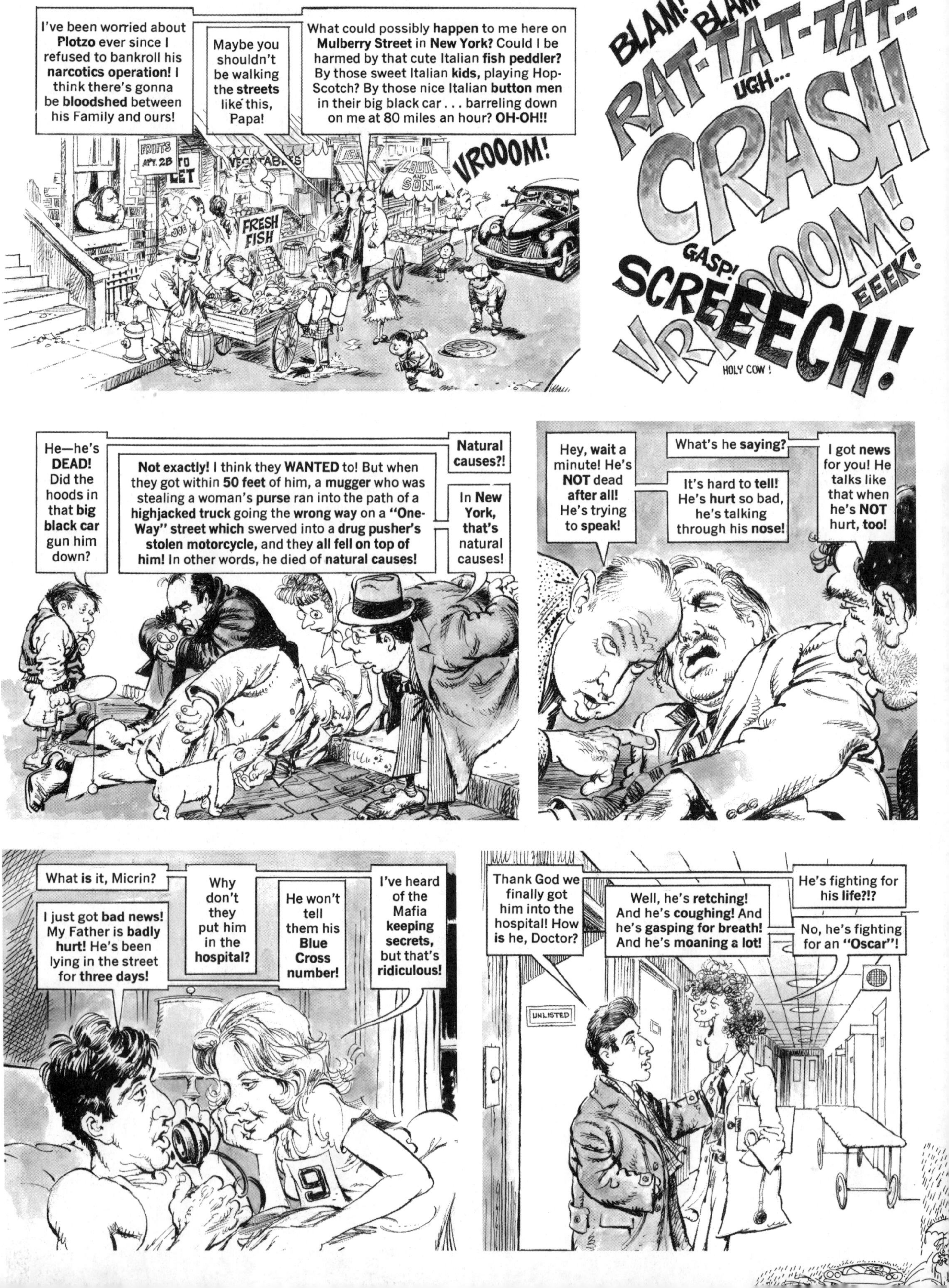

I've been worried about **Plotzo** ever since I refused to bankroll his **narcotics operation!** I think there's gonna be **bloodshed** between his Family and ours!
Maybe you shouldn't be walking the **streets** like this, Papa!
What could possibly **happen** to me here on **Mulberry Street** in **New York?** Could I be harmed by that cute Italian **fish peddler?** By those sweet Italian **kids,** playing Hop-Scotch? By those nice Italian **button men** in their big black car . . . barreling down on me at 80 miles an hour? **OH-OH!!**
FRUITS
APT. 2B
TO LET
FRESH FISH
LOUIE AND SON INC.
VROOOM!
BLAM! BLAM!
RAT-TAT-TAT...
UGH...
CRASH
VROOOM!
GASP!
SCREEECH!
EEEK!
HOLY COW!
He—he's **DEAD!** Did the hoods in that **big black car** gun him down?
Not exactly! I think they **WANTED** to! But when they got within **50 feet** of him, a **mugger** who was stealing a woman's **purse** ran into the path of a **highjacked truck** going the **wrong way** on a **"One-Way" street** which swerved into a **drug pusher's stolen motorcycle,** and they **all fell on top of him!** In other words, he died of **natural causes!**
Natural causes?!
In **New York, that's** natural causes!
Hey, **wait** a minute! He's **NOT** dead **after all!** He's trying to **speak!**
What's he **saying?**
It's hard to **tell!** He's **hurt** so bad, he's talking through his **nose!**
I got **news** for you! He talks like that when he's **NOT** hurt, **too!**
What **is it,** Micrin?
I just got **bad news!** My Father is **badly hurt!** He's been lying in the street for **three days!**
Why don't they put him in the **hospital?**
He won't tell them his **Blue Cross number!**
I've heard of the Mafia **keeping secrets,** but that's **ridiculous!**
Thank God we finally got him into the hospital! How **is** he, Doctor?
Well, he's **retching!** And he's **coughing!** And he's **gasping for breath!** And he's **moaning a lot!**
He's fighting for his **life?!?**
No, he's fighting for an **"Oscar"!**
UNLISTED

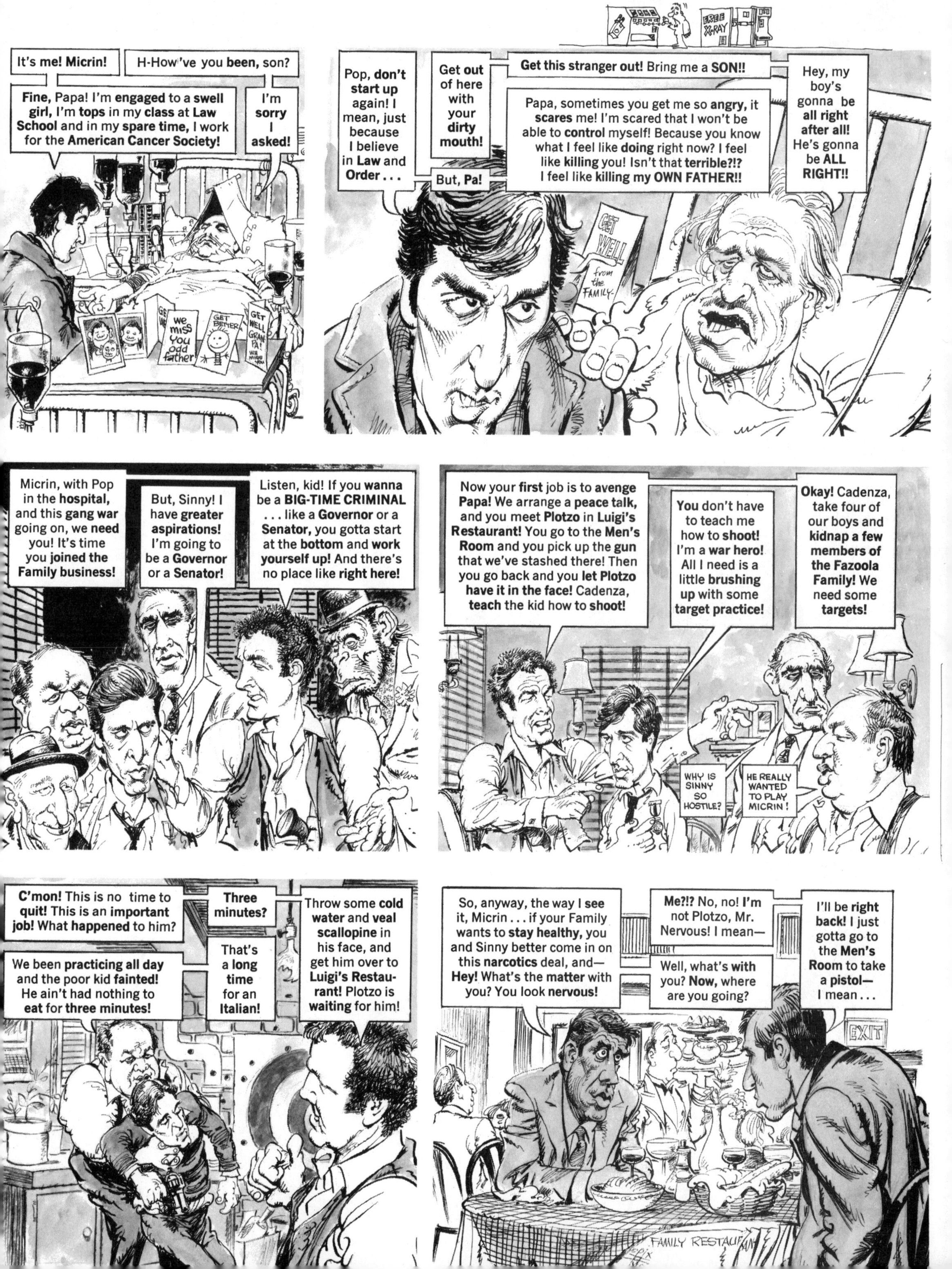
FREE X-RAY
It's me! **Micrin!**
H-How've you **been,** son?
Fine, Papa! I'm **engaged** to a **swell girl,** I'm **tops** in my **class** at **Law School** and in my **spare time,** I work for the **American Cancer Society!**
I'm **sorry** I **asked!**
we miss You odd father
GET BETTER
GET WELL GRAN PA!
Pop, **don't start up** again! I mean, just because I believe in **Law** and **Order . . .**
Get out of here with your **dirty mouth!**
But, **Pa!**
Get this stranger out! Bring me a **SON!!**
Papa, sometimes you get me so **angry,** it **scares** me! I'm scared that I won't be able to **control** myself! Because you know what I feel like **doing** right now? I feel like **killing** you! Isn't that **terrible?!?** I feel like **killing** my **OWN FATHER!!**
Hey, my boy's gonna be **all right after all!** He's gonna be **ALL RIGHT!!**
GET WELL from the FAMILY
Micrin, with Pop in the **hospital,** and this **gang war** going on, we **need** you! It's time you **joined the Family business!**
But, Sinny! I have **greater aspirations!** I'm going to be a **Governor** or a **Senator!**
Listen, kid! If you **wanna** be a **BIG-TIME CRIMINAL** . . . like a **Governor** or a **Senator,** you gotta start at the **bottom** and **work yourself up!** And there's no place like **right here!**
Now your **first** job is to **avenge Papa!** We arrange a **peace talk,** and you meet **Plotzo** in **Luigi's Restaurant!** You go to the **Men's Room** and you pick up the **gun** that we've stashed there! Then you go back and you **let Plotzo have it in the face!** Cadenza, **teach** the kid how to **shoot!**
You don't have to teach me how to **shoot!** I'm a **war hero!** All I need is a little **brushing up** with some **target practice!**
Okay! Cadenza, take four of our boys and **kidnap a few members of the Fazoola Family!** We need some **targets!**
WHY IS SINNY SO HOSTILE?
HE REALLY WANTED TO PLAY MICRIN!
C'mon! This is no time to **quit!** This is an **important job!** What **happened** to him?
We been **practicing all day** and the poor kid **fainted!** He ain't had nothing to **eat** for **three minutes!**
Three minutes?
That's a **long** time for an **Italian!**
Throw some **cold water** and **veal scallopine** in his face, and get him over to **Luigi's Restaurant!** Plotzo is **waiting** for him!
So, anyway, the way I **see** it, Micrin . . . if your Family wants to **stay healthy,** you and Sinny better come in on this **narcotics** deal, and— **Hey!** What's the **matter** with you? You look **nervous!**
Me?!? No, no! **I'm** not Plotzo, Mr. Nervous! I mean—
Well, what's **with** you? **Now,** where are you going?
I'll be **right back!** I just gotta go to the **Men's Room** to take a **pistol—** I mean . . .
EXIT
FAMILY RESTAURANT

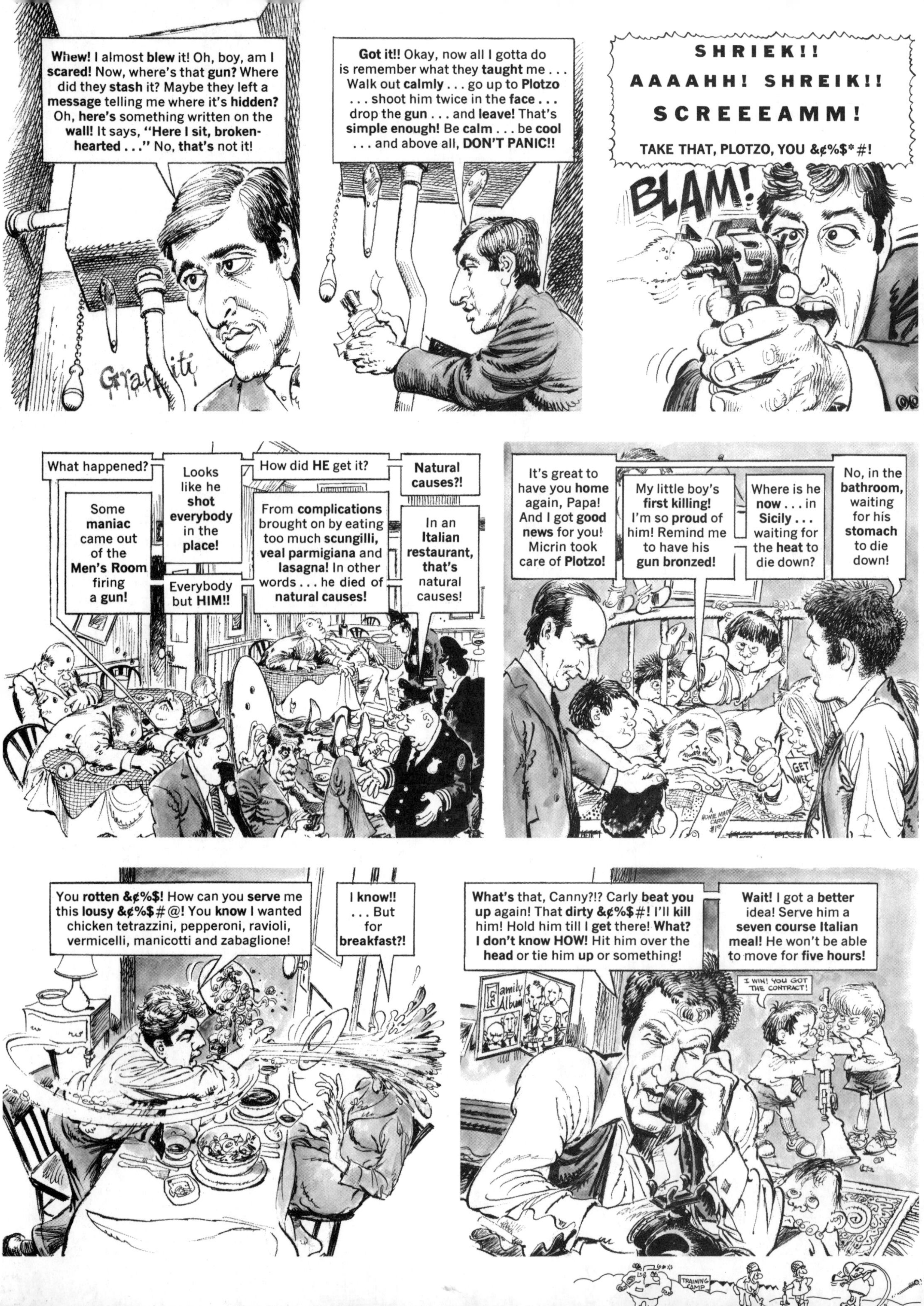

Whew! I almost blew it! Oh, boy, am I scared! Now, where's that gun? Where did they stash it? Maybe they left a message telling me where it's hidden? Oh, here's something written on the wall! It says, "Here I sit, broken-hearted . . ." No, that's not it!
Graffiti
Got it!! Okay, now all I gotta do is remember what they taught me . . . Walk out calmly . . . go up to Plotzo . . . shoot him twice in the face . . . drop the gun . . . and leave! That's simple enough! Be calm . . . be cool . . . and above all, DON'T PANIC!!
SHRIEK!!
AAAAHH! SHREIK!!
SCREEEAMM!
TAKE THAT, PLOTZO, YOU &¢%$*#!
BLAM!
What happened?
Some maniac came out of the Men's Room firing a gun!
Looks like he shot everybody in the place!
Everybody but HIM!!
How did HE get it?
From complications brought on by eating too much scungilli, veal parmigiana and lasagna! In other words . . . he died of natural causes!
Natural causes?!
In an Italian restaurant, that's natural causes!
It's great to have you home again, Papa! And I got good news for you! Micrin took care of Plotzo!
My little boy's first killing! I'm so proud of him! Remind me to have his gun bronzed!
Where is he now . . . in Sicily . . . waiting for the heat to die down?
No, in the bathroom, waiting for his stomach to die down!
GET WE
A HOME MADE CARD
You rotten &¢%$! How can you serve me this lousy &¢%$#@! You know I wanted chicken tetrazzini, pepperoni, ravioli, vermicelli, manicotti and zabaglione!
I know!! . . . But for breakfast?!
What's that, Canny?!? Carly beat you up again! That dirty &¢%$#! I'll kill him! Hold him till I get there! What? I don't know HOW! Hit him over the head or tie him up or something!
Wait! I got a better idea! Serve him a seven course Italian meal! He won't be able to move for five hours!
Family Album
I WIN! YOU GOT THE CONTRACT!
TRAINING CAMP

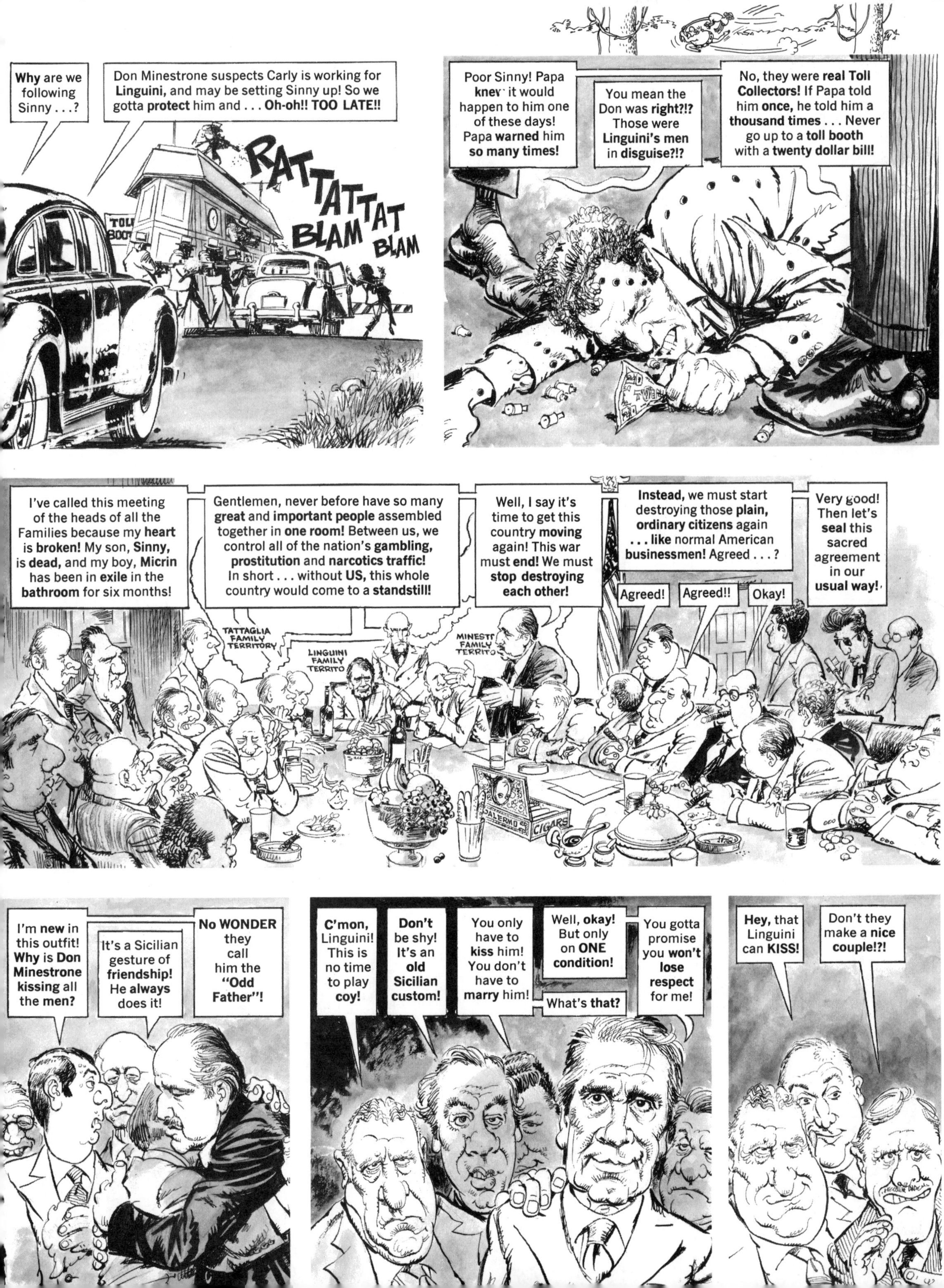
Why are we following Sinny . . .?
Don Minestrone suspects Carly is working for Linguini, and may be setting Sinny up! So we gotta protect him and . . . Oh-oh!! TOO LATE!!
RATTATTAT
BLAM
BLAM
Poor Sinny! Papa knew it would happen to him one of these days! Papa warned him so many times!
You mean the Don was right?!? Those were Linguini's men in disguise?!?
No, they were real Toll Collectors! If Papa told him once, he told him a thousand times . . . Never go up to a toll booth with a twenty dollar bill!
I've called this meeting of the heads of all the Families because my heart is broken! My son, Sinny, is dead, and my boy, Micrin has been in exile in the bathroom for six months!
Gentlemen, never before have so many great and important people assembled together in one room! Between us, we control all of the nation's gambling, prostitution and narcotics traffic! In short . . . without US, this whole country would come to a standstill!
TATTAGLIA FAMILY TERRITORY
LINGUINI FAMILY TERRITO
MINESTI FAMILY TERRITO
Well, I say it's time to get this country moving again! This war must end! We must stop destroying each other!
Instead, we must start destroying those plain, ordinary citizens again . . . like normal American businessmen! Agreed . . . ?
Agreed!
Agreed!!
Okay!
Very good! Then let's seal this sacred agreement in our usual way!
PALERMO
CIGARS
I'm new in this outfit! Why is Don Minestrone kissing all the men?
It's a Sicilian gesture of friendship! He always does it!
No WONDER they call him the "Odd Father"!
C'mon, Linguini! This is no time to play coy!
Don't be shy! It's an old Sicilian custom!
You only have to kiss him! You don't have to marry him!
Well, okay! But only on ONE condition!
What's that?
You gotta promise you won't lose respect for me!
Hey, that Linguini can KISS!
Don't they make a nice couple!?!

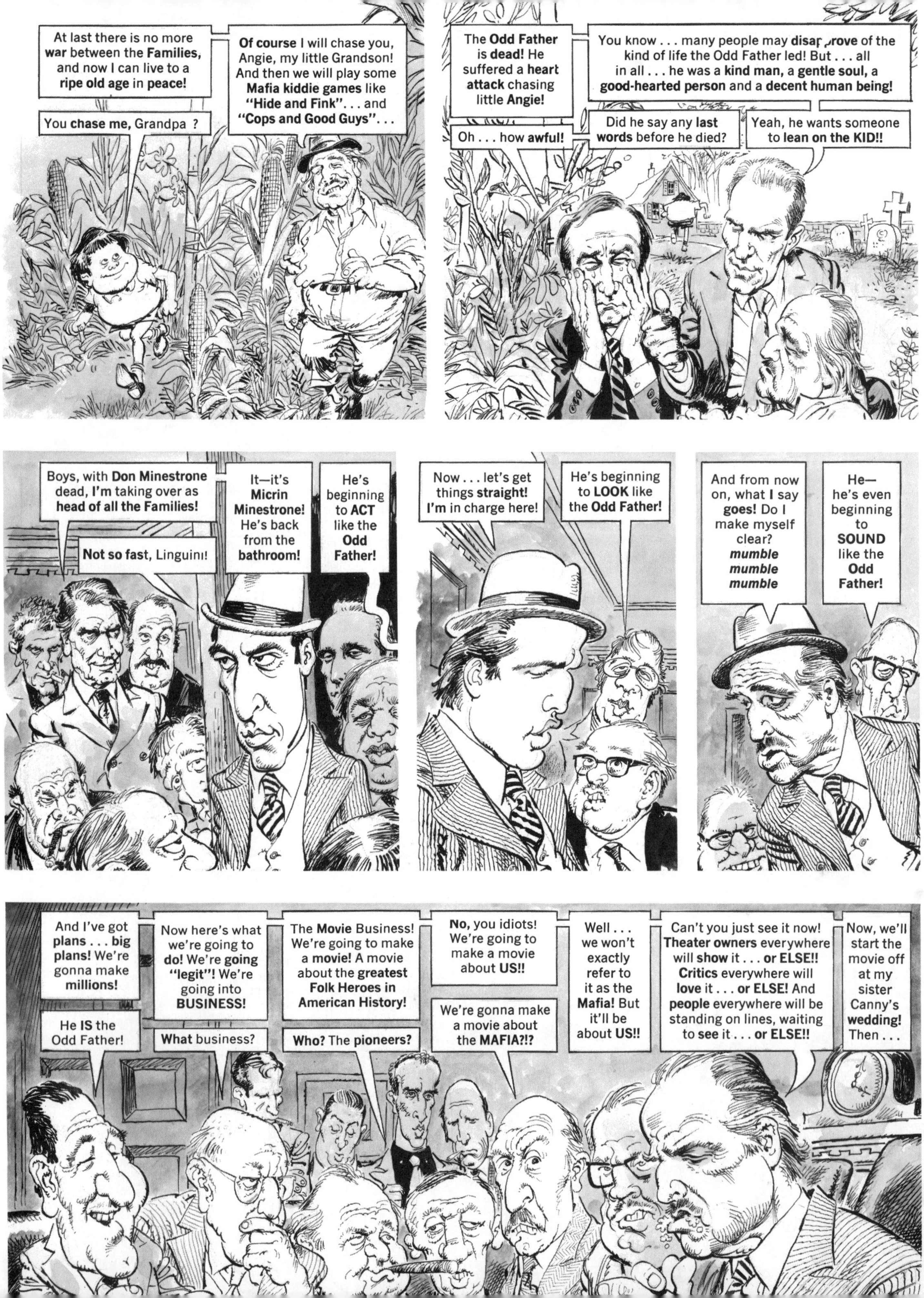

At last there is no more war between the Families, and now I can live to a ripe old age in peace!
You chase me, Grandpa ?
Of course I will chase you, Angie, my little Grandson! And then we will play some Mafia kiddie games like "Hide and Fink" . . . and "Cops and Good Guys" . . .
The Odd Father is dead! He suffered a heart attack chasing little Angie!
Oh . . . how awful!
You know . . . many people may disapprove of the kind of life the Odd Father led! But . . . all in all . . . he was a kind man, a gentle soul, a good-hearted person and a decent human being!
Did he say any last words before he died?
Yeah, he wants someone to lean on the KID!!
Boys, with Don Minestrone dead, I'm taking over as head of all the Families!
Not so fast, Linguini!
It—it's Micrin Minestrone! He's back from the bathroom!
He's beginning to ACT like the Odd Father!
Now . . . let's get things straight! I'm in charge here!
He's beginning to LOOK like the Odd Father!
And from now on, what I say goes! Do I make myself clear? mumble mumble mumble
He—he's even beginning to SOUND like the Odd Father!
And I've got plans . . . big plans! We're gonna make millions!
He IS the Odd Father!
Now here's what we're going to do! We're going "legit"! We're going into BUSINESS!
What business?
The Movie Business! We're going to make a movie! A movie about the greatest Folk Heroes in American History!
Who? The pioneers?
No, you idiots! We're going to make a movie about US!!
We're gonna make a movie about the MAFIA?!?
Well . . . we won't exactly refer to it as the Mafia! But it'll be about US!!
Can't you just see it now! Theater owners everywhere will show it . . . or ELSE!! Critics everywhere will love it . . . or ELSE! And people everywhere will be standing on lines, waiting to see it . . . or ELSE!!
Now, we'll start the movie off at my sister Canny's wedding! Then . . .

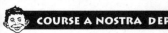

Editor's Note: William "The Gofer" Gaylord joined the Calamari Crime Family as Capo Di Tutti Interni or "Intern of Interns." During his three months as a Mafioso summer intern, William witnessed events and lived through adventures that no typical summer intern ever experienced. In a publishing coup, MAD has obtained the diary that Gaylord kept during that fun-filled time. Originally scribbled on the back of soiled napkins, brown paper dropoff bags and bloodstained towels, the editors can't guarantee 100% accuracy for the following presentation. If this sounds like a cowardly, contrived copout, you're damn right!

BLOOD, HONOR & THREE CREDITS

My Internship With The Calamari Crime Family

A Diary With Pictures By William "The Gofer" Gaylord

June 18 First Day!

My Mafia internship began this morning with a swearing in ceremony at the Calamari Social Club in Brooklyn. Tony "Lazy Eye" Rigatoni, who is in charge of both the interns and the temps, says to me: "Give me your pointing finger." "Lazy Eye" needed a couple of chances before he was able to prick the correct finger and draw blood. He then says, "Look straight into my eyes and swear your allegiance on pain of death." Between trying to achieve the "eyes" part and the frightening finality of his words, both my tear ducts and bladder discharged their contents.

Tony places a pinkie ring onto the table. He then declares, "William Gaylord, from hence on forward to be known as 'The Gofer,' you shall wear this pinkie ring with pride. Congratulations—now go fetch me a glass of chianti. With all your bleeding and crying and pants wetting, I need a drink!"

I later learned that before me, that same pinkie ring belonged to intern Tommy "The Paper Clip" Finochiaro. He was killed the previous summer because he left someone called "The Red Spine" on hold too long. Something to remember!

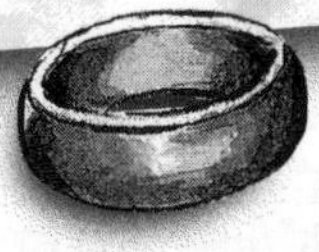

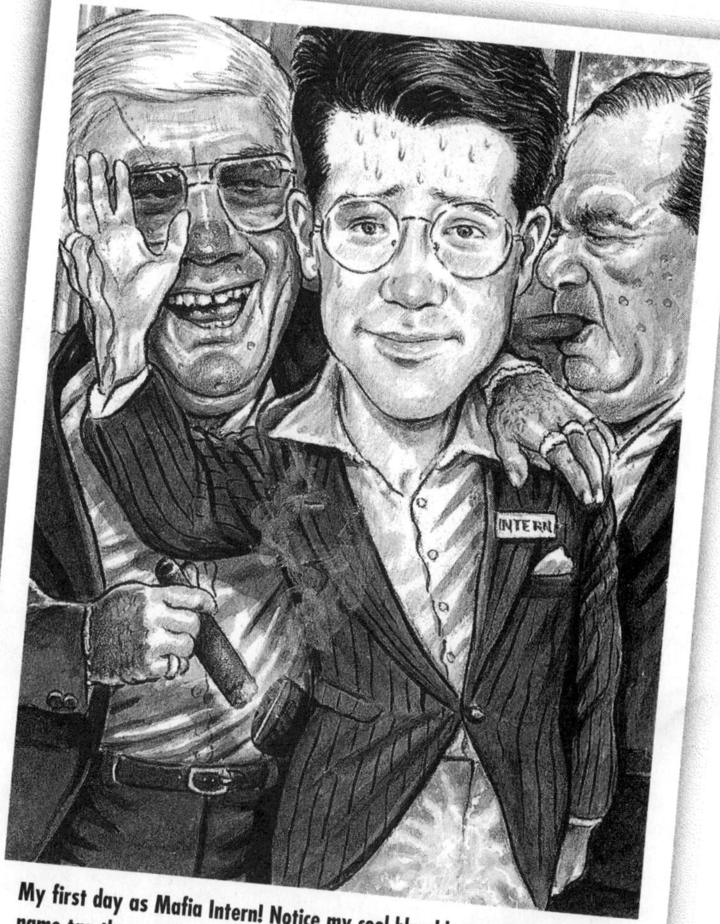
INTERN

My first day as Mafia Intern! Notice my cool blue blazer, pinkie ring and name tag that reads: INTERN! Try not to notice my stained khaki slacks!

ARTIST: DREW FRIEDMAN WRITER: J. MICHAEL SHADE

BLOOD, HONOR & THREE CREDITS

My Internship With The Calamari Crime Family

June 24 It's Already Hectic!

Today I had a very busy day! In the morning I edited extortion notices until my eyes were blurry. Later in the afternoon I stayed busy by xeroxing death threats until my hands were aching. So much work to do! And to think that I'm doing it all for free!

June 28 My First Major Assignment!

Jimmy "Phlegm" Fettucini decided today that I would perform the infamous "Kiss of Death" on Ricky "Canker Sore" Capellini.

So, impressing the gangsters who stood by and merely watched, I walked straight up to Ricky, kissed him on the lips and declared, "You have just received the kiss of death!"

I hope Don Calamari doesn't mind that when I went out to pick up his dry cleaning I also stopped at the drugstore to get myself some Blistex.

PEOPLE TO SHOOT TODAY:
"CLAMS" CASINO
FRANKIE "TOOTH PICK" SANTO PADRE
UNCLE CARMINE

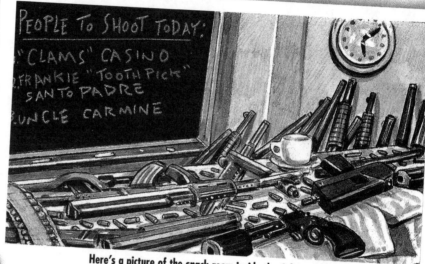

Here's a picture of the snack room inside the Calamari club. The "People To Shoot Today" chalkboard was my idea!

June 29 My Second Major Assignment!

I am so lucky to be in an organization where I am given major responsibilities to perform!

Like this afternoon, I was told that a spectacular bank robbery would be going down soon! As the intern for the Family, I was given the task of renting the getaway car for as little money as possible! After three hours of haggling, I was able to negotiate for a four-door sedan with a huge trunk for machine guns, bags of stolen money and potential hostages. Best of all it was a smoke-free car! Success!

July 6 Whistle While You Work!

Another busy day! In the morning I spent many hours polishing the Family's guns and waxing the Family's knives! There's going to be a gang war later this weekend and I felt that it might be appropriate if our Family projected a nice, clean image for the public to witness!

Appearances do count!

July 15 Another Clever Idea!

Mixed cement by hand this afternoon after the gigantic mixer broke down (a body got wedged between the blades). Later went to the market and bought dead fish to be sent to the Family's enemies. The first batch of fish quickly went bad and started to stink, so I returned and bought frozen fish sticks. Finding frozen fish sticks on your doorstep probably isn't as scary as finding a fresh fish, but who would complain?

I DIDN'T DO IT

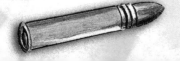

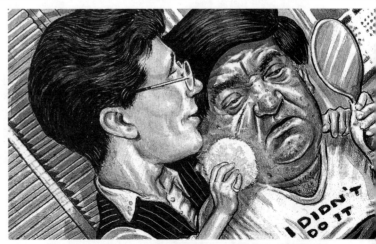

Here I am applying makeup to Sal "The Rug" Fusilli for his appearance before a police lineup. The "I Didn't Do It" T-shirt was my idea!

July 24 This Job Is Neat!

I'm starting to gain a reputation for my intelligence! Today I stood in the corner of the club and held up cue cards with quotes from popular gangster movies printed on them. Because of this, no one in the Family will ever be at a loss for something interesting to say.

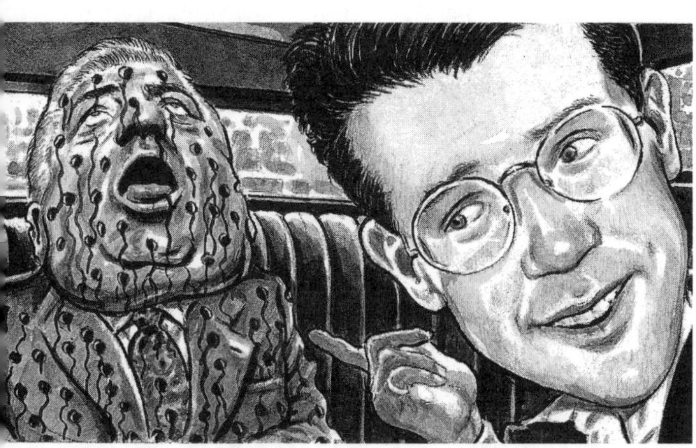

Me next to Nunzio "The Mouth" Puttanesca as he was about to be driven to some New Jersey swampland. Just moments before I held up a cue card with "Tell Don Calamari it wasn't personal – only business" written on it.

August 1 I Make A New Friend!

Guido "The Putz" Scungilli came up to me this morning and asked if he could change his name to Guido "The Winner" Scungilli. After searching through the database of nicknames I had set up on the computer, I discovered there was already a "Winner," but that plenty of other nicknames were still available, such as "The Charming," "The Attractive" and "The Cunning" to name a few.

Guido ultimately chose "The Attractive" and, after changing his name tag accordingly, now struts around the city with a more upbeat attitude.

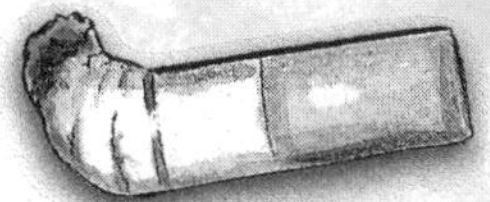

August 4 Play Ball!

I was just put in charge of organizing the Calamari Family softball team! I couldn't find anyone to play, but I did manage to locate hundreds of baseball bats and enough T-shirts, most with bullet holes, to go around.

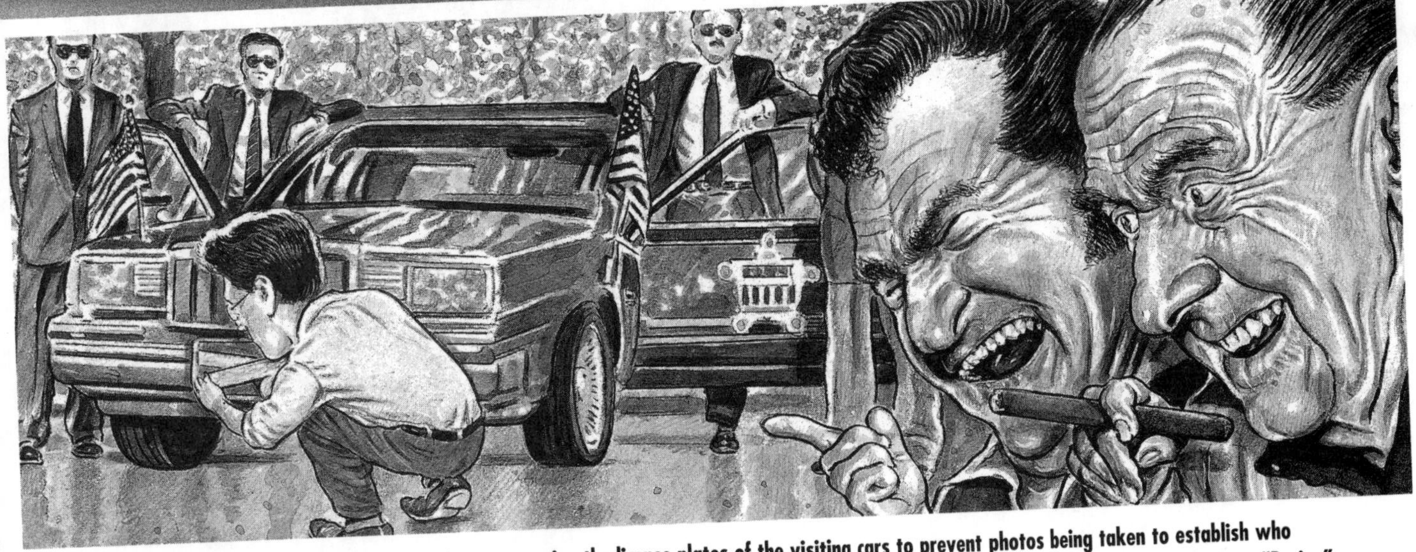

At the Calamari Family Picnic. I'm the one covering the license plates of the visiting cars to prevent photos being taken to establish who attended. Luca "Fazool" Fagioli got a kick out of my covering the plates of an F.B.I. car, too! "This kid kills me," he said. To which Marv "Brains" Turetsky, the Family accountant replied, "Careful, Luca. It just might happen." Everyone roared! Chalk up another Brownie Point for yours truly!

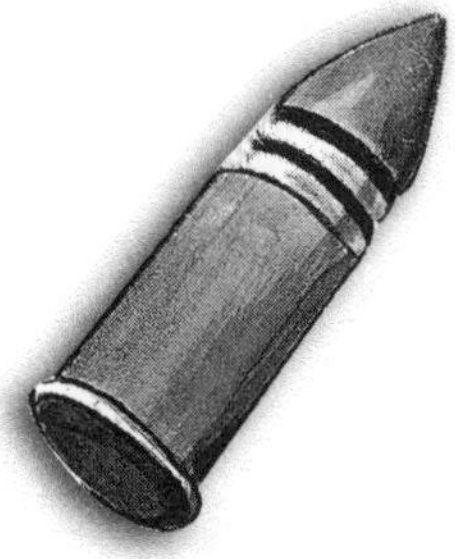

August 12 Goodbye Tony!

Some sad news today: Tony "Lazy Eye" Rigatoni was killed after he inadvertently stared down the Godfather. The poor guy didn't even see it coming!

I was told to dispose of his body by leaving it in the trunk of a rented car. The Godfather was pleased I saved money by getting a compact, and when I told him that this one was a smoker's rental to help cover the stench of the decaying body, he laughed! "This little strunz is all right," he said. I've learned that praise like this isn't easily come by from him! It was the proudest moment of my life!

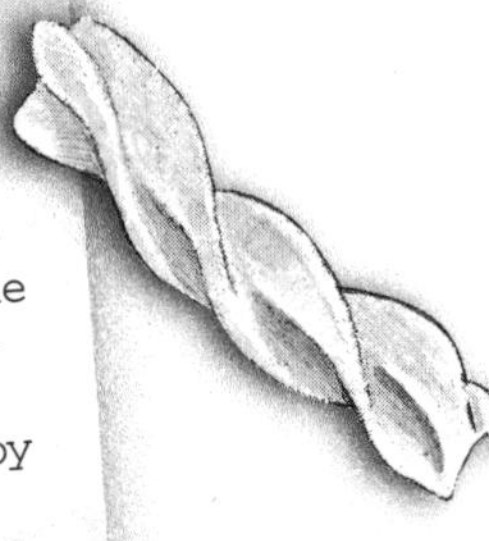

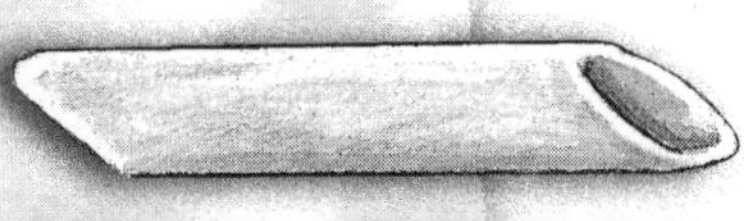

BLOOD, HONOR & THREE CREDITS

My Internship With The Calamari Crime Family

August 17 Busy, Busy, Busy!

I'm exhausted! All morning I kept busy by entering ransom notes, collection schedules and other business matters into the computer. When I finished, I was ordered to blow up the computer to destroy all the evidence. Sometimes I don't understand Family logic. But as the Godfather explained to me, "Mine is not to question why, mine is just to do and fuhgeddaboutit!"

August 21 A Business Opportunity!

With the internship quickly coming to an end, I find myself searching for meaningful things to do. Yesterday, I stood on the sidewalk and sold people phony memberships into the Mafia (complete with a fake certificate and an imitation mug shot).

The tourists were eating them up until Angie "The Frog" Zucchini realized there was a buck to be made and offered to buy me out for a slice of pizza. I told him no. He then said, "'Lazy Eye' has been asking about you visiting him soon, if you know what I mean!"

The pizza was delicious.

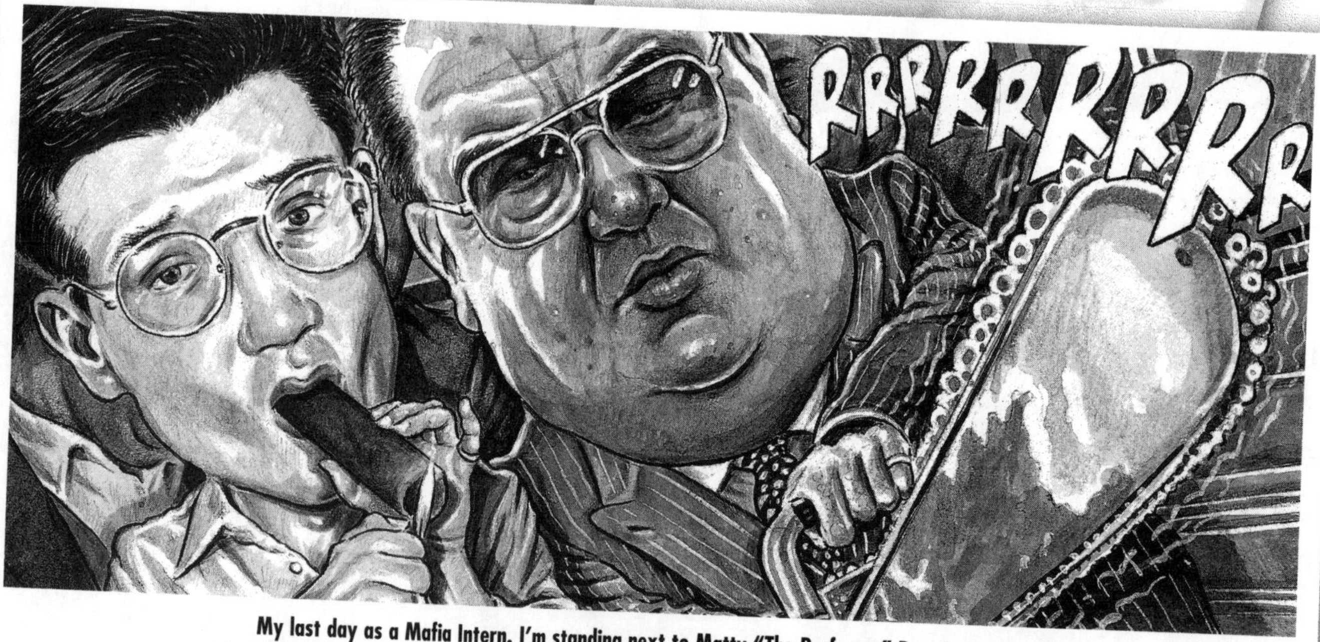
RRRRRRRRR

My last day as a Mafia Intern. I'm standing next to Matty "The Professor" Prosciutto. Matty later "suggested" to the dean of my university that I deserved school credit for my internship. It was an offer the dean couldn't refuse. In fact, he threw in three extra credits for "life — and death — experiences."

August 28 Last Day!

The Family threw a huge farewell party for me this afternoon! Charlie "Rough Stuff" Parmesan handed me the recommendation that I had previously asked him to write, but he did so by cutting thousands of individual words from the newspaper and then pasting them onto a piece of cardboard. He later told me that he didn't want to be held accountable.

The Family then led me to the back door and mentioned that they looked forward to seeing me again in the future, but "not in court, or else." I waved good-bye, as did everyone else, including Jimmy "One Finger" Spedini, who was either very sad to see me go, or very happy to give me the finger!

What a summer!

William "The Gofer" Gaylord

DON MARTIN DEPT.

ONE FINE EVENING ON A BROOKLYN STREET

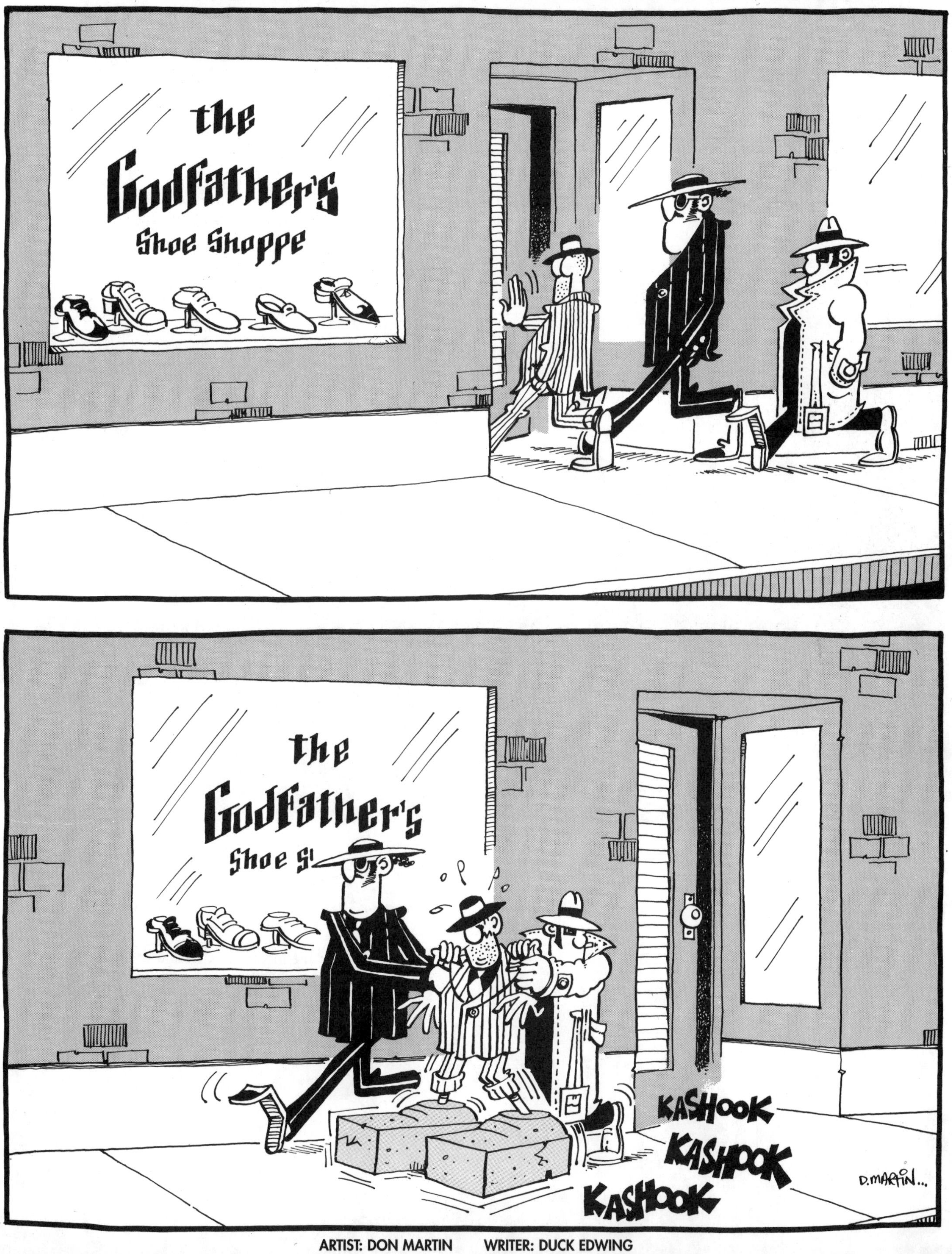
the Godfather's Shoe Shoppe
the Godfather's Shoe S
KASHOOK
KASHOOK
KASHOOK
D.MARTIN...

ARTIST: DON MARTIN WRITER: DUCK EDWING

ARE YOU TALKIN' TO ME — AT $100 AN HOUR? DEPT.

In 1972, MAD spoofed *The Godfather.* In 1974, we parodied *The Godfather Part II.* And just when we thought we were finished, they pulled us back in with *The Godfather Part III!* Recently, there's been a different kind of mobster movie — it's about a wiseguy in crisis. In *The Godfather* they went to the mattresses, in this film they're going to the couches! Seems like they're just begging us to...

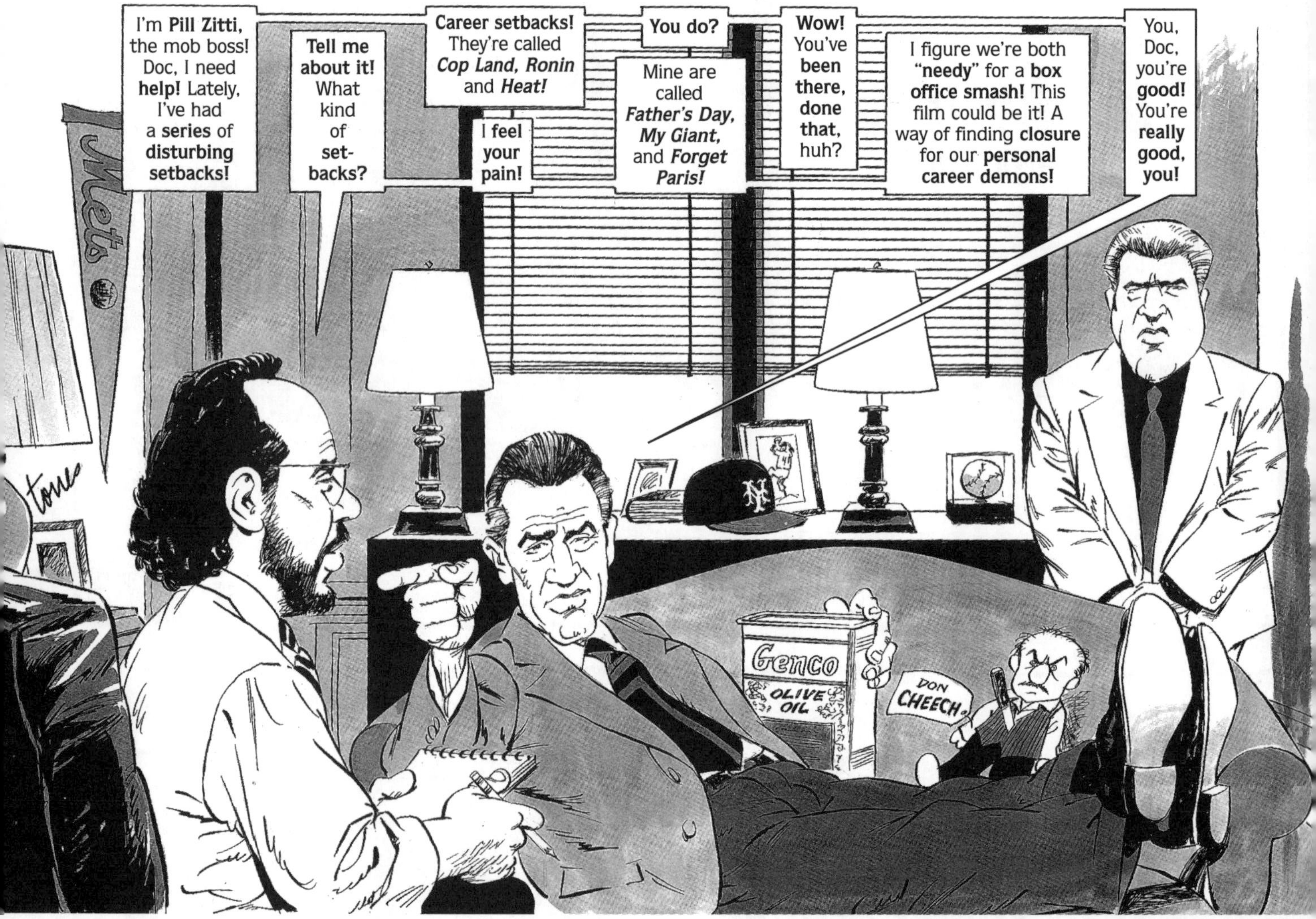
I'm **Pill Zitti,** the mob boss! Doc, I need **help!** Lately, I've had a **series** of **disturbing setbacks!**
Tell me about it! What kind of **set-backs?**
Career setbacks! They're called ***Cop Land, Ronin*** and ***Heat!***
I feel your pain!
You do?
Mine are called ***Father's Day, My Giant,*** and ***Forget Paris!***
Wow! You've **been there, done that,** huh?
I figure we're both **"needy"** for a **box office smash!** This film could be it! A way of finding **closure** for our **personal career demons!**
You, Doc, you're **good!** You're **really good,** you!
Mets
Genco OLIVE OIL
DON CHEECH

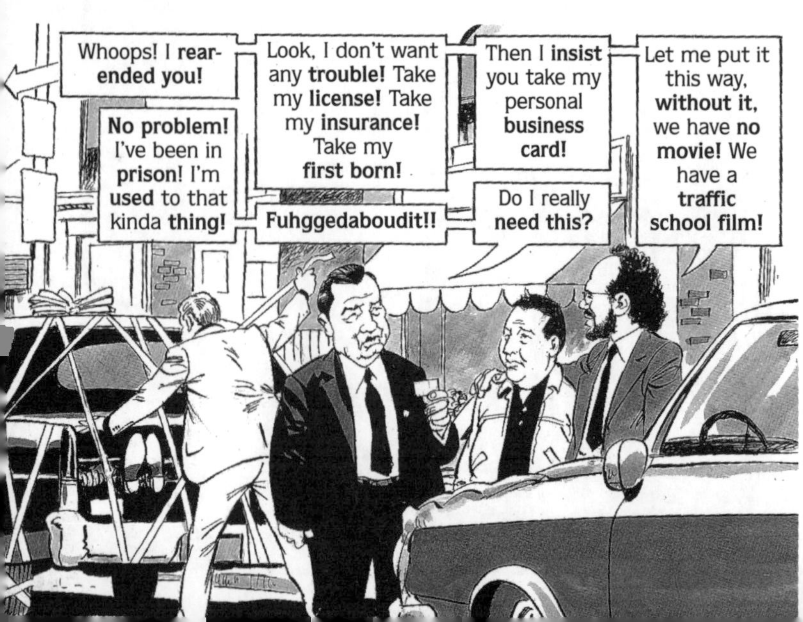
Whoops! I **rear-ended you!**
No problem! I've been in **prison!** I'm **used** to that kinda **thing!**
Look, I don't want any **trouble!** Take my **license!** Take my **insurance!** Take my **first born!**
Fuhggedaboudit!!
Then I **insist** you take my personal **business card!**
Do I really need this?
Let me put it this way, **without it,** we have **no movie!** We have a **traffic school film!**

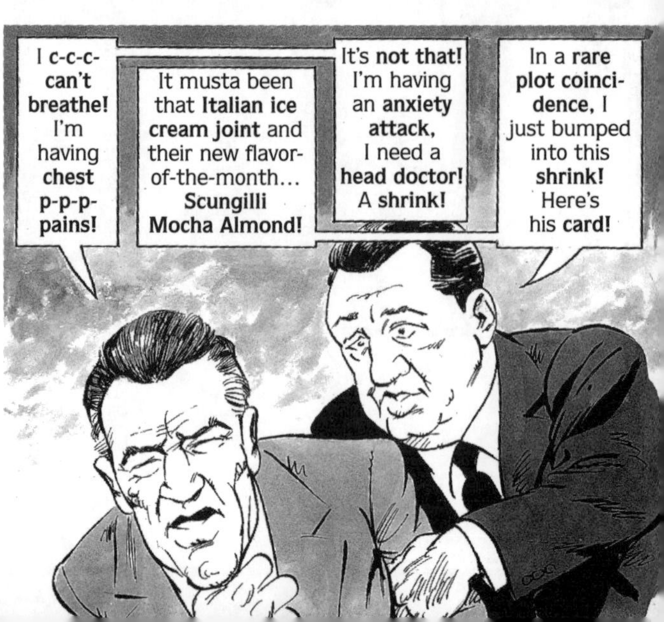
I c-c-c-can't breathe! I'm having **chest p-p-p-pains!**
It musta been that **Italian ice cream joint** and their new flavor-of-the-month... **Scungilli Mocha Almond!**
It's **not that!** I'm having an **anxiety attack,** I need a **head doctor!** A **shrink!**
In a **rare plot coinci-dence,** I just bumped into this **shrink!** Here's his **card!**

satirize this

ARTIST: ANGELO TORRES WRITER: JOSH GORDON

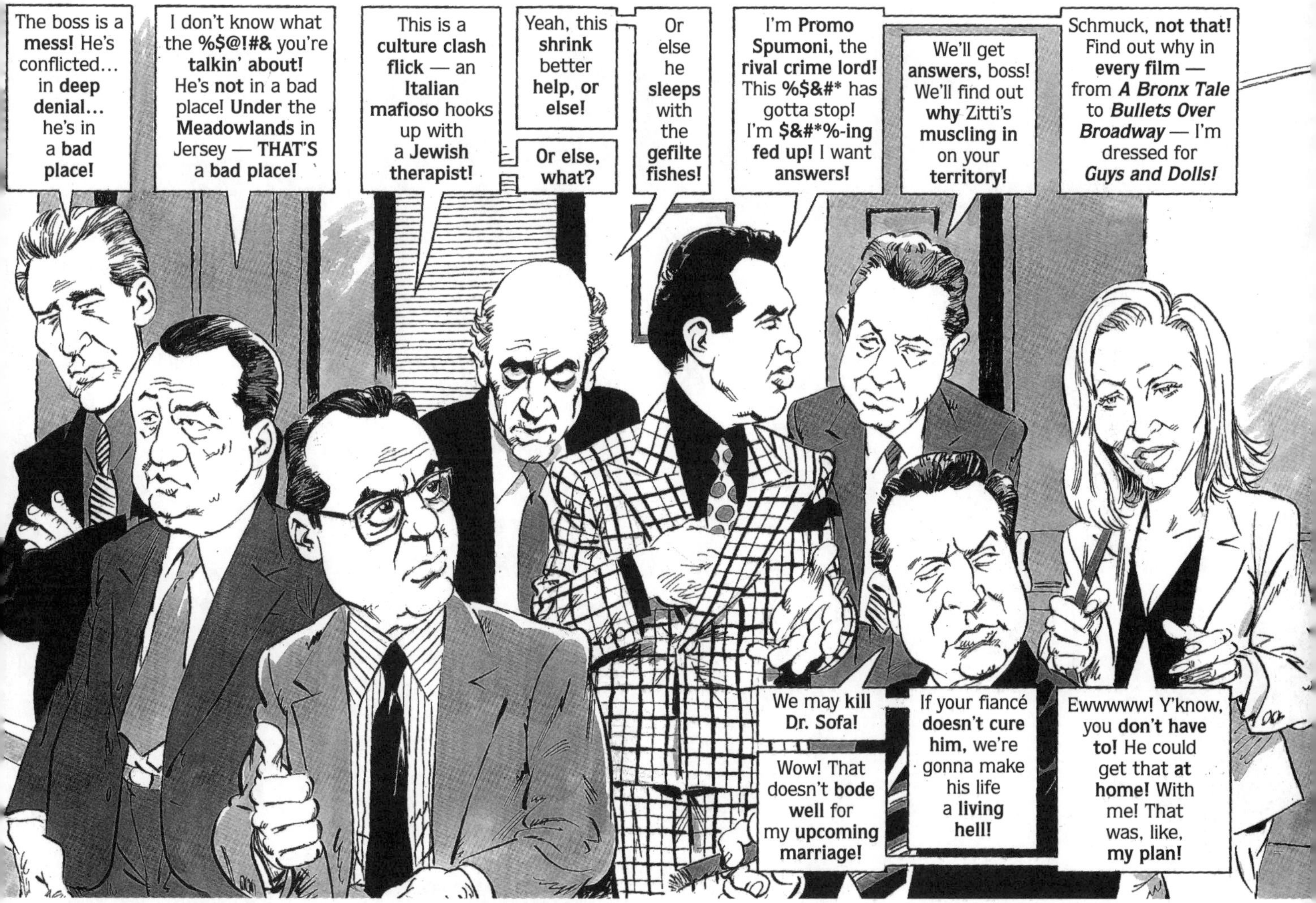

The boss is a mess! He's conflicted… in deep denial… he's in a bad place!
I don't know what the %$@!#& you're talkin' about! He's not in a bad place! Under the Meadowlands in Jersey — THAT'S a bad place!
This is a culture clash flick — an Italian mafioso hooks up with a Jewish therapist!
Yeah, this shrink better help, or else!
Or else, what?
Or else he sleeps with the gefilte fishes!
I'm Promo Spumoni, the rival crime lord! This %$&#* has gotta stop! I'm $&#*%-ing fed up! I want answers!
We'll get answers, boss! We'll find out why Zitti's muscling in on your territory!
Schmuck, not that! Find out why in every film — from A Bronx Tale to Bullets Over Broadway — I'm dressed for Guys and Dolls!
We may kill Dr. Sofa!
Wow! That doesn't bode well for my upcoming marriage!
If your fiancé doesn't cure him, we're gonna make his life a living hell!
Ewwwww! Y'know, you don't have to! He could get that at home! With me! That was, like, my plan!

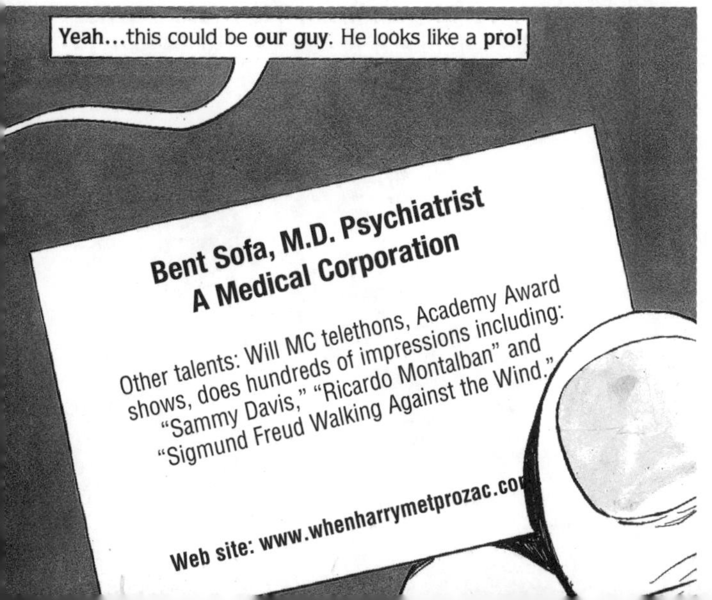

Yeah…this could be our guy. He looks like a pro!
Bent Sofa, M.D. Psychiatrist
A Medical Corporation
Other talents: Will MC telethons, Academy Award shows, does hundreds of impressions including: "Sammy Davis," "Ricardo Montalban" and "Sigmund Freud Walking Against the Wind."
Web site: www.whenharrymetprozac.co

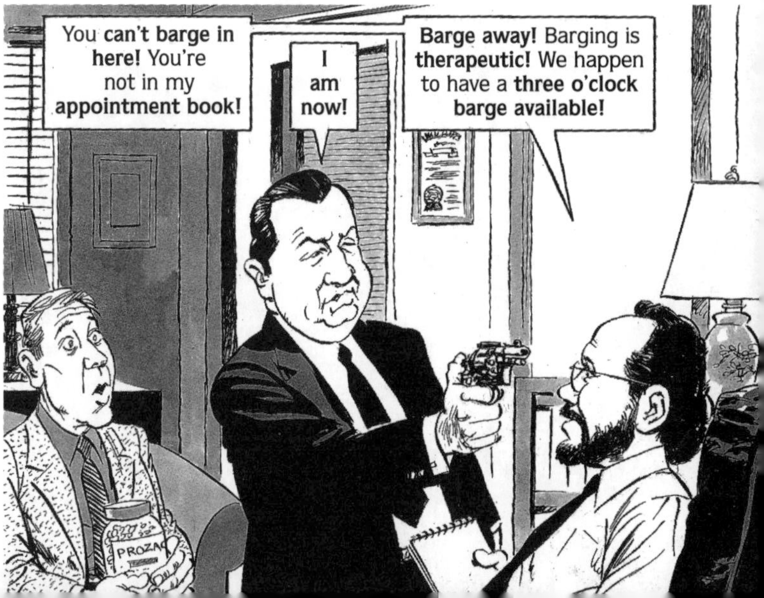

You can't barge in here! You're not in my appointment book!
I am now!
Barge away! Barging is therapeutic! We happen to have a three o'clock barge available!
PROZAC

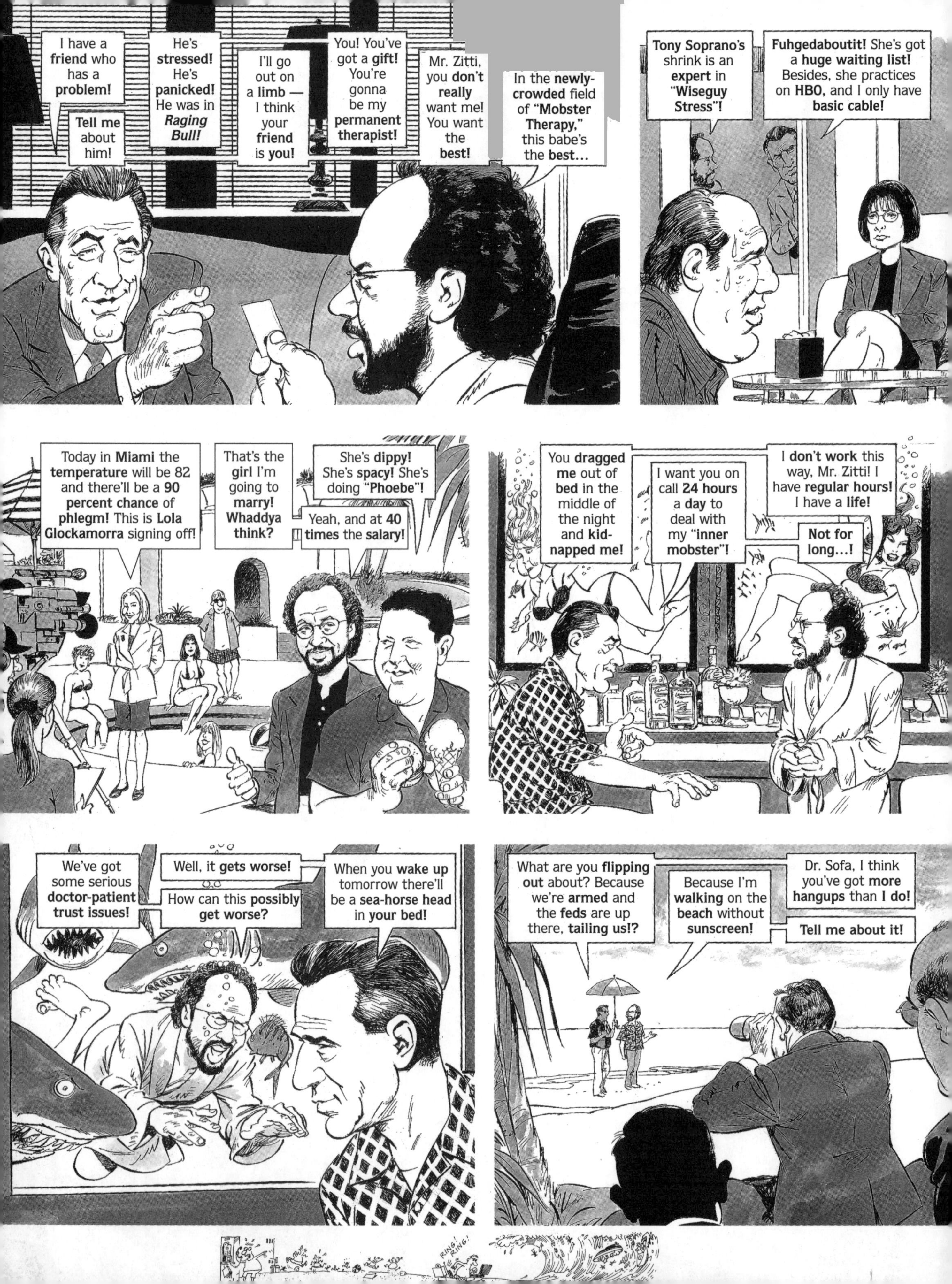

I have a **friend** who has a **problem!**
Tell me about him!
He's **stressed!** He's **panicked!** He was in ***Raging Bull!***
I'll go out on a **limb** — I think your **friend** is **you!**
You! You've got a **gift!** You're gonna be my **permanent therapist!**
Mr. Zitti, you **don't really** want me! You want the **best!**
In the **newly-crowded** field of **"Mobster Therapy,"** this babe's the **best...**
Tony Soprano's shrink is an **expert** in **"Wiseguy Stress"!**
Fuhgedaboutit! She's got a **huge waiting list!** Besides, she practices on **HBO,** and I only have **basic cable!**
Today in **Miami** the **temperature** will be 82 and there'll be a **90 percent chance** of **phlegm!** This is **Lola Glockamorra** signing off!
That's the **girl** I'm going to **marry! Whaddya think?**
She's **dippy!** She's **spacy!** She's doing **"Phoebe"**!
Yeah, and at **40 times** the **salary!**
You **dragged me** out of **bed** in the middle of the night and **kid-napped me!**
I want you on call **24 hours** a **day** to deal with my **"inner mobster"!**
I **don't work** this way, Mr. Zitti! I have **regular hours!** I have a **life!**
Not for long...!
We've got some serious **doctor-patient trust issues!**
Well, it **gets worse!**
How can this **possibly get worse?**
When you **wake up** tomorrow there'll be a **sea-horse head** in **your bed!**
What are you **flipping out** about? Because we're **armed** and the **feds** are up there, **tailing us!?**
Because I'm **walking** on the **beach** without **sunscreen!**
Dr. Sofa, I think you've got **more hangups** than **I do!**
Tell me about it!
RING! RING!

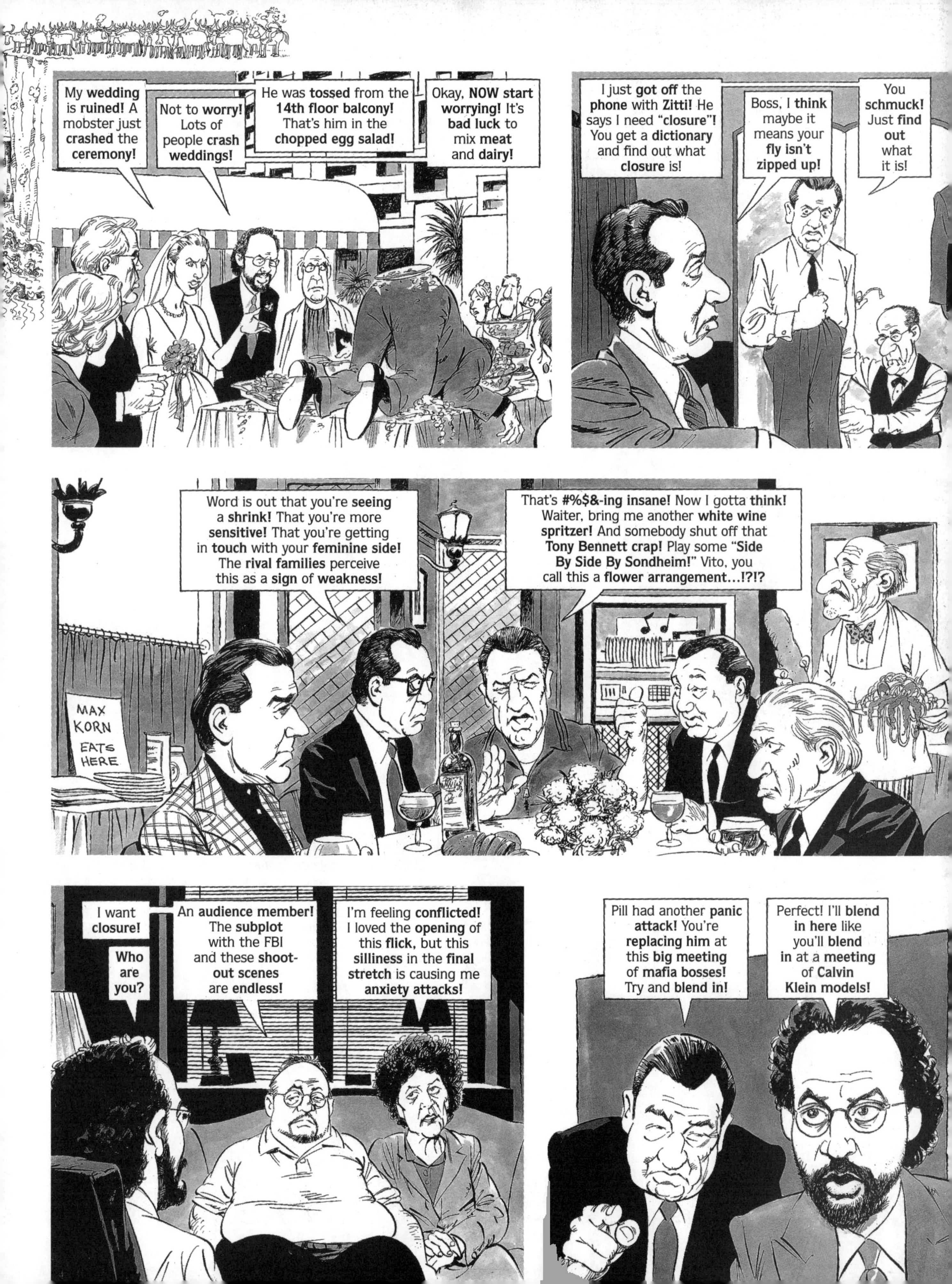
My wedding is ruined! A mobster just crashed the ceremony!
Not to worry! Lots of people crash weddings!
He was tossed from the 14th floor balcony! That's him in the chopped egg salad!
Okay, NOW start worrying! It's bad luck to mix meat and dairy!
I just got off the phone with Zitti! He says I need "closure"! You get a dictionary and find out what closure is!
Boss, I think maybe it means your fly isn't zipped up!
You schmuck! Just find out what it is!
Word is out that you're seeing a shrink! That you're more sensitive! That you're getting in touch with your feminine side! The rival families perceive this as a sign of weakness!
That's #%$&-ing insane! Now I gotta think! Waiter, bring me another white wine spritzer! And somebody shut off that Tony Bennett crap! Play some "Side By Side By Sondheim!" Vito, you call this a flower arrangement...!?!?
MAX KORN EATS HERE
I want closure!
Who are you?
An audience member! The subplot with the FBI and these shoot-out scenes are endless!
I'm feeling conflicted! I loved the opening of this flick, but this silliness in the final stretch is causing me anxiety attacks!
Pill had another panic attack! You're replacing him at this big meeting of mafia bosses! Try and blend in!
Perfect! I'll blend in here like you'll blend in at a meeting of Calvin Klein models!

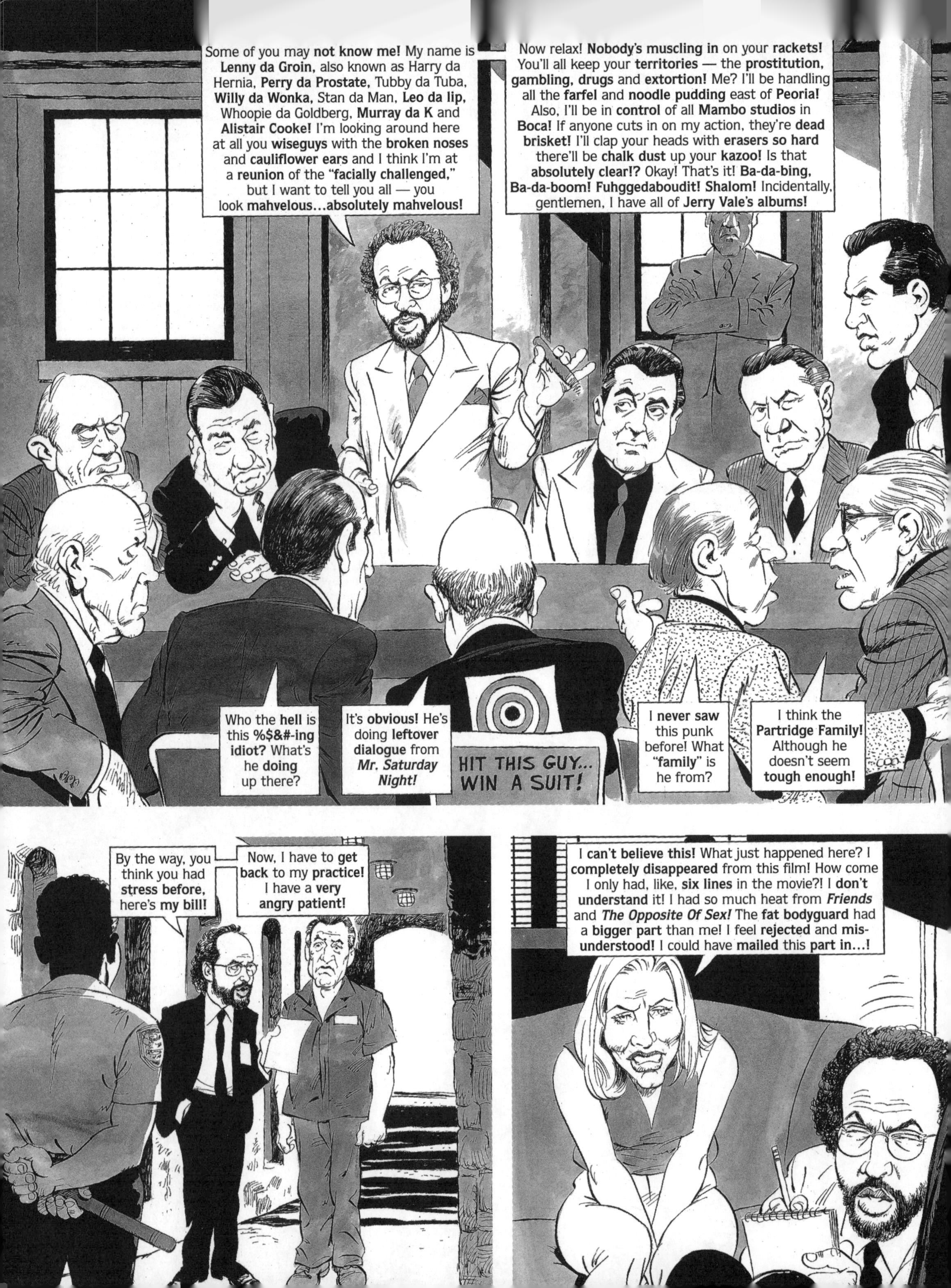
Some of you may not know me! My name is Lenny da Groin, also known as Harry da Hernia, Perry da Prostate, Tubby da Tuba, Willy da Wonka, Stan da Man, Leo da lip, Whoopie da Goldberg, Murray da K and Alistair Cooke! I'm looking around here at all you wiseguys with the broken noses and cauliflower ears and I think I'm at a reunion of the "facially challenged," but I want to tell you all — you look mahvelous…absolutely mahvelous!
Now relax! Nobody's muscling in on your rackets! You'll all keep your territories — the prostitution, gambling, drugs and extortion! Me? I'll be handling all the farfel and noodle pudding east of Peoria! Also, I'll be in control of all Mambo studios in Boca! If anyone cuts in on my action, they're dead brisket! I'll clap your heads with erasers so hard there'll be chalk dust up your kazoo! Is that absolutely clear!? Okay! That's it! Ba-da-bing, Ba-da-boom! Fuhggedaboudit! Shalom! Incidentally, gentlemen, I have all of Jerry Vale's albums!
Who the hell is this %$&#-ing idiot? What's he doing up there?
It's obvious! He's doing leftover dialogue from Mr. Saturday Night!
HIT THIS GUY… WIN A SUIT!
I never saw this punk before! What "family" is he from?
I think the Partridge Family! Although he doesn't seem tough enough!
By the way, you think you had stress before, here's my bill!
Now, I have to get back to my practice! I have a very angry patient!
I can't believe this! What just happened here? I completely disappeared from this film! How come I only had, like, six lines in the movie?! I don't understand it! I had so much heat from Friends and The Opposite Of Sex! The fat bodyguard had a bigger part than me! I feel rejected and misunderstood! I could have mailed this part in…!

SHTICK 'EM UP! DEPT.

If you live in a big city . . . or a small town, for that matter . . . the odds are that sooner or later you're gonna be mugged! So, as a public service, MAD offers these lines of dialogue calculated to

BLUFF THAT MUGGER!

ARTIST: BRUCE DAY WRITER: E. NELSON BRIDWELL

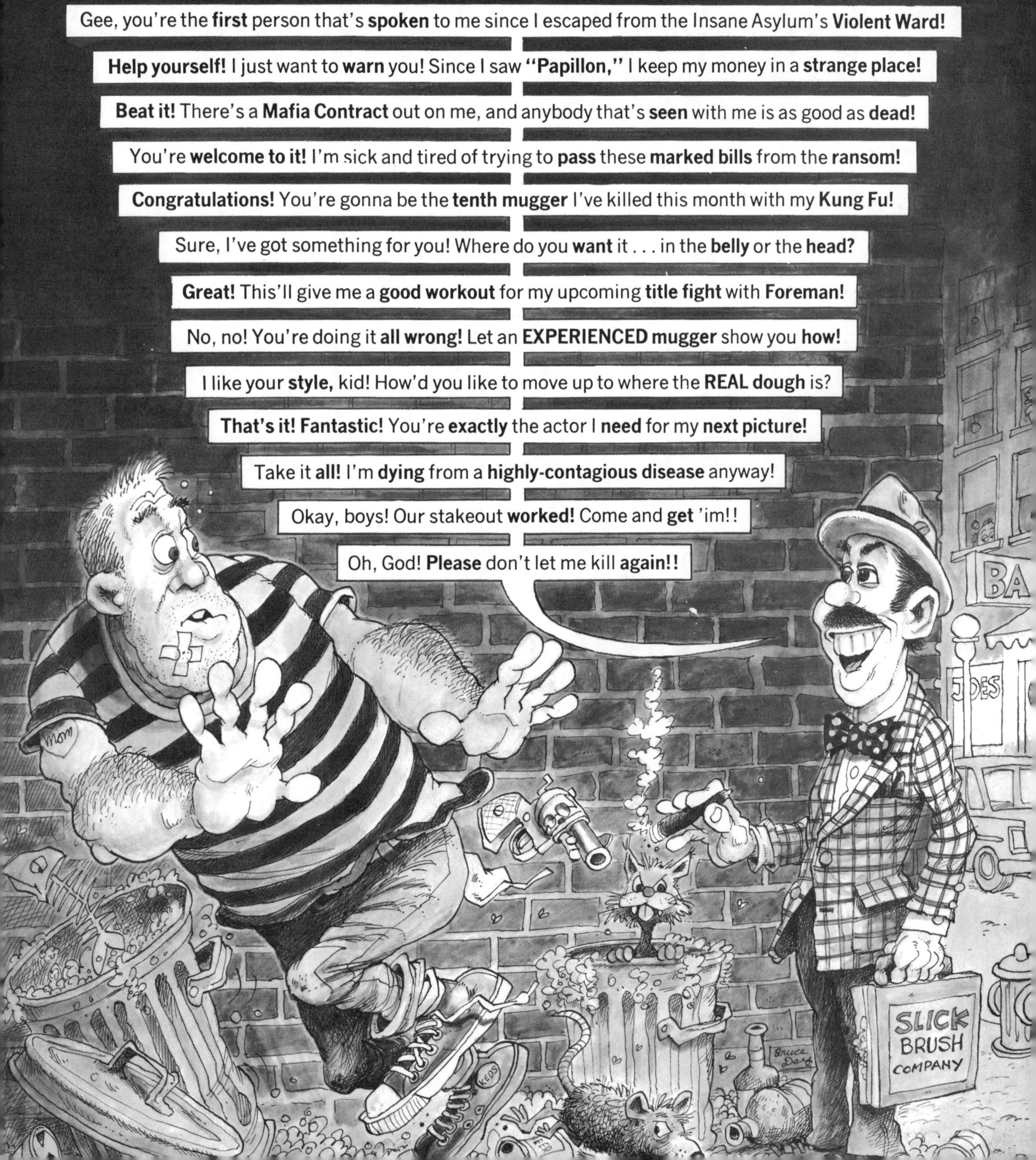
Gee, you're the **first** person that's **spoken** to me since I escaped from the Insane Asylum's **Violent Ward!**
Help yourself! I just want to **warn** you! Since I saw **"Papillon,"** I keep my money in a **strange place!**
Beat it! There's a **Mafia Contract** out on me, and anybody that's **seen** with me is as good as **dead!**
You're **welcome to it!** I'm sick and tired of trying to **pass** these **marked bills** from the **ransom!**
Congratulations! You're gonna be the **tenth mugger** I've killed this month with my **Kung Fu!**
Sure, I've got something for you! Where do you **want** it . . . in the **belly** or the **head?**
Great! This'll give me a **good workout** for my upcoming **title fight** with **Foreman!**
No, no! You're doing it **all wrong!** Let an **EXPERIENCED mugger** show you **how!**
I like your **style,** kid! How'd you like to move up to where the **REAL dough** is?
That's it! Fantastic! You're **exactly** the actor I **need** for my **next picture!**
Take it **all!** I'm **dying** from a **highly-contagious disease** anyway!
Okay, boys! Our stakeout **worked!** Come and **get** 'im!!
Oh, God! **Please** don't let me kill **again!!**
Mom
KEDS
SLICK BRUSH COMPANY

How do you let potential buyers know about your product or service? You advertise that's how! But there are some people who can't advertise their products or ser

IF THE UNDERW WERE ALLOWE

ARTIST: JACK RICKARD

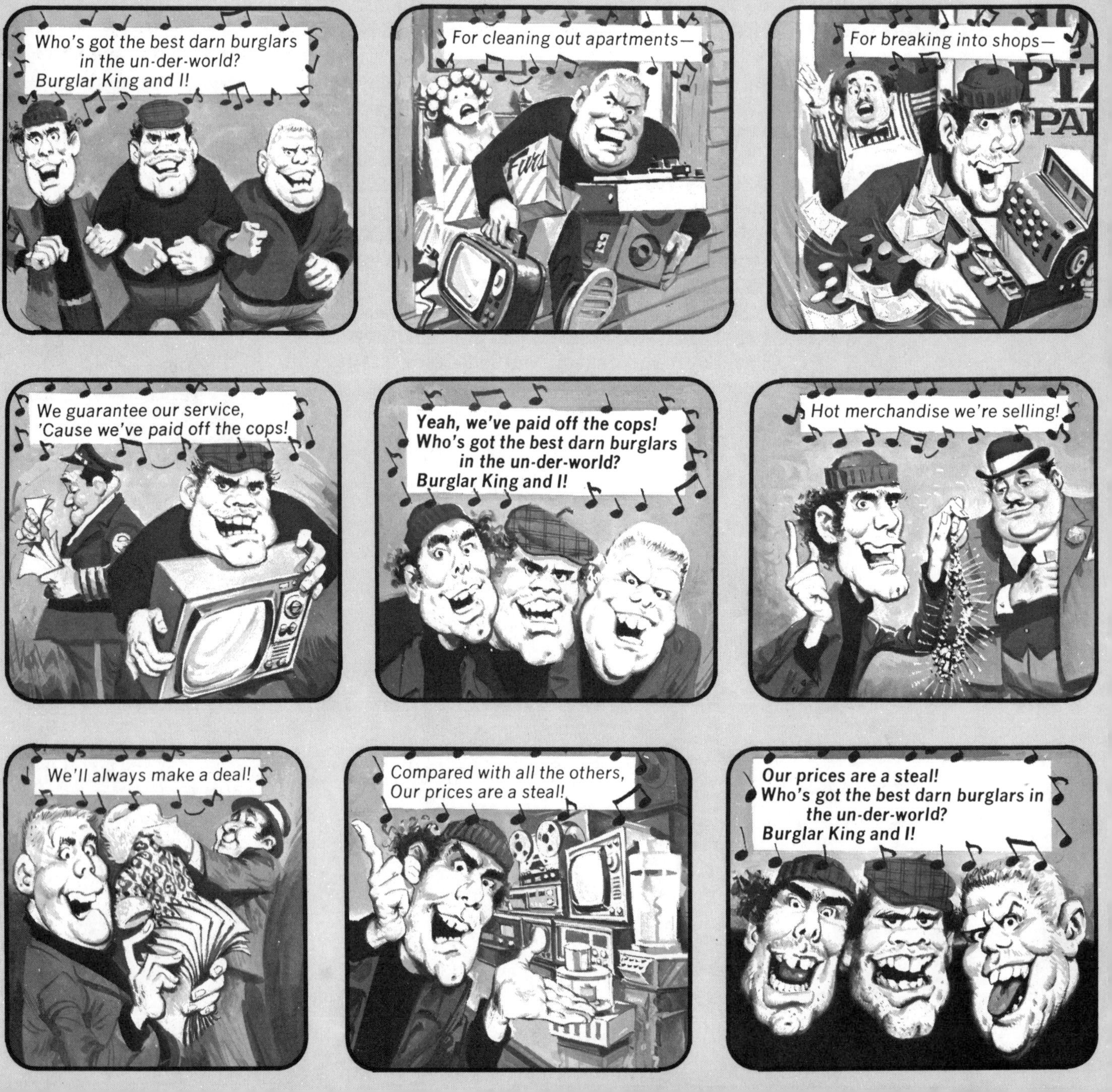

Who's got the best darn burglars in the un-der-world? Burglar King and I!
For cleaning out apartments—
For breaking into shops—
We guarantee our service, 'Cause we've paid off the cops!
Yeah, we've paid off the cops! Who's got the best darn burglars in the un-der-world? Burglar King and I!
Hot merchandise we're selling!
We'll always make a deal!
Compared with all the others, Our prices are a steal!
Our prices are a steal! Who's got the best darn burglars in the un-der-world? Burglar King and I!

vices . . . namely crooks, mobsters and other creeps who operate outside the law! So let's take a look (and this is how MAD creates a premise) at what we'd have . . .

ORLD ...AND OTHER ILLEGAL KINDS OF OPERATIONS TO ADVERTISE

WRITER: FRANK JACOBS

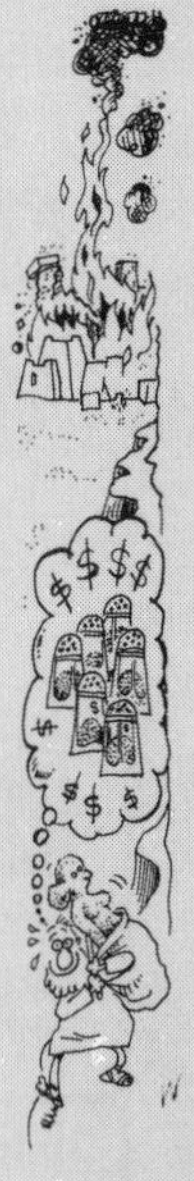

10 REASONS WHY YOU SHOULD LET J. & R. BILK HANDLE YOUR TAX RETURN

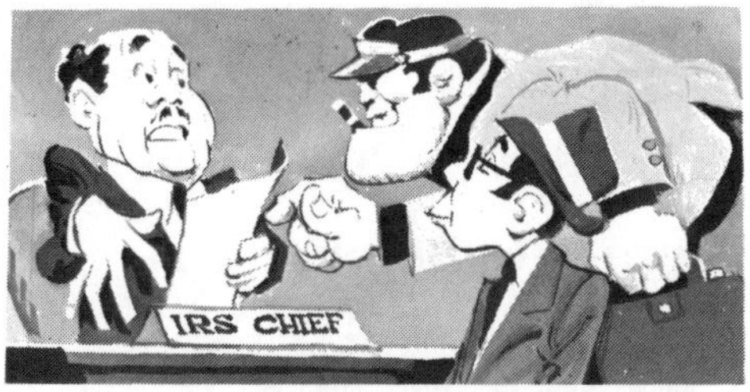
IRS CHIEF

1. We create deductions which are impossible to trace.
2, We jam I.R.S. computers with a lot of bewildering data.
3. We threaten anyone who questions your return.
4. We bribe shamelessly.
5. We furnish receipts for our services 12 times what you actually pay and completely deductible.
6. We provide up to 9 children whom you can claim as exemptions.
7. We supply iron-clad proof that you are incapable of making a living.
8. We are adept at doubletalk.
9. We furnish evidence that your business is actually a non-profit organization.
10. If all else fails, we furnish you with a new identity in a foreign country.

J. & R. BILK

Efficient, Dependable, Devious

Are Bills Piling Up . . . And Getting You Down?

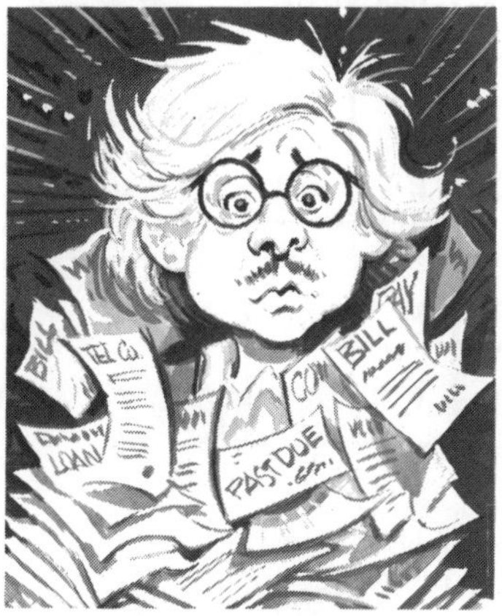
BILL
PAST DUE
LOAN

You Can Pay Them All With MONEY From MANNY!

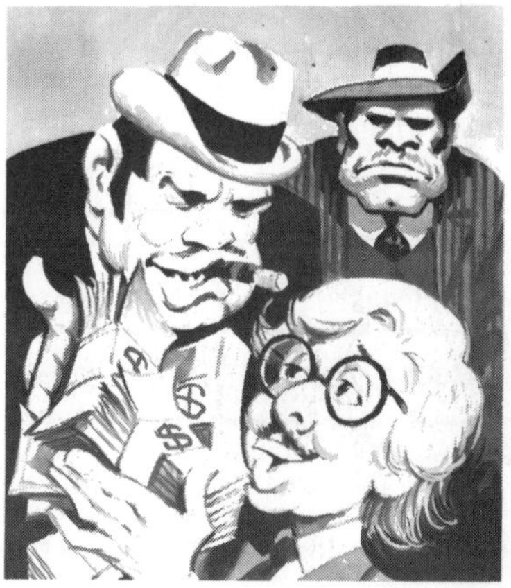

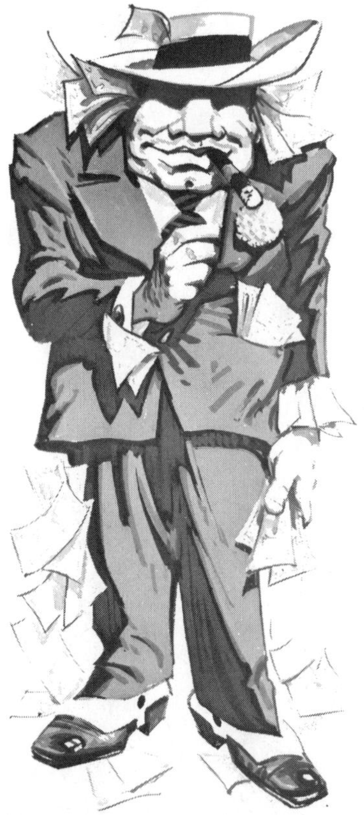

Just imagine yourself <u>debt-free!</u> Without any red tape. Without any nosy bankers. Without putting up your car or house as collateral. How?

MONEY FROM MANNY!

Manny doesn't make you sign long, complex loan forms. Manny doesn't check credit ratings. Manny doesn't know from Federal Lending Laws. Manny KNOWS you'll pay him back . . . because Manny's only collateral is YOU! And you can bet your LIFE on that!

MANNY'S ONE-STOP

LOAN SHARKING SERVICE

A Member Of The Mafia Group

WHEN YOU'RE BUYING A HOT CAR

COMPARE

WALLY'S STEAL-A-CAR

WITH ALL THE OTHERS!!

	Wally's	Chicago Louie	Pete's Discount	Hot Harry	Thrifty Heist
Choice of Make & Model	YES	NO	NO	NO	NO
Forged Registration	YES	NO	YES	NO	YES
Untraceable Plates	YES	YES	NO	NO	NO
New Paint Job	YES	NO	YES	YES	NO
Driven Less Than 10,000 Miles	YES	NO	NO	NO	NO
Respectable First Owner	YES	NO	NO	NO	NO
AM-FM Radio	YES	YES	NO	YES	NO

Ten Thousand Satisfied Customers Can't Be Wrong!

Why Is Wally Number One? Because He Steals Only The Best And Passes Up The Rest!

If you've got the CASH . . .

Wally's Steal-A-Car has got the DEAL!

Some Lawyers Offer Promises

MURRAY THE MOUTHPIECE GETS RESULTS!

Charge: Assault and Armed Robbery for hijacking a 197-car freight train across state lines.
Verdict: Suspended sentence for disorderly conduct.
Lawyer: Murray the Mouthpiece.

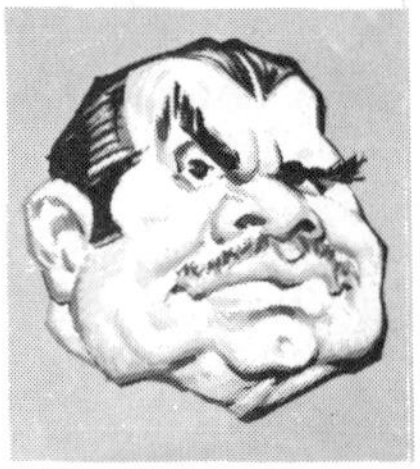

Tailpipe Izzie

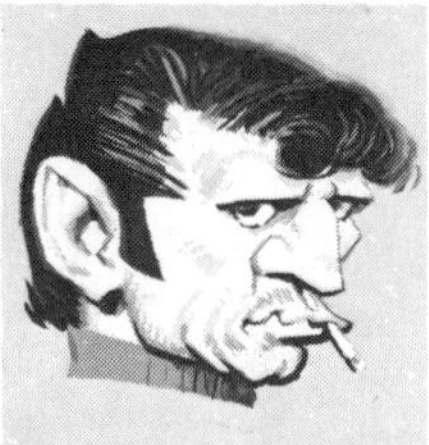

Rocco the Gimp

Charge: 1st-Degree Murder for wiping out a family of four.
Verdict: $50 fine for loitering.
Lawyer: Murray the Mouthpiece.

Charge: Manslaughter for clubbing a crippled newsdealer after guning him down in a stolen car.
Verdict: Loss of driver's license for one year.
Lawyer: Murray the Mouthpiece.

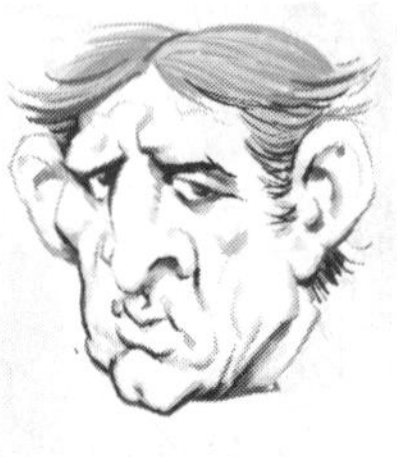

Weasel Wally

When There's A Loophole In The Law, MURRAY FINDS IT!

MURRAY

The Mouthpiece Crooks Get Off On

Tired of Arguing With Your Business Partner?

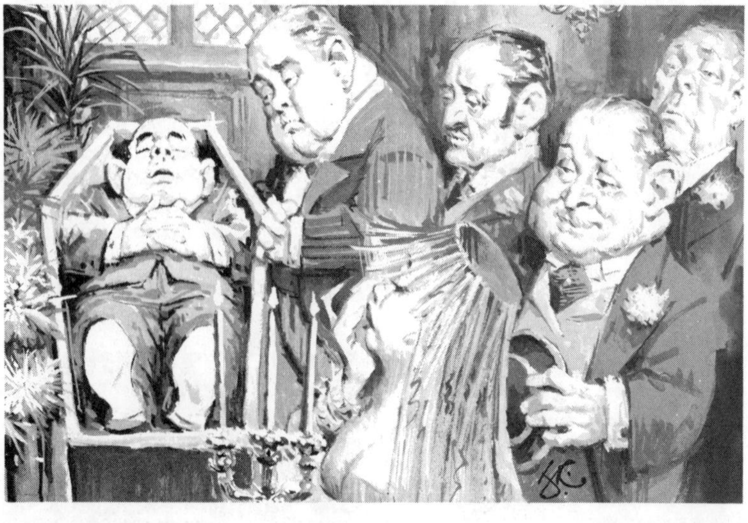

Rudy's Removals Can Help You

BE YOUR OWN BOSS!

Sometimes, one business isn't big enough for two partners. When this happens, it's time to call in Rudy's Removals. Quietly, discreetly, efficiently, we solve your problem by removing the source—your partner. This leaves you free to run things your way and double your share of the business profits.

Isn't It Time That You Took A Shot With Rudy?

Ask About Our Low-Cost Corporate Package Deal, In Which We Remove An Entire Board Of Directors!

RUDY'S REMOVALS

"The Businessman's Best Friend"
Estimates Cheerfully Given

THE ADVENTURES OF ARTIE

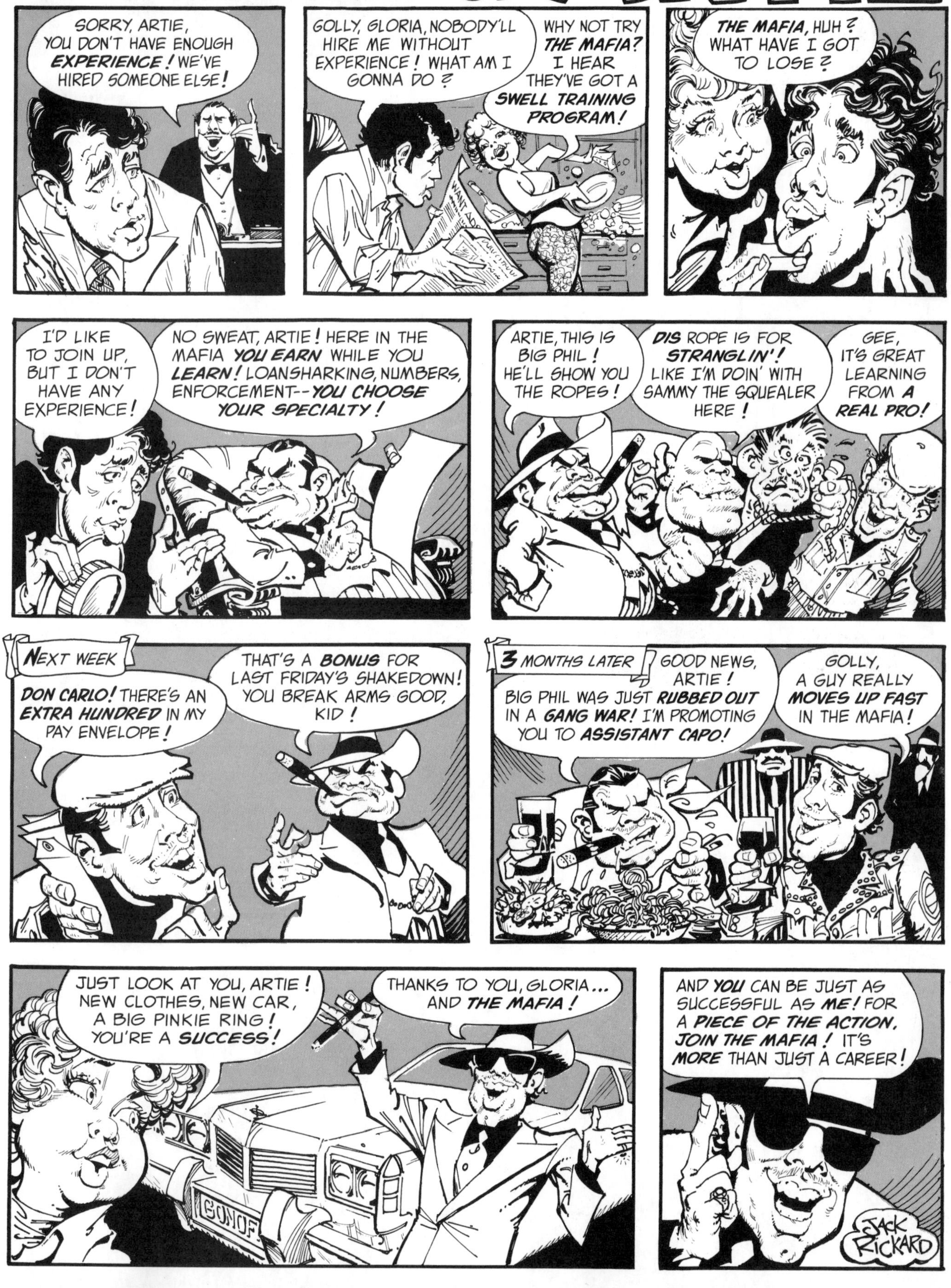
SORRY, ARTIE, YOU DON'T HAVE ENOUGH EXPERIENCE! WE'VE HIRED SOMEONE ELSE!
GOLLY, GLORIA, NOBODY'LL HIRE ME WITHOUT EXPERIENCE! WHAT AM I GONNA DO?
WHY NOT TRY THE MAFIA? I HEAR THEY'VE GOT A SWELL TRAINING PROGRAM!
THE MAFIA, HUH? WHAT HAVE I GOT TO LOSE?
I'D LIKE TO JOIN UP, BUT I DON'T HAVE ANY EXPERIENCE!
NO SWEAT, ARTIE! HERE IN THE MAFIA YOU EARN WHILE YOU LEARN! LOANSHARKING, NUMBERS, ENFORCEMENT--YOU CHOOSE YOUR SPECIALTY!
ARTIE, THIS IS BIG PHIL! HE'LL SHOW YOU THE ROPES!
DIS ROPE IS FOR STRANGLIN'! LIKE I'M DOIN' WITH SAMMY THE SQUEALER HERE!
GEE, IT'S GREAT LEARNING FROM A REAL PRO!
NEXT WEEK
DON CARLO! THERE'S AN EXTRA HUNDRED IN MY PAY ENVELOPE!
THAT'S A BONUS FOR LAST FRIDAY'S SHAKEDOWN! YOU BREAK ARMS GOOD, KID!
3 MONTHS LATER
GOOD NEWS, ARTIE! BIG PHIL WAS JUST RUBBED OUT IN A GANG WAR! I'M PROMOTING YOU TO ASSISTANT CAPO!
GOLLY, A GUY REALLY MOVES UP FAST IN THE MAFIA!
JUST LOOK AT YOU, ARTIE! NEW CLOTHES, NEW CAR, A BIG PINKIE RING! YOU'RE A SUCCESS!
THANKS TO YOU, GLORIA... AND THE MAFIA!
GONOF
AND YOU CAN BE JUST AS SUCCESSFUL AS ME! FOR A PIECE OF THE ACTION, JOIN THE MAFIA! IT'S MORE THAN JUST A CAREER!
JACK RICKARD

"FAMILY" REUNION DEPT.

When last we saw the beloved Minestrone Family three years (and a couple of hundred bodies, and several Academy Awards, and $100 million in box office grosses) ago, God had made Vino, the original Odd Father, an offer he couldn't refuse and called him to that "Great Pizzeria In The Sky," and Micrin, Vino's youngest son, had taken over. We pick up the action again with Micrin Minestrone as Head of the Family and determined to prove that *he* can play . . .

THE O
PA

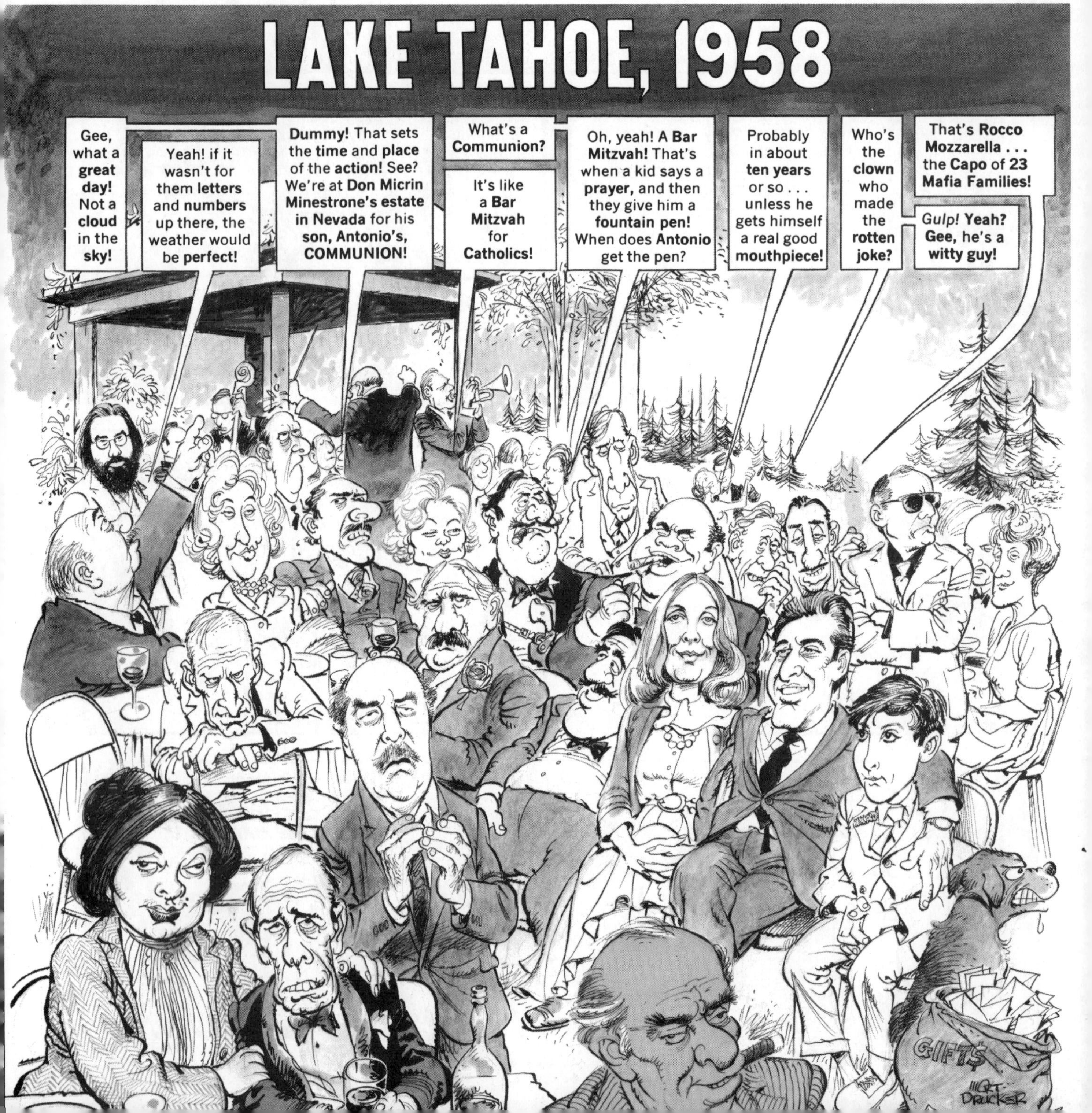
LAKE TAHOE, 1958
Gee, what a **great day!** Not a **cloud** in the **sky!**
Yeah! if it wasn't for them **letters** and **numbers** up there, the weather would be **perfect!**
Dummy! That sets the **time** and **place** of the **action!** See? We're at **Don Micrin Minestrone's estate in Nevada** for his **son, Antonio's, COMMUNION!**
What's a **Communion?**
It's like a **Bar Mitzvah** for **Catholics!**
Oh, yeah! A **Bar Mitzvah!** That's when a kid says a **prayer,** and then they give him a **fountain pen!** When does **Antonio** get the pen?
Probably in about **ten years** or so . . . unless he gets himself a real good **mouthpiece!**
Who's the **clown** who made the **rotten joke?**
That's **Rocco Mozzarella . . .** the **Capo** of **23 Mafia Families!**
Gulp! **Yeah? Gee,** he's a **witty guy!**
GIFTS
MORT DRUCKER

OD FATHER
RT, TOO!

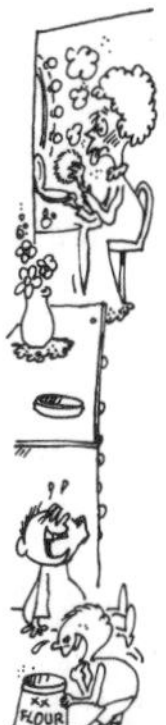

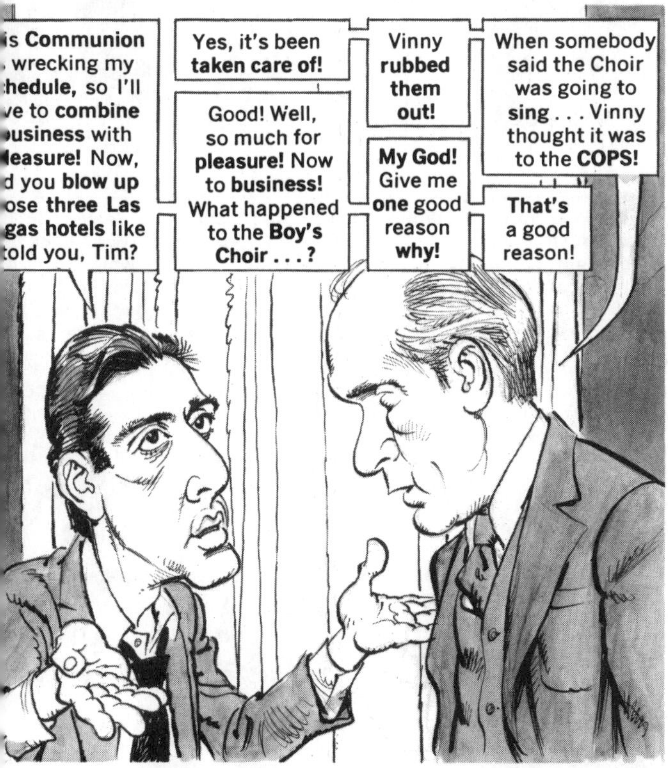
is Communion wrecking my hedule, so I'll ve to combine business with leasure! Now, d you blow up ose three Las gas hotels like told you, Tim?
Yes, it's been taken care of!
Good! Well, so much for pleasure! Now to business! What happened to the Boy's Choir . . . ?
Vinny rubbed them out!
My God! Give me one good reason why!
When somebody said the Choir was going to sing . . . Vinny thought it was to the COPS!
That's a good reason!

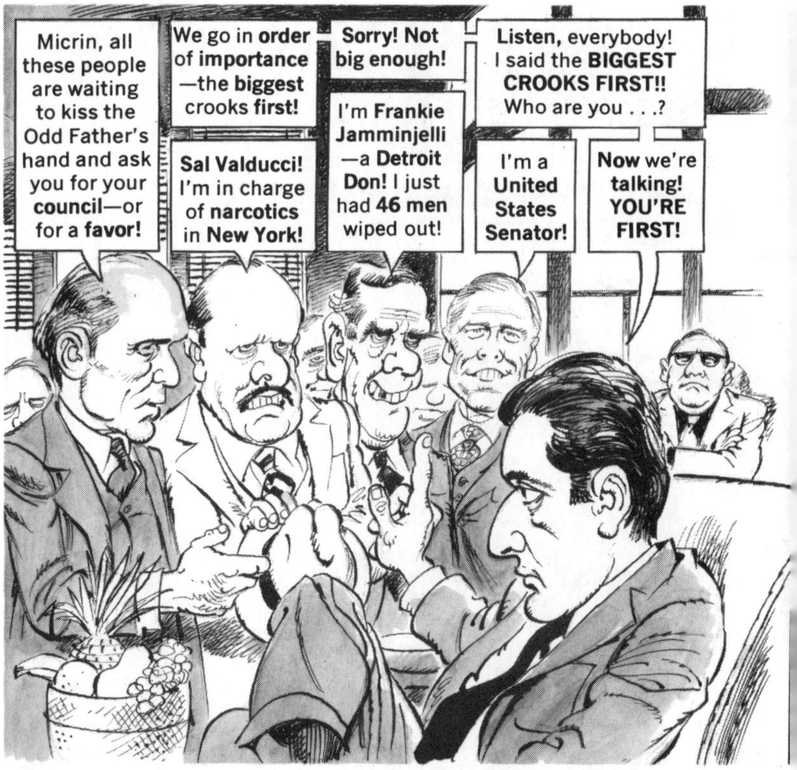
Micrin, all these people are waiting to kiss the Odd Father's hand and ask you for your council—or for a favor!
We go in order of importance—the biggest crooks first!
Sal Valducci! I'm in charge of narcotics in New York!
Sorry! Not big enough!
I'm Frankie Jamminjelli—a Detroit Don! I just had 46 men wiped out!
Listen, everybody! I said the BIGGEST CROOKS FIRST!! Who are you . . .?
I'm a United States Senator!
Now we're talking! YOU'RE FIRST!

ARTIST: MORT DRUCKER WRITER: LARRY SIEGEL

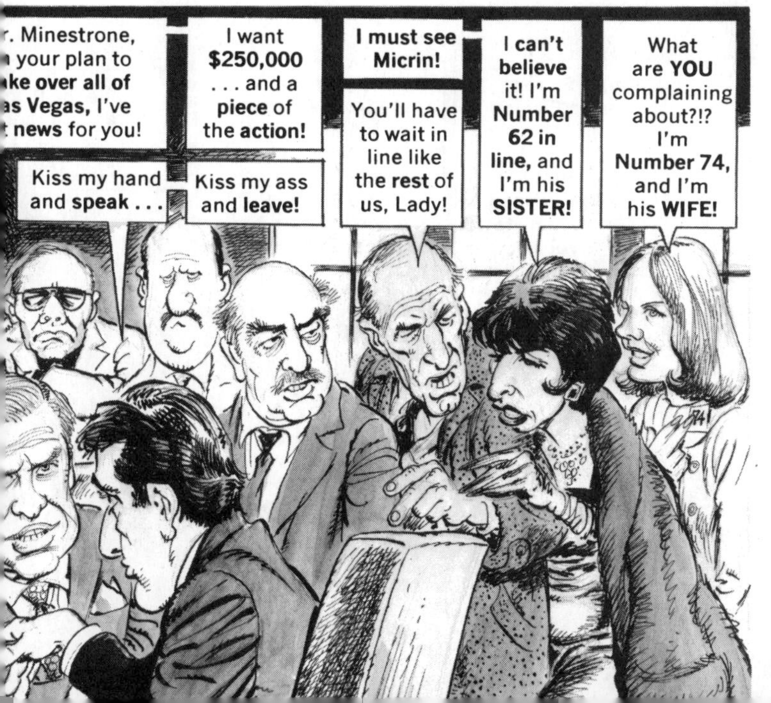
r. Minestrone, your plan to ake over all of as Vegas, I've t news for you!
Kiss my hand and speak . . .
I want $250,000 . . . and a piece of the action!
Kiss my ass and leave!
I must see Micrin!
You'll have to wait in line like the rest of us, Lady!
I can't believe it! I'm Number 62 in line, and I'm his SISTER!
What are YOU complaining about?!? I'm Number 74, and I'm his WIFE!

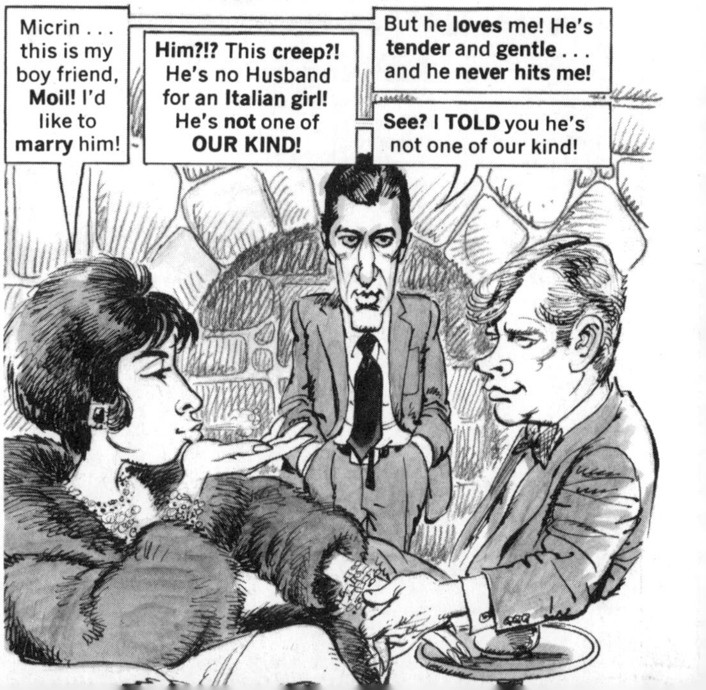
Micrin . . . this is my boy friend, Moil! I'd like to marry him!
Him?!? This creep?! He's no Husband for an Italian girl! He's not one of OUR KIND!
But he loves me! He's tender and gentle . . . and he never hits me!
See? I TOLD you he's not one of our kind!

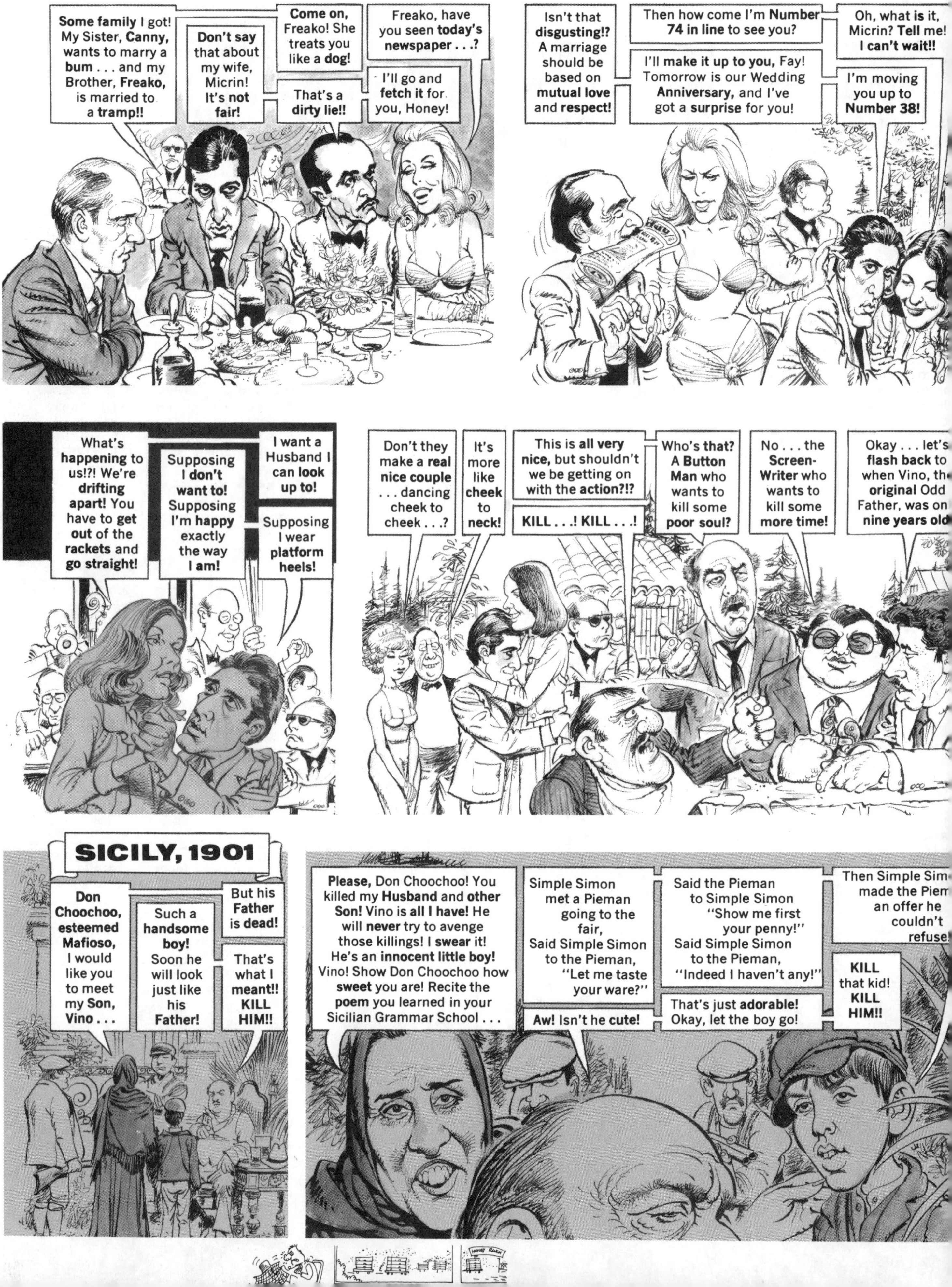
Some family I got! My Sister, Canny, wants to marry a bum . . . and my Brother, Freako, is married to a tramp!!
Don't say that about my wife, Micrin! It's not fair!
Come on, Freako! She treats you like a dog!
That's a dirty lie!!
Freako, have you seen today's newspaper . . .?
I'll go and fetch it for you, Honey!
Isn't that disgusting!? A marriage should be based on mutual love and respect!
Then how come I'm Number 74 in line to see you?
I'll make it up to you, Fay! Tomorrow is our Wedding Anniversary, and I've got a surprise for you!
Oh, what is it, Micrin? Tell me! I can't wait!!
I'm moving you up to Number 38!
What's happening to us!?! We're drifting apart! You have to get out of the rackets and go straight!
Supposing I don't want to! Supposing I'm happy exactly the way I am!
I want a Husband I can look up to!
Supposing I wear platform heels!
Don't they make a real nice couple . . . dancing cheek to cheek . . .?
It's more like cheek to neck!
This is all very nice, but shouldn't we be getting on with the action?!?
KILL . . .! KILL . . .!
Who's that? A Button Man who wants to kill some poor soul?
No . . . the Screen-Writer who wants to kill some more time!
Okay . . . let's flash back to when Vino, th original Odd Father, was on nine years old
SICILY, 1901
Don Choochoo, esteemed Mafioso, I would like you to meet my Son, Vino . . .
Such a handsome boy! Soon he will look just like his Father!
But his Father is dead!
That's what I meant!! KILL HIM!!
Please, Don Choochoo! You killed my Husband and other Son! Vino is all I have! He will never try to avenge those killings! I swear it! He's an innocent little boy! Vino! Show Don Choochoo how sweet you are! Recite the poem you learned in your Sicilian Grammar School . . .
Simple Simon met a Pieman going to the fair, Said Simple Simon to the Pieman, "Let me taste your ware?"
Aw! Isn't he cute!
Said the Pieman to Simple Simon "Show me first your penny!" Said Simple Simon to the Pieman, "Indeed I haven't any!"
That's just adorable! Okay, let the boy go!
Then Simple Sim made the Piem an offer he couldn't refuse!
KILL that kid! KILL HIM!!

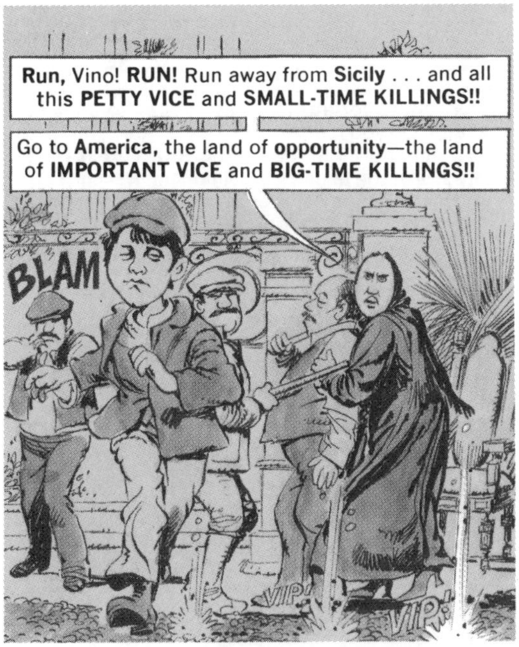
Run, Vino! RUN! Run away from Sicily . . . and all this PETTY VICE and SMALL-TIME KILLINGS!!
Go to America, the land of opportunity—the land of IMPORTANT VICE and BIG-TIME KILLINGS!!
BLAM
VIP
VIP
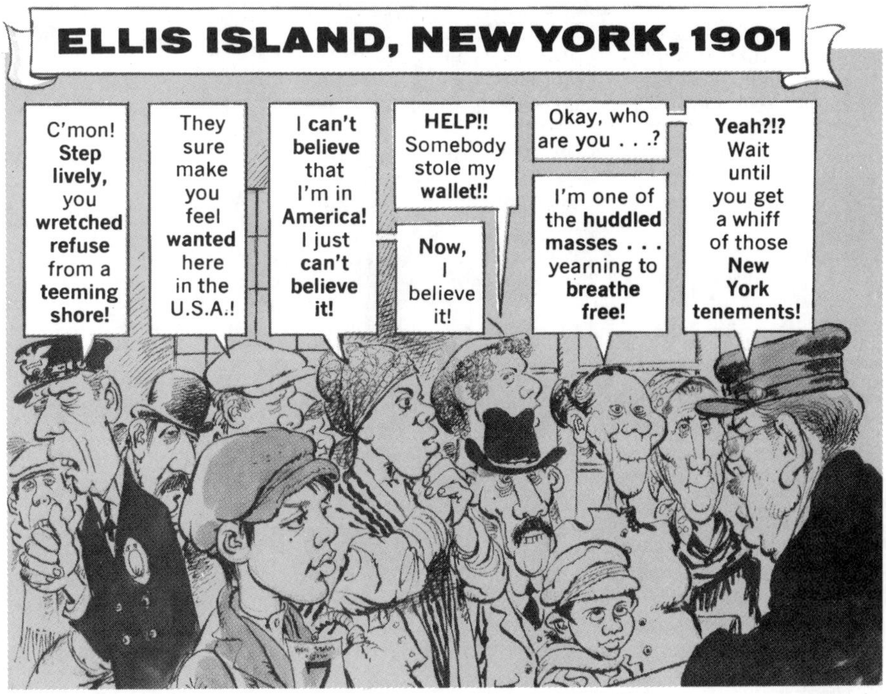
ELLIS ISLAND, NEW YORK, 1901
C'mon! Step lively, you wretched refuse from a teeming shore!
They sure make you feel wanted here in the U.S.A.!
I can't believe that I'm in America! I just can't believe it!
HELP!! Somebody stole my wallet!!
Now, I believe it!
Okay, who are you . . .?
I'm one of the huddled masses . . . yearning to breathe free!
Yeah?!? Wait until you get a whiff of those New York tenements!
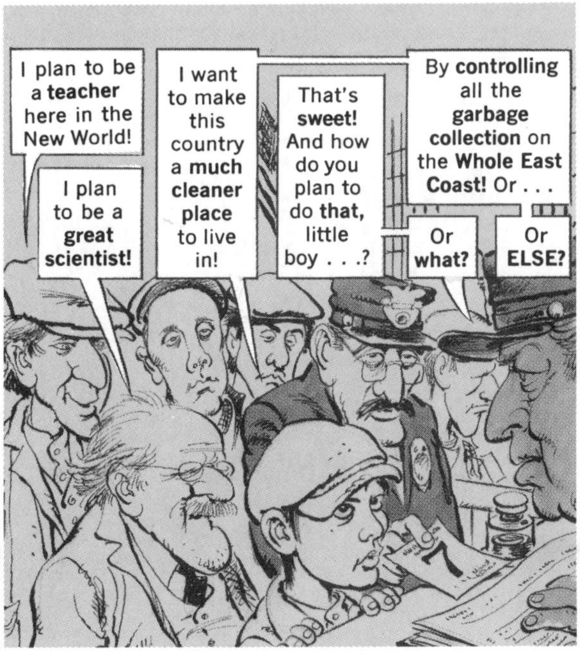
I plan to be a teacher here in the New World!
I plan to be a great scientist!
I want to make this country a much cleaner place to live in!
That's sweet! And how do you plan to do that, little boy . . .?
By controlling all the garbage collection on the Whole East Coast! Or . . .
Or what?
Or ELSE?
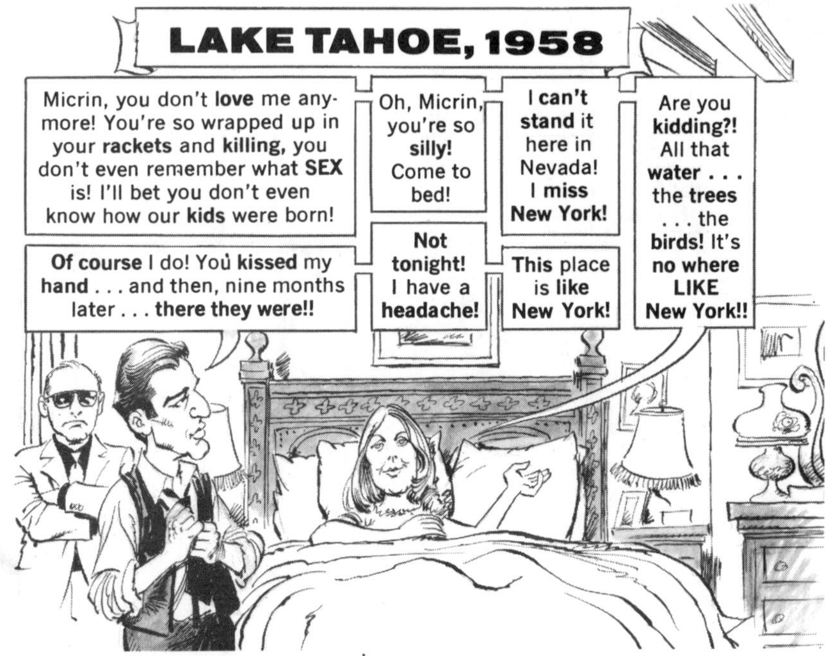
LAKE TAHOE, 1958
Micrin, you don't love me any-more! You're so wrapped up in your rackets and killing, you don't even remember what SEX is! I'll bet you don't even know how our kids were born!
Of course I do! You kissed my hand . . . and then, nine months later . . . there they were!!
Oh, Micrin, you're so silly! Come to bed!
Not tonight! I have a headache!
I can't stand it here in Nevada! I miss New York!
This place is like New York!
Are you kidding?! All that water . . . the trees . . . the birds! It's no where LIKE New York!!
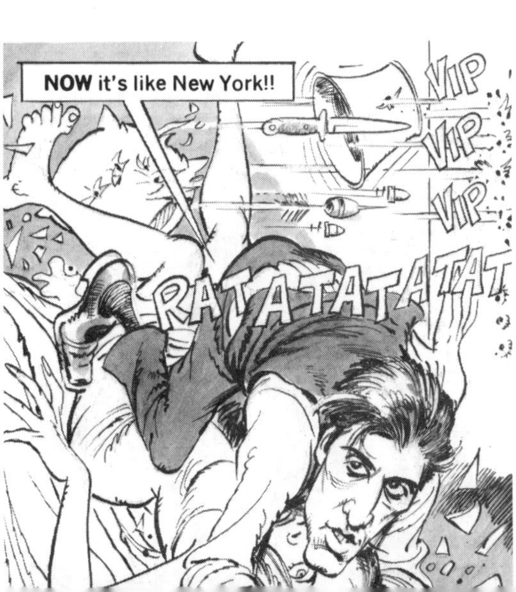
NOW it's like New York!!
VIP
VIP
VIP
RATATATATAT
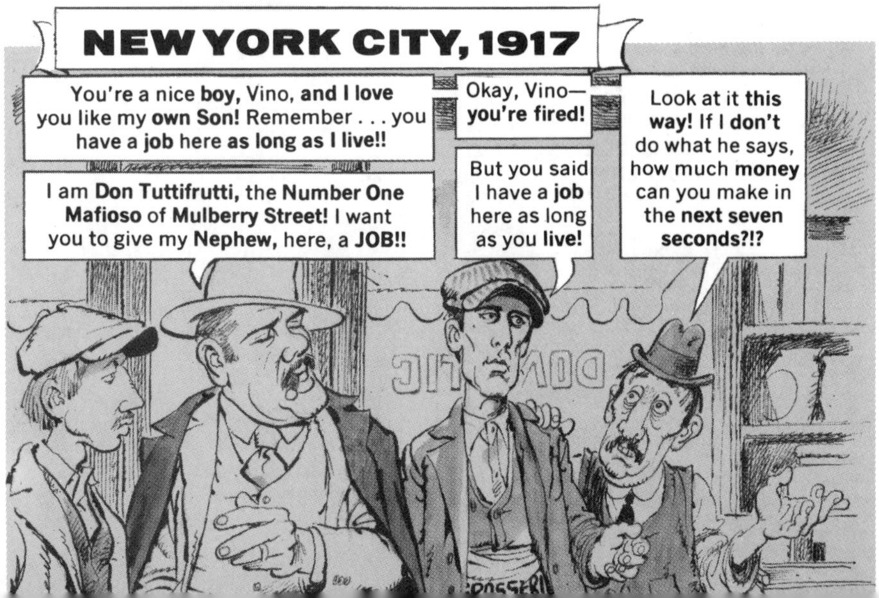
NEW YORK CITY, 1917
You're a nice boy, Vino, and I love you like my own Son! Remember . . . you have a job here as long as I live!!
I am Don Tuttifrutti, the Number One Mafioso of Mulberry Street! I want you to give my Nephew, here, a JOB!!
Okay, Vino—you're fired!
But you said I have a job here as long as you live!
Look at it this way! If I don't do what he says, how much money can you make in the next seven seconds?!?

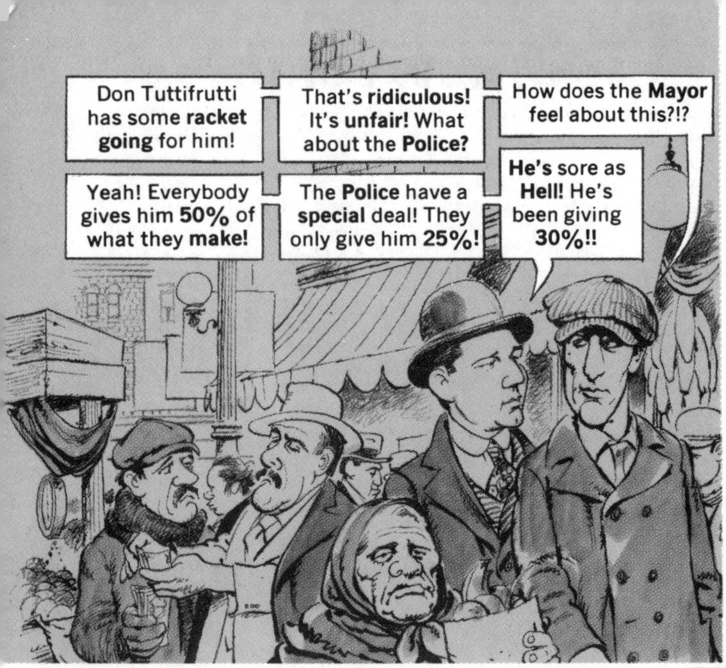
Don Tuttifrutti has some racket going for him!
Yeah! Everybody gives him 50% of what they make!
That's ridiculous! It's unfair! What about the Police?
The Police have a special deal! They only give him 25%!
How does the Mayor feel about this?!?
He's sore as Hell! He's been giving 30%!!

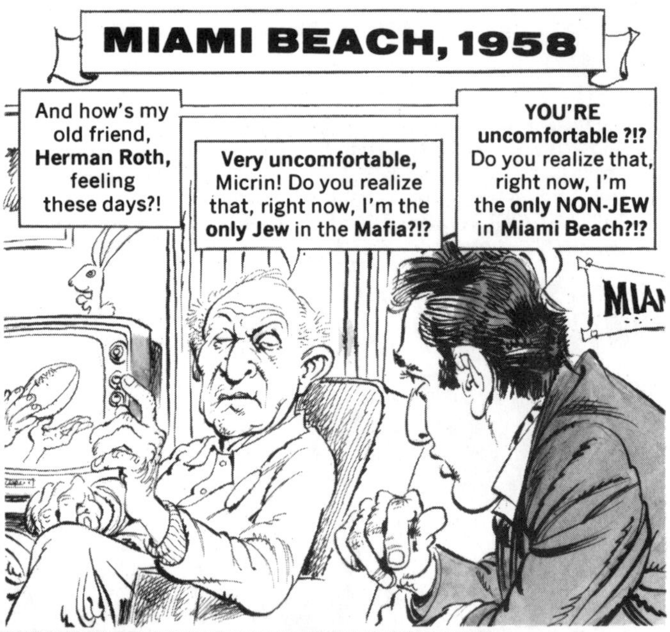
MIAMI BEACH, 1958
And how's my old friend, Herman Roth, feeling these days?!
Very uncomfortable, Micrin! Do you realize that, right now, I'm the only Jew in the Mafia?!?
YOU'RE uncomfortable ?!? Do you realize that, right now, I'm the only NON-JEW in Miami Beach?!?

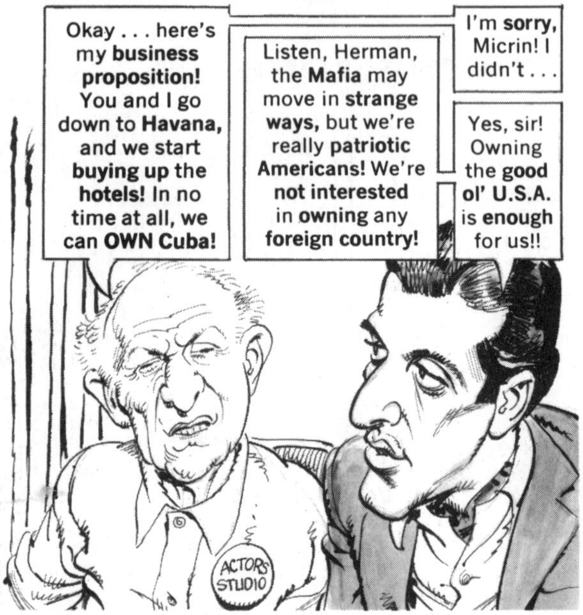
Okay . . . here's my business proposition! You and I go down to Havana, and we start buying up the hotels! In no time at all, we can OWN Cuba!
Listen, Herman, the Mafia may move in strange ways, but we're really patriotic Americans! We're not interested in owning any foreign country!
I'm sorry, Micrin! I didn't . . .
Yes, sir! Owning the good ol' U.S.A. is enough for us!!
ACTORS STUDIO

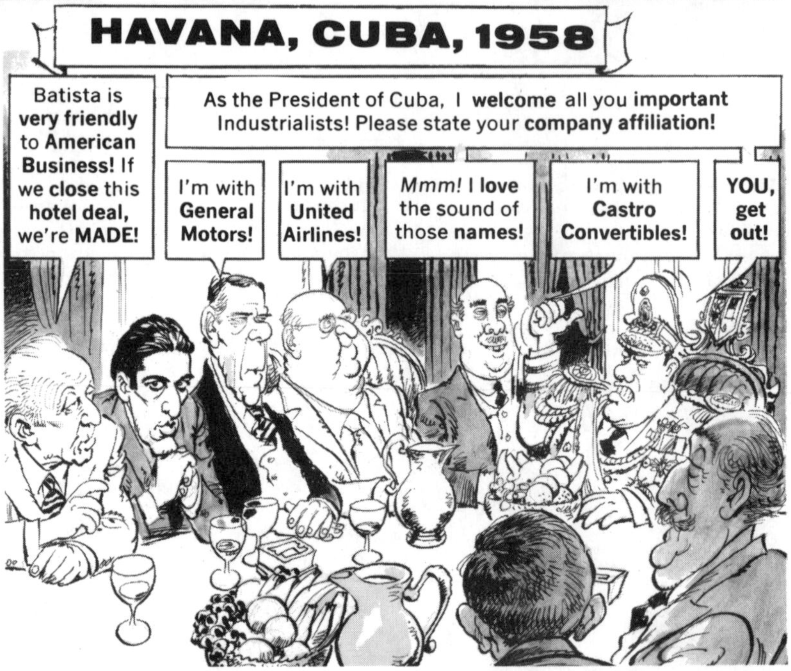
HAVANA, CUBA, 1958
Batista is very friendly to American Business! If we close this hotel deal, we're MADE!
As the President of Cuba, I welcome all you important Industrialists! Please state your company affiliation!
I'm with General Motors!
I'm with United Airlines!
Mmm! I love the sound of those names!
I'm with Castro Convertibles!
YOU, get out!

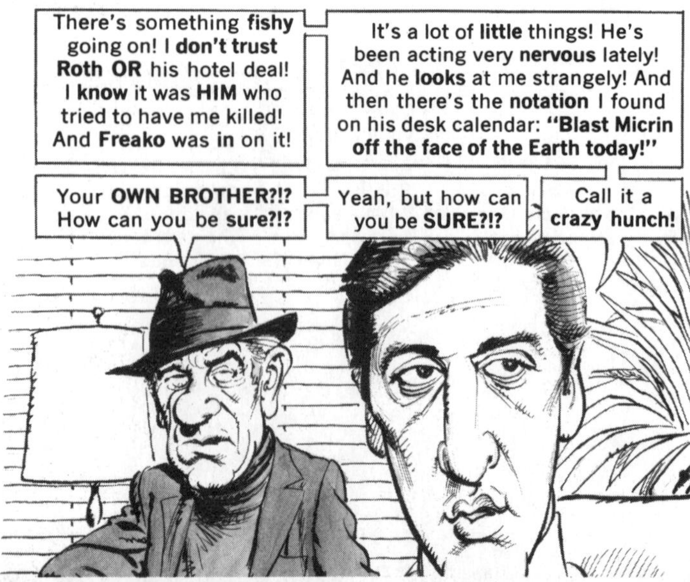
There's something fishy going on! I don't trust Roth OR his hotel deal! I know it was HIM who tried to have me killed! And Freako was in on it!
It's a lot of little things! He's been acting very nervous lately! And he looks at me strangely! And then there's the notation I found on his desk calendar: "Blast Micrin off the face of the Earth today!"
Your OWN BROTHER?!? How can you be sure?!?
Yeah, but how can you be SURE?!?
Call it a crazy hunch!

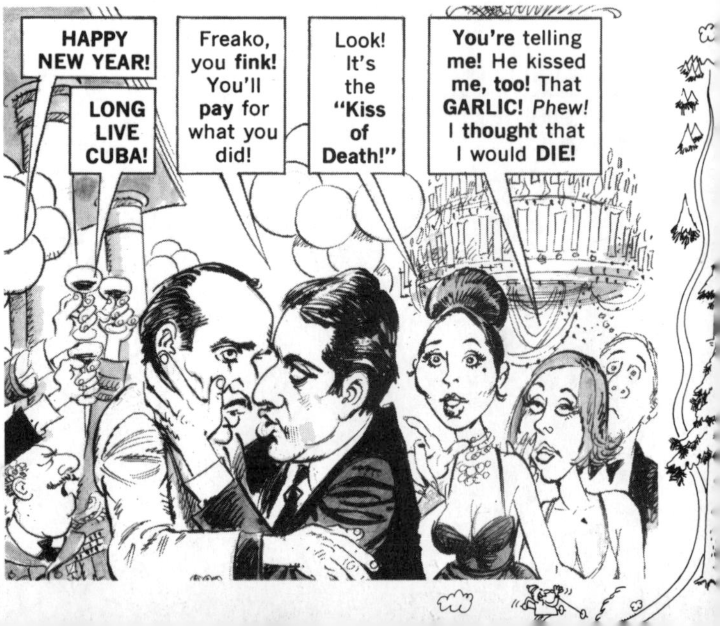
HAPPY NEW YEAR!
LONG LIVE CUBA!
Freako, you fink! You'll pay for what you did!
Look! It's the "Kiss of Death!"
You're telling me! He kissed me, too! That GARLIC! Phew! I thought that I would DIE!

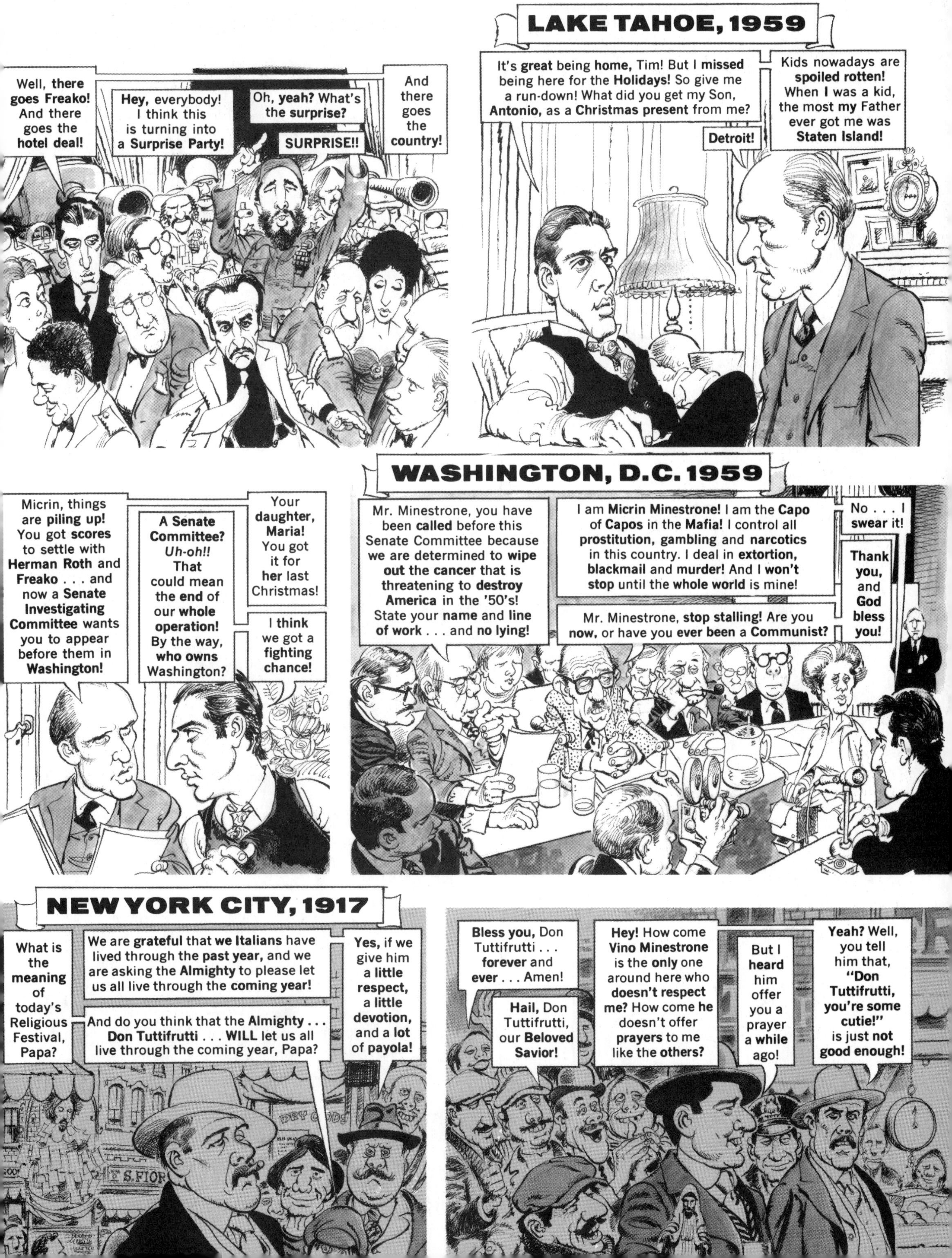
Well, there goes Freako! And there goes the hotel deal!
Hey, everybody! I think this is turning into a Surprise Party!
Oh, yeah? What's the surprise?
SURPRISE!!
And there goes the country!
LAKE TAHOE, 1959
It's great being home, Tim! But I missed being here for the Holidays! So give me a run-down! What did you get my Son, Antonio, as a Christmas present from me?
Detroit!
Kids nowadays are spoiled rotten! When I was a kid, the most my Father ever got me was Staten Island!
Micrin, things are piling up! You got scores to settle with Herman Roth and Freako . . . and now a Senate Investigating Committee wants you to appear before them in Washington!
A Senate Committee? Uh-oh!! That could mean the end of our whole operation! By the way, who owns Washington?
Your daughter, Maria! You got it for her last Christmas!
I think we got a fighting chance!
WASHINGTON, D.C. 1959
Mr. Minestrone, you have been called before this Senate Committee because we are determined to wipe out the cancer that is threatening to destroy America in the '50's! State your name and line of work . . . and no lying!
I am Micrin Minestrone! I am the Capo of Capos in the Mafia! I control all prostitution, gambling and narcotics in this country. I deal in extortion, blackmail and murder! And I won't stop until the whole world is mine!
Mr. Minestrone, stop stalling! Are you now, or have you ever been a Communist?
No . . . I swear it!
Thank you, and God bless you!
NEW YORK CITY, 1917
What is the meaning of today's Religious Festival, Papa?
We are grateful that we Italians have lived through the past year, and we are asking the Almighty to please let us all live through the coming year!
And do you think that the Almighty . . . Don Tuttifrutti . . . WILL let us all live through the coming year, Papa?
Yes, if we give him a little respect, a little devotion, and a lot of payola!
Bless you, Don Tuttifrutti . . . forever and ever . . . Amen!
Hail, Don Tuttifrutti, our Beloved Savior!
Hey! How come Vino Minestrone is the only one around here who doesn't respect me? How come he doesn't offer prayers to me like the others?
But I heard him offer you a prayer a while ago!
Yeah? Well, you tell him that, "Don Tuttifrutti, you're some cutie!" is just not good enough!

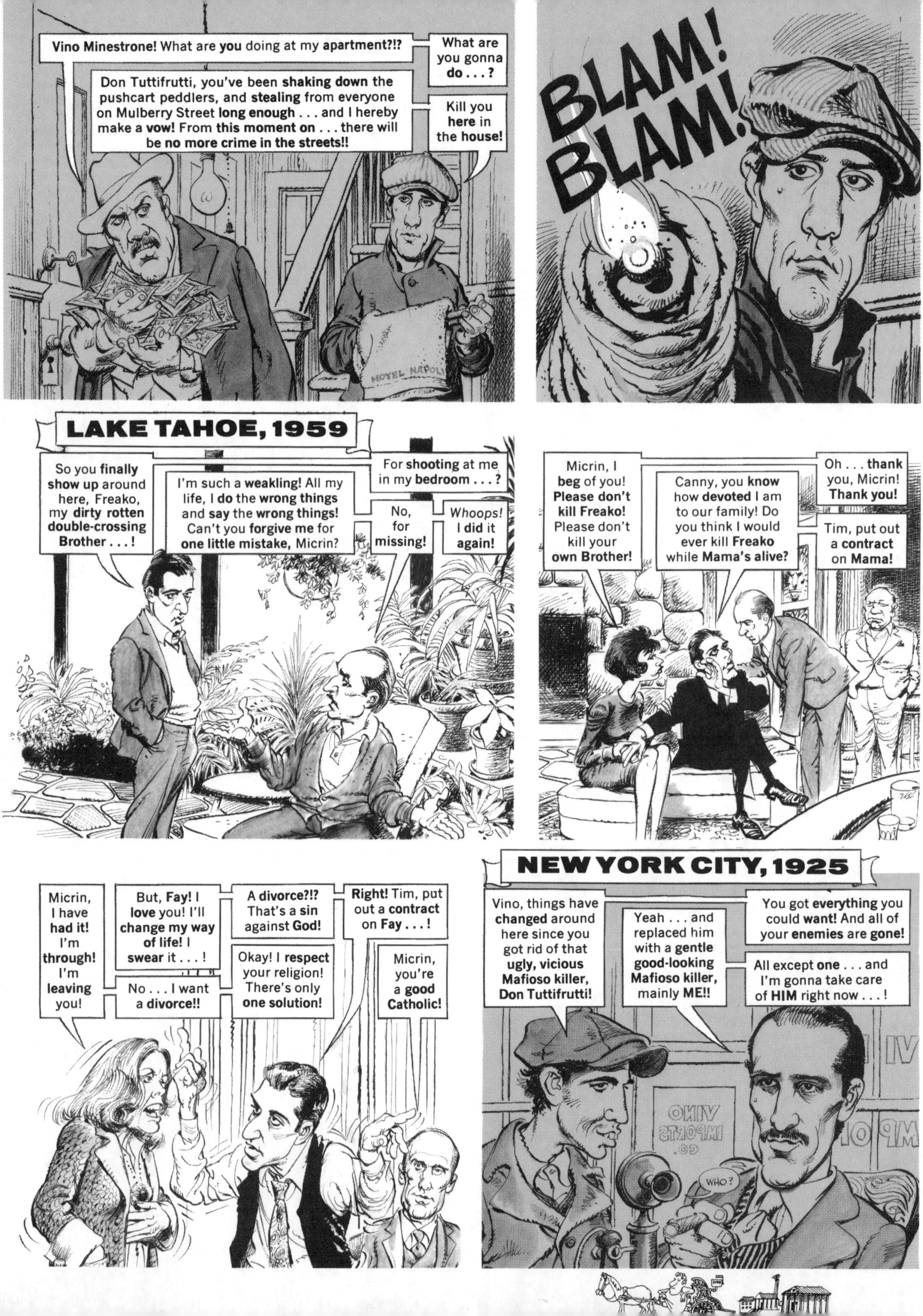
Vino Minestrone! What are you doing at my apartment?!?
Don Tuttifrutti, you've been shaking down the pushcart peddlers, and stealing from everyone on Mulberry Street long enough . . . and I hereby make a vow! From this moment on . . . there will be no more crime in the streets!!
What are you gonna do . . . ?
Kill you here in the house!
HOTEL NAPOLI
BLAM! BLAM!
LAKE TAHOE, 1959
So you finally show up around here, Freako, my dirty rotten double-crossing Brother . . . !
I'm such a weakling! All my life, I do the wrong things and say the wrong things! Can't you forgive me for one little mistake, Micrin?
For shooting at me in my bedroom . . . ?
No, for missing!
Whoops! I did it again!
Micrin, I beg of you! Please don't kill Freako! Please don't kill your own Brother!
Canny, you know how devoted I am to our family! Do you think I would ever kill Freako while Mama's alive?
Oh . . . thank you, Micrin! Thank you!
Tim, put out a contract on Mama!
Micrin, I have had it! I'm through! I'm leaving you!
But, Fay! I love you! I'll change my way of life! I swear it . . . !
No . . . I want a divorce!!
A divorce?!? That's a sin against God!
Okay! I respect your religion! There's only one solution!
Right! Tim, put out a contract on Fay . . . !
Micrin, you're a good Catholic!
NEW YORK CITY, 1925
Vino, things have changed around here since you got rid of that ugly, vicious Mafioso killer, Don Tuttifrutti!
Yeah . . . and replaced him with a gentle good-looking Mafioso killer, mainly ME!!
You got everything you could want! And all of your enemies are gone!
All except one . . . and I'm gonna take care of HIM right now . . . !
WHO?

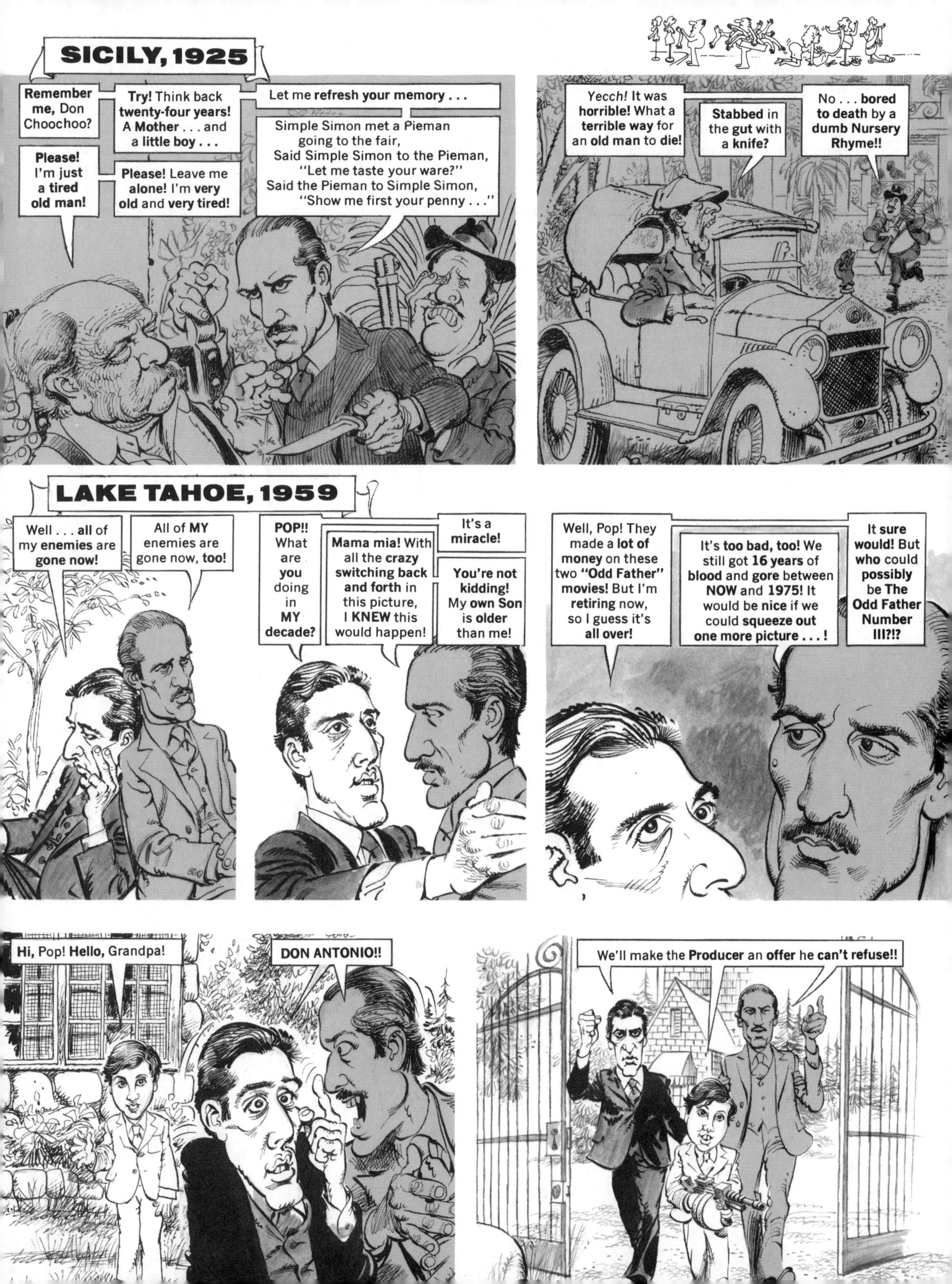
SICILY, 1925
Remember me, Don Choochoo?
Please! I'm just a tired old man!
Try! Think back twenty-four years! A Mother . . . and a little boy . . .
Please! Leave me alone! I'm very old and very tired!
Let me refresh your memory . . .
Simple Simon met a Pieman going to the fair, Said Simple Simon to the Pieman, "Let me taste your ware?" Said the Pieman to Simple Simon, "Show me first your penny . . ."
Yecch! It was horrible! What a terrible way for an old man to die!
Stabbed in the gut with a knife?
No . . . bored to death by a dumb Nursery Rhyme!!
LAKE TAHOE, 1959
Well . . . all of my enemies are gone now!
All of MY enemies are gone now, too!
POP!! What are you doing in MY decade?
Mama mia! With all the crazy switching back and forth in this picture, I KNEW this would happen!
It's a miracle!
You're not kidding! My own Son is older than me!
Well, Pop! They made a lot of money on these two "Odd Father" movies! But I'm retiring now, so I guess it's all over!
It's too bad, too! We still got 16 years of blood and gore between NOW and 1975! It would be nice if we could squeeze out one more picture . . . !
It sure would! But who could possibly be The Odd Father Number III?!?
Hi, Pop! Hello, Grandpa!
DON ANTONIO!!
We'll make the Producer an offer he can't refuse!!

"WHERE'S THE THIEF?" DEPT.

The phone company urges us to avoid shopper's nerves and aching feet by letting our fingers do the walking through the Yellow Pages. That seems like a reasonable suggestion. But suppose the business we need to transact is a bit illegal, like engaging a hit man to blow away a rich uncle. People offering such services don't advertise, or even hang out signs. The only way to locate a gunman for hire is by asking around, which can lead to all sorts of complications. It's a sad truth of our times that no one can find a crook easily except another crook. What is clearly needed is a means of putting the average citizen in touch with his neighborhood bookie, arsonist or all-purpose hoodlum. In MAD's opinion, what works for legitimate business should work equally well in the realm of the illegit, which leads us to conjure up this vision of...

THE CRIMINALS' YELLOW PAGES

ARTIST: GEORGE WOODBRIDGE

WRITER: TOM KOCH

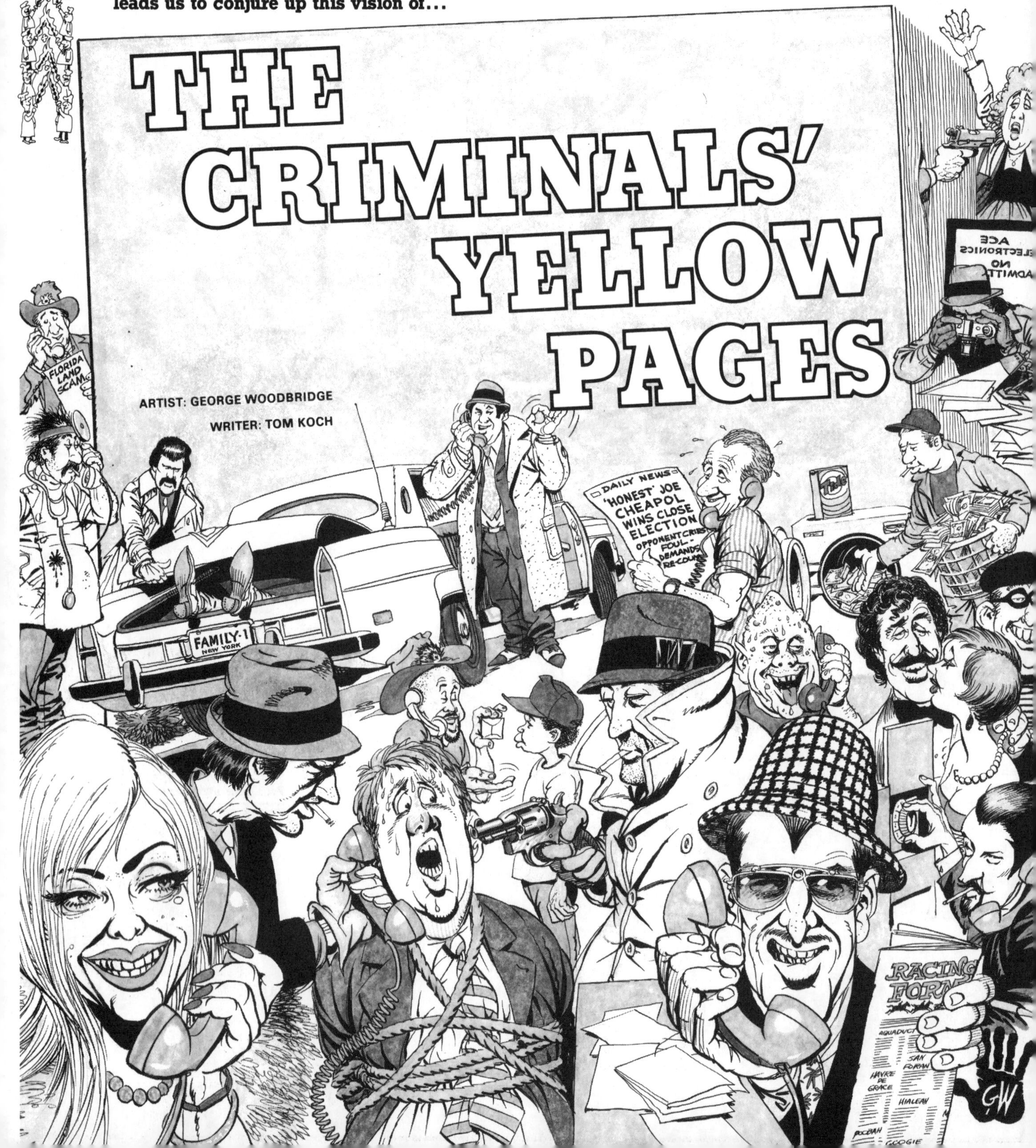
FLORIDA LAND SCAM
DAILY NEWS
'HONEST' JOE CHEAPOL WINS CLOSE ELECTION
OPPONENT CRIES FOUL- DEMANDS RE-COUN
FAMILY-1 NEW YORK
RACING FORM
AQUADUCT
HAVRE DE GRACE
HIALEAH
GOOGIE
GW

▶ Accountants—Crooked

FITTERMAN, "FOUR EYES"

EMBEZZLEMENTS COVERED UP
LEDGERS BURNED
DIRTY MONEY LAUNDERED

"Serving The Financial Needs Of The Underworld's Top Scum Since 1957."

2157 E. Fiduciary . **BO**okjuggle 2148

▶ Arsonists

FIREBUGS ANONYMOUS

Why Pay A Professional Torch To Set Your Blaze When Our Psychopaths Will Do It For Kicks?

1449 N. Flamegiggle **BU**rnbaby 1313

IMPRUDENTIAL FIRE INSURANCE COLLECTION CO.

ROCKY UMBUFSKY, PROP.
Just Call And Say,
"I Want To Buy A Piece Of The Rock."

728 Gasoline Alley **SM**okybear 9904

▶ Bookmakers

BIG NATHAN'S BARBER SHOP

3 CHAIRS - 7 BOOKIES - NO WAITING
We're Open From 9-to-5 Paying Off At 5-to-2

7829 E. Pimlico . **PO**intspread 8829

CITY HALL LOBBY CIGAR STAND

Football Pools - Baseball Bets - Basketball Parlays
(Sometimes We Even Sell Cigars)

City Hall, Law & Order Plaza . . . . **HI**ghroller 1021

▶ Bootleggers

MAFIOSO LIQUOR DISTRIBUTORS

We Specialize In The Sale Of Sickening Booze To Minors.
Call For Location Of A School Playground Retailer Near You.

Capone Memorial Bldg. . . . . **GO**dfather 8800

HIDDEN VALLEY DISTILLERS

HIGH POWERED MOONSHINE
AT ROCK BOTTOM PRICES

★Old Shopsmell Varnish Remover
★White Lightning Barrel Dregs
★150-Proof Antifreeze
Order A Case And Paralyze Your Whole Family

Box 14,
Petrified Forest . . . **RO**tgut 4420

▶ Bribery—Offered & Accepted

Abscam Associates
Congressional
Office Bldg . . . . **BI**gbucks 4147

ARNOLD THE ARRANGER

LET ME HELP YOU BUY AS MANY LEGISLATORS, COPS OR BUILDING INSPECTORS AS YOUR SITUATION REQUIRES.

Wholesale Rates For Bribes By The Dozen

We Accept Unmarked Cash, Gold Bullion Or Mastercharge

1816A Watergate
Towers . . . . **WH**eelerdealer 5656

Benchwarmer, Judge Uriah L.
Hall of Justice . . . . . **NO**oseknot 2133

(See My Display Ad This Page)

▶ Charities—Phony

FRAIL ORPHANS' SUMMER CAMP FUND

Donate $50 To Our Unscrupulous Racket, And We'll Give You A Receipt For $200 To Show The I.R.S.

Office—166 N. Fasttalk,
Room 304 . . . **SI**lvertongue 6399
Summer Camp—166 N. Fasttalk,
Room 304 Closet
SIlvertongue 8721

▶ Cops On The Take

DRUMMOND, SGT. TOPDOG—CHICAGO P.D.

6827 N. Lake Shore Drive,
Chicago . Toll Free 1-800-555-6820

NINTH PRECINCT NIGHT SHIFT

Ask About Our Low Fees For
★Fixing Traffic Tickets
★Losing Search Warrants
★Ignoring Felonies

Stationhouse
Basement . . . . . . **BU**mfuzz 1888

▶ Counterfeiters

Collector's Item Counterfeiting Co.
217 W. Sotheby . . . . . **FA**kemore 0111

(See Our Display Ad This Page)

DAVE'S DISCOUNT CURRENCY CO.

Stretch Your Weekly Paycheck By Trading It For Our Bargain Priced Funny Money

3371 N. Printers
Row . . . . **SA**wbuck 0771

▶ Delinquents—Adult

UNTERMEYER, MAD DOG

NOW ACCEPTING ASSIGNMENTS FOR 1993 WHEN I'LL BE BACK OUT ON THE STREETS

Cell Block J,
San Quentin . . . **SL**ammer 9662

(If The Warden Answers, Hang Up!)

Whip & Chain Motorcycle Club
642 N. Sadism. . . . . **CR**ossbones 1414

DON'T RISK DOING HARD TIME!

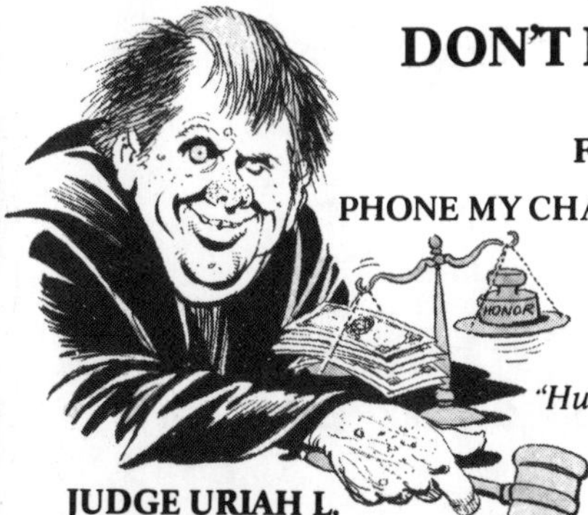
HONOR

Buy A Criminal Court Judge For Less Than You Might Think!

PHONE MY CHAMBERS FOR CURRENT BRIBERY RATES ON
–Plea Copping
–Mistrials
–Case Dismissals
–Outright Acquittals

"Hundreds Of Guilty Satisfied Customers Roaming The Streets Today"

HALL OF JUSTICE (Ha-ha)
NOOSEKNOT 2133

JUDGE URIAH L. BENCHWARMER

Vicious Vinnie Says:
"TAKE CARE OF ALL THOSE MONTHLY BILLS WITH ONE CONVENIENT DAILY PAYMENT."

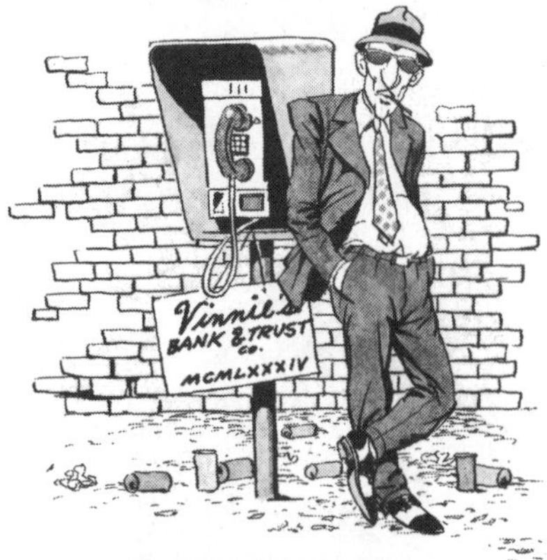
Vinnie's
BANK & TRUST CO.
MCMLXXXIV

No Credit Investigations
No Salary Garnishments
No Broken Bones (If You Pay By 6 P.M.)

VINNIE'S BANK & TRUST CO.

PHONE
VIgorish 0017

CALL NOW!
(But Only If You're Too Desperate To Ask How Much I Charge.)

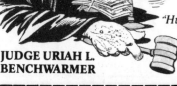

▶ Delinquents—Juvenile

MANGLER MULEBOCK & ASSOCIATES

Don't Try Beating Up The Playground Bully Alone!
Hire A Mob Of First Rate Punks To Help You!

5166 N. Vicious Circle . . . . **BO**necrunch 0192

Umbridge, Mervin (The Ox), 2119 W. Temperfit . . . **BI**gbruiser 5842

▶ Disguises—Temporary & Permanent

GRINDER, DR. BORIS (FORMERLY LICENSED M.D.)

PLASTIC SURGERY FOR THE HUNTED
I Turned Ma Barker Into Leonard Nimoy,
And I Can Work Similar Miracles For You.

3427 N. Skingraft **BL**oodspurt 0442

▶ Extortionists

WILFRED THE WEASEL

I'LL KEEP MY MOUTH SHUT ABOUT YOU
FOR AS LITTLE AS $10 A WEEK!
BUY PEACE OF MIND NOW.

Mrs. Rumsey's Rooming House . **TR**ueflake 4468

▶ Forgery

RUDY'S HOUSE OF REPLICAS

YOUR HEADQUARTERS FOR AUTHENTIC LOOKING
DRIVER'S LICENSES, PASSPORTS & DIPLOMAS
Also Overnight Service On Art Masterpiece Reproduction Orders

4804 N. Inkstain . . . **CO**pycat 9932

▶ Getaway Cars—Rental & Drivers

MAVIS RENT-A-CHASE

We're All Parole Violators,
So We Drive Faster!

5116 E. Tiresqueal . . . . . **IN**dy 0082

WHITEY THE WHEELMAN

NO CAPER IS SUCCESSFUL IF YOU CAN'T LEAVE THE SCENE
Unbeatable Buicks Untraceable License Plates

707 W. Vroooooom . . **LE**adfoot 8791

▶ Hijackers

Cooper, D.B., Guess Where! . . . . . **HI**ghjumper 0655

THRILLING TRAVEL TOURS, UNINC.

Make Your Next Vacation An Exciting "Holiday At Gunpoint."
Regular Hijackings To Cuba, Libya & Dallas-Fort Worth.

414 N. Jetsetter . . . . . **BO**eing 0707

▶ Killers—Hired

MR. DAVE OF DETROIT

I SPECIALIZE IN SPOUSE ELIMINATION
& BUSINESS COMPETITOR DISPOSAL
"A Solution To Your Problem
Is Only A Phone Call Away."

Ask-No-Questions Hotel . . . . **BL**owaway 2284

▶ Killers—Pathological

LUMBUFSKY, LOONY LEONARD

If Your Intended Victim Is A Woman Over Fifty Who Whines,
Then She'll Remind Me Of My Mother, And I'll Gladly Knock Her Off.

Attic over 316 W. 28th St. . **DI**ngaling 1130

Ralph The Ripper, 352 W. Fogbound Walk . . . . **EV**ersharp 8849

(See My Display Ad This Page)

▶ Loan Sharks

Vinnie's Bank & Trust Co., P.O. Box 5186 . . . . **VI**gorish 0017

(See My Display Ad This Page)

ARNOLD'S ARSENAL
YOUR HEADQUARTERS FOR FIREPOWER

Low Prices On Good Used Artillery From

Captured	Bankrupt	Retired
Guerrillas	Countries	Terrorists

Whether You're Planning A Stick-up Or Invading El Salvador, Cannons Speak Louder Than Saturday Night Specials.

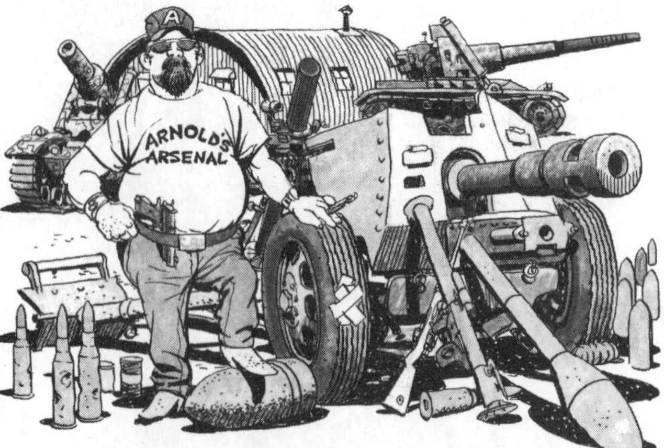
ARNOLD'S ARSENAL

ARNOLD'S ARSENAL
402 N. Kaboooooom **HO**witzer 6628

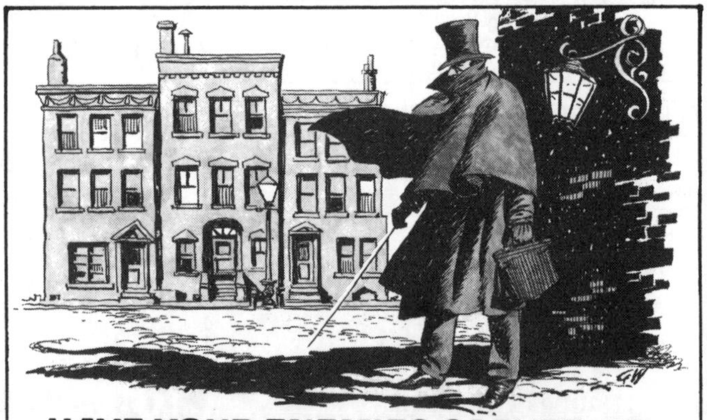

HAVE YOUR ENEMIES CARVED UP BY A FULL SERVICE LUNATIC

Simple Slashings
Or Total Dismemberment

• • •

Ominous Footsteps
And Maniacal Drooling

• • •

Special Discount
During Full Moon

RALPH THE RIPPER
352 W. Fogbound Walk **EV**ersharp 8849

▶ **Merchandise—Hot**

APEX TV, FUR, JEWELRY & SMALL APPLIANCE CO.

Helping You Keep Up With The Joneses By Selling You What We Stole From The Joneses

Pier 14
Warehouse . . . **DO**orjimmy 5507

DRIVE-BY-NIGHT AUTO SALES

SLIGHTLY USED CARS
WITH BRAND NEW SERIAL NUMBERS

Garage Behind 5816
Southwest Hwy . . **HO**twires 7228

▶ **Protection**

EAST SIDE SYNDICATE

Let Our Representative In Your Area Help You Work Out A Financial Plan To Protect Yourself Against Us.

2322 Guarded Mansion
Road . . . . **MO**bster 6631

▶ **Quack Cures**

TERMINAL SPRINGS SANITARIUM

Put A Sickly Relative In Our Steam Bath For Just Two Weeks
And Watch Your Problems Disappear.

4043 S. Unpaved
Road . . . . **GR**aveside 1163

▶ **Safecrackers**

NOODLEMAN, NIMBLE FINGERS

Blowing Up A Building To Open Its Safe Attracts Unwanted Attention.
Let Me Help You Enjoy
The Advantages Of Silent Theft.

1628 E. Tumbler **CO**mbination 61-8-44

▶ **Senseless Violence**

Army Of The 32nd Of July,
911 W. Fruitcake . . **UN**derground 0444

(See Our Ad Under "Terrorism")

▶ **Smugglers**

EXOTIC IMPORTING CO.

HARD-TO-FIND FOREIGN ITEMS
★SOUTH AFRICAN IVORY
★SOUTH AMERICAN PARROTS
★SOUTH HONDURAS BEAN PICKERS

Hidden Runway
Airport . . . . . **BO**rdersneak 3155

▶ **Telephone Bugs—Illegal**

C.I.A. VETERANS' WIRETAP SERVICE

Why Pay For Cable TV When It's More Entertaining
To Eavesdrop On Your Neighbors' Private Conversations?

1253 N.
Shady Lane . . . **DE**epthroat 4338

▶ **Telephone Calls—Obscene**

WEIRDNY, MUNGO J.

COLORFUL VOCABULARY
HEAVY BREATHING
Hire Me To Call The Girl Of Your Dreams
And Tell Her Exactly What You Have In Mind
"Se Habla Español"

1804 E. Sicko . . . . . **DI**altone 4347

▶ **Terrorism**

ARMY OF THE 32ND OF JULY

ENLIST NOW TO HELP RID THE WORLD OF WELSH MINERS, IRISH TENORS, GREEK RESTAURANTS & DALMATIAN PUPPIES
Phone For A Recorded Message About These & Others We Hate

911 W. Fruitcake **UN**derground 0444

COMMITTEE FOR A FREE NEW JERSEY

WE SPECIALIZE IN BOMBING NEWARK & TRENTON,
BUT WILL CONSIDER OUT-OF-STATE DEMOLITION.

Our Lady of
Hoboken Hall . . . . . **TU**nnelview 3185

▶ **Vandalism—Wholesale**

ANGRY AUGIE

TOPS IN TRASHING SINCE 1974

School Burnings	Subway Defacings	Home Wreckings

877 N. Brainwarp . **SL**ashpillow 0144

Disturbed Students Of P.S. 168,
Locker #2643 . . **UN**derachiever -3738

SMUTTY SPRAY PAINT SERVICE

Choose From Our Wide Selection Of Four Letter Words!
Have Your Enemy's Property Defaced This Very Night!

5177 Macho Mall . . **#&$!)$#** 2166

▶ **Weapons—Illegal**

Arnold's Arsenal,
402 N. Kabooooooom . . **HO**witzer 6628

(See Our Display Ad This Page)

MISS MELANIE'S NITROGLYCERIN BOUTIQUE

IMPORTED & DOMESTIC EXPLOSIVES
FOR THE DISCRIMINATING HOUSEWIFE
"Only TNT Destroys The Evidence
As It Destroys Your Husband"

414 S. Mayhem . . . . **SK**yhigh 2200

Next time you or your business needs to reach out and put the touch on someone, consult these Yellow Pages.

DON'T BUY EXPENSIVE OLD COINS!
LET US MAKE YOU CHEAP NEW ONES.

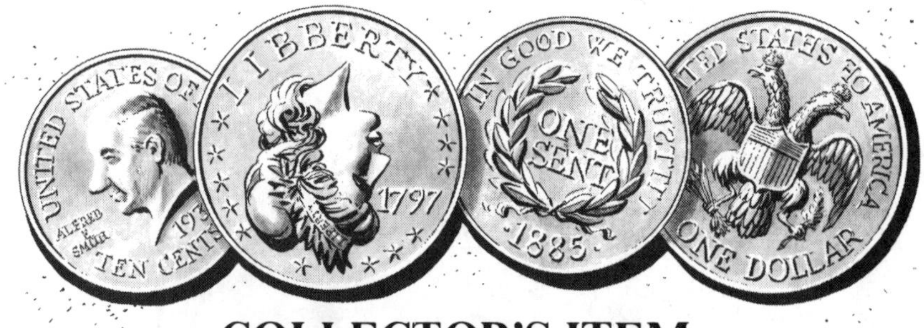
UNITED STATES OF
TEN CENTS
1797
ONE SENT
1885
ONE DOLLAR

COLLECTOR'S ITEM COUNTERFEITING CO.

UNDETECTABLE REPLICAS FOR THE HOBBYIST

★ Rare U.S. Gold, Silver & Copper
★ Even Scarcer Misprinted Currency
★ Truly Unique Postage Stamps With Errors

ORDER AS FEW AS 100 OR AS MANY AS A CARLOAD

217 W. Sotheby . . . . **FA**kemore 0111

SNORT SUBJECT DEPT.

Some time ago, a promising young film star rose to new heights portraying a brilliant Italian-American college graduate who takes over a huge criminal empire. Now, more than ten years later, this same film star sinks to new lows portraying a sick, amoral Cuban junkie who takes over another huge criminal empire. In real life, this would be called "degeneracy." In Hollywood, this is called "progress." Anyway, here's our version of–

SCAR

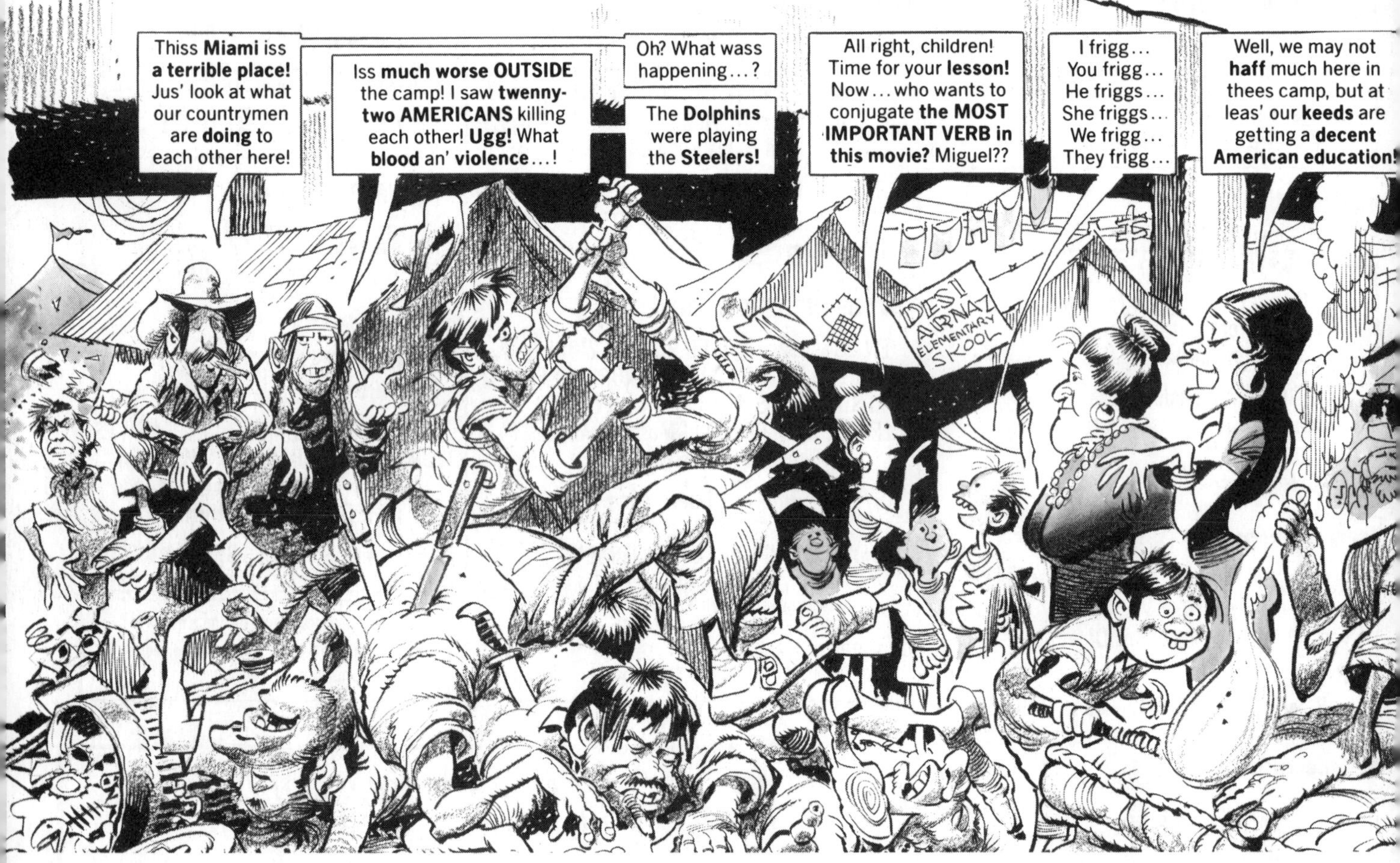

Thiss **Miami** iss **a terrible place!** Jus' look at what our countrymen are **doing** to each other here!
Iss **much worse OUTSIDE** the camp! I saw **twenny-two AMERICANS** killing each other! **Ugg!** What **blood** an' **violence**...!
Oh? What wass happening...?
The **Dolphins** were playing the **Steelers!**
All right, children! Time for your **lesson!** Now... who wants to conjugate **the MOST IMPORTANT VERB in this movie?** Miguel??
I frigg... You frigg... He friggs... She friggs... We frigg... They frigg...
Well, we may not **haff** much here in thees camp, but at leas' our **keeds** are getting a **decent American education!**
DESI ARNAZ ELEMENTARY SKOOL

ARTIST: JACK DAV

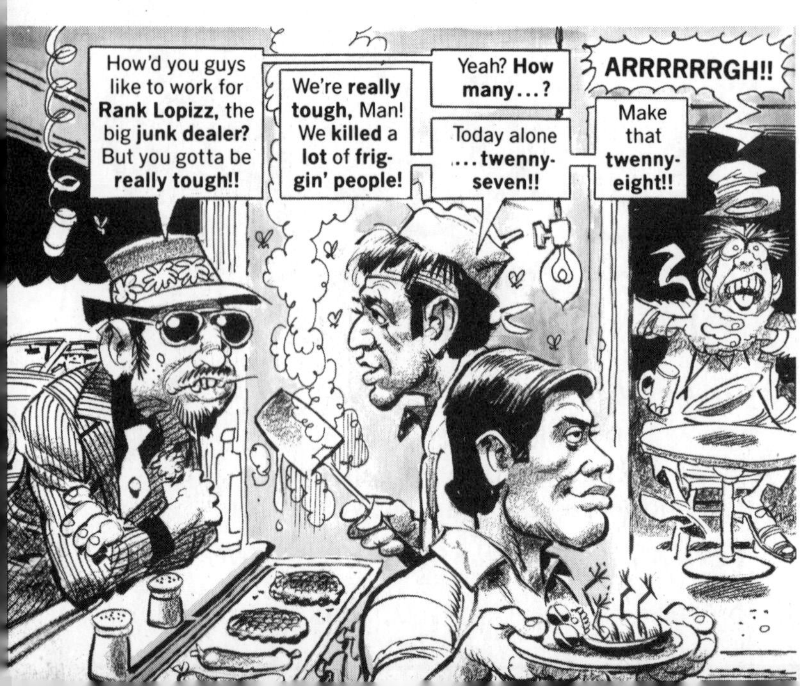

How'd you guys like to work for **Rank Lopizz,** the big **junk dealer?** But you gotta be **really tough!!**
We're **really tough,** Man! We **killed** a **lot** of **frig-gin' people!**
Yeah? **How many...?**
Today alone **....twenny-seven!!**
ARRRRRRGH!!
Make that **twenny-eight!!**

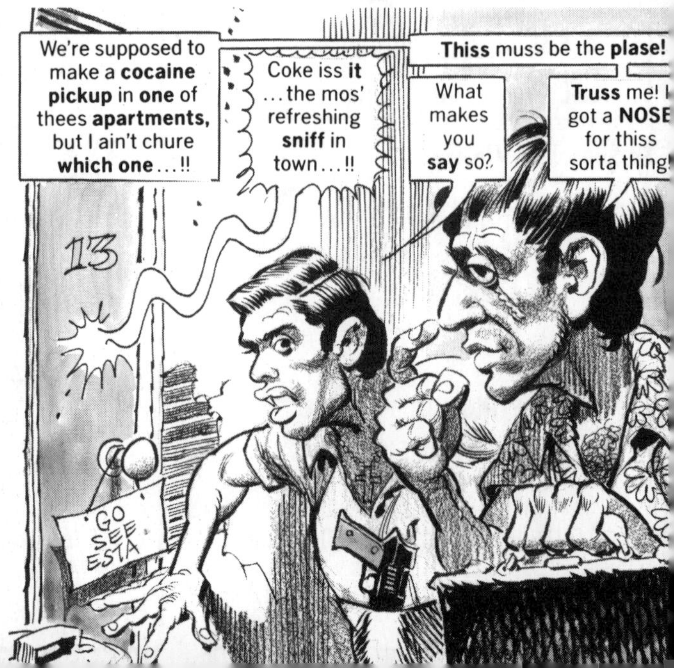

We're supposed to make a **cocaine pickup** in **one** of **thees apartments,** but I ain't chure **which one**...!!
Coke iss **it** ...the mos' refreshing **sniff** in town...!!
Thiss muss be the **plase!**
What makes you **say** so?
Truss me! I got a **NOSE** for thiss sorta thing
13
GO SEE ESTA

RED FACE

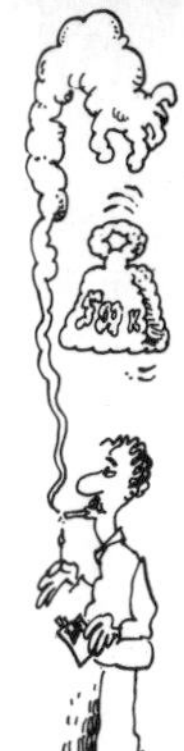

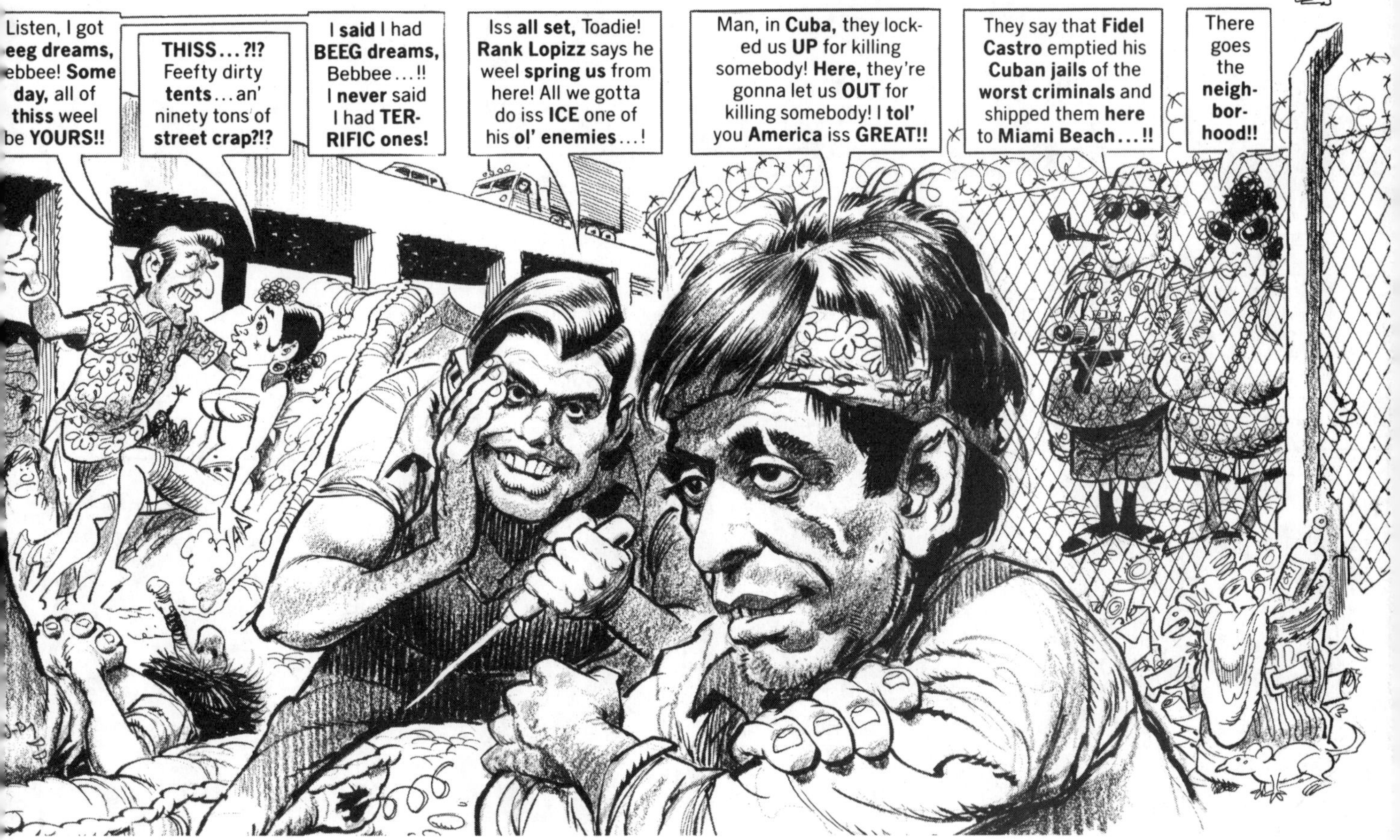

Listen, I got eeg dreams, ebbee! Some day, all of thiss weel be YOURS!!
THISS...?!? Feefty dirty tents... an' ninety tons of street crap?!?
I said I had BEEG dreams, Bebbee...!! I never said I had TERRIFIC ones!
Iss all set, Toadie! Rank Lopizz says he weel spring us from here! All we gotta do iss ICE one of his ol' enemies...!
Man, in Cuba, they locked us UP for killing somebody! Here, they're gonna let us OUT for killing somebody! I tol' you America iss GREAT!!
They say that Fidel Castro emptied his Cuban jails of the worst criminals and shipped them here to Miami Beach...!!
There goes the neighborhood!!

RITER: LARRY SIEGEL

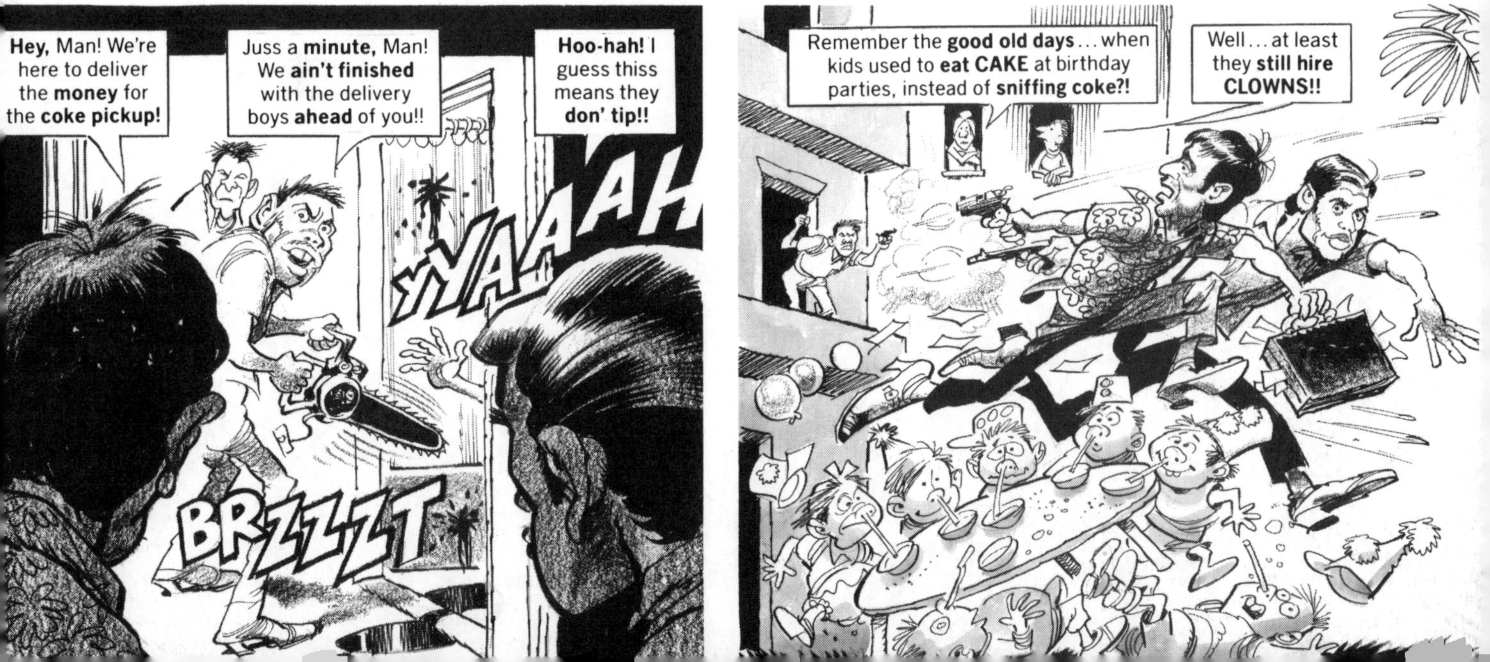

Hey, Man! We're here to deliver the money for the coke pickup!
Juss a minute, Man! We ain't finished with the delivery boys ahead of you!!
Hoo-hah! I guess thiss means they don' tip!!
YYAAAH
BRZZZT
Remember the good old days... when kids used to eat CAKE at birthday parties, instead of sniffing coke?!
Well... at least they still hire CLOWNS!!

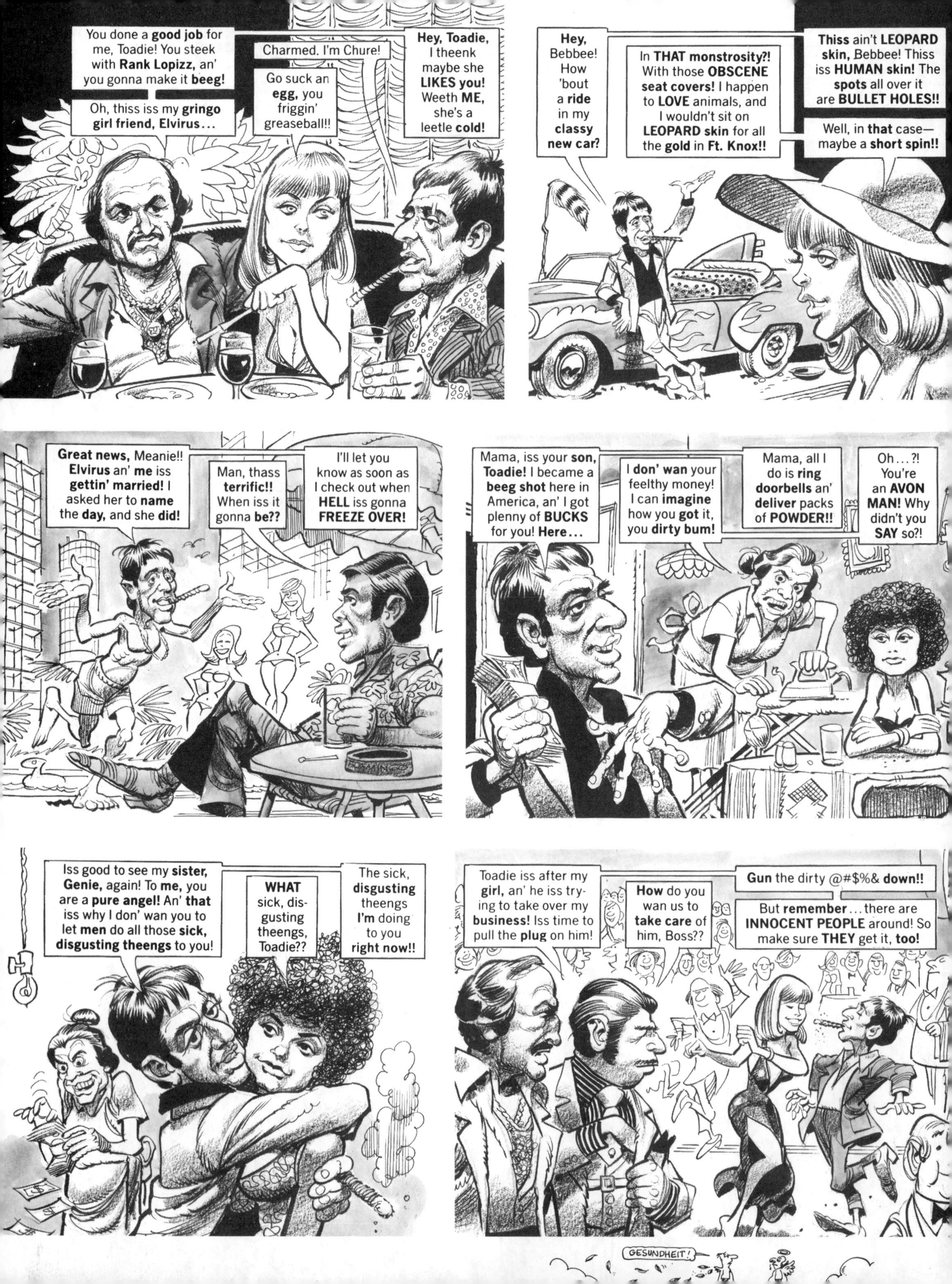
You done a good job for me, Toadie! You steek with Rank Lopizz, an' you gonna make it beeg!
Oh, thiss iss my gringo girl friend, Elvirus...
Charmed. I'm Chure!
Go suck an egg, you friggin' greaseball!!
Hey, Toadie, I theenk maybe she LIKES you! Weeth ME, she's a leetle cold!
Hey, Bebbee! How 'bout a ride in my classy new car?
In THAT monstrosity?! With those OBSCENE seat covers! I happen to LOVE animals, and I wouldn't sit on LEOPARD skin for all the gold in Ft. Knox!!
Thiss ain't LEOPARD skin, Bebbee! Thiss iss HUMAN skin! The spots all over it are BULLET HOLES!!
Well, in that case—maybe a short spin!!
Great news, Meanie!! Elvirus an' me iss gettin' married! I asked her to name the day, and she did!
Man, thass terrific!! When iss it gonna be??
I'll let you know as soon as I check out when HELL iss gonna FREEZE OVER!
Mama, iss your son, Toadie! I became a beeg shot here in America, an' I got plenny of BUCKS for you! Here...
I don' wan your feelthy money! I can imagine how you got it, you dirty bum!
Mama, all I do is ring doorbells an' deliver packs of POWDER!!
Oh...?! You're an AVON MAN! Why didn't you SAY so?!
Iss good to see my sister, Genie, again! To me, you are a pure angel! An' that iss why I don' wan you to let men do all those sick, disgusting theengs to you!
WHAT sick, disgusting theengs, Toadie??
The sick, disgusting theengs I'm doing to you right now!!
Toadie iss after my girl, an' he iss trying to take over my business! Iss time to pull the plug on him!
How do you wan us to take care of him, Boss??
Gun the dirty @#$%& down!!
But remember... there are INNOCENT PEOPLE around! So make sure THEY get it, too!
GESUNDHEIT!

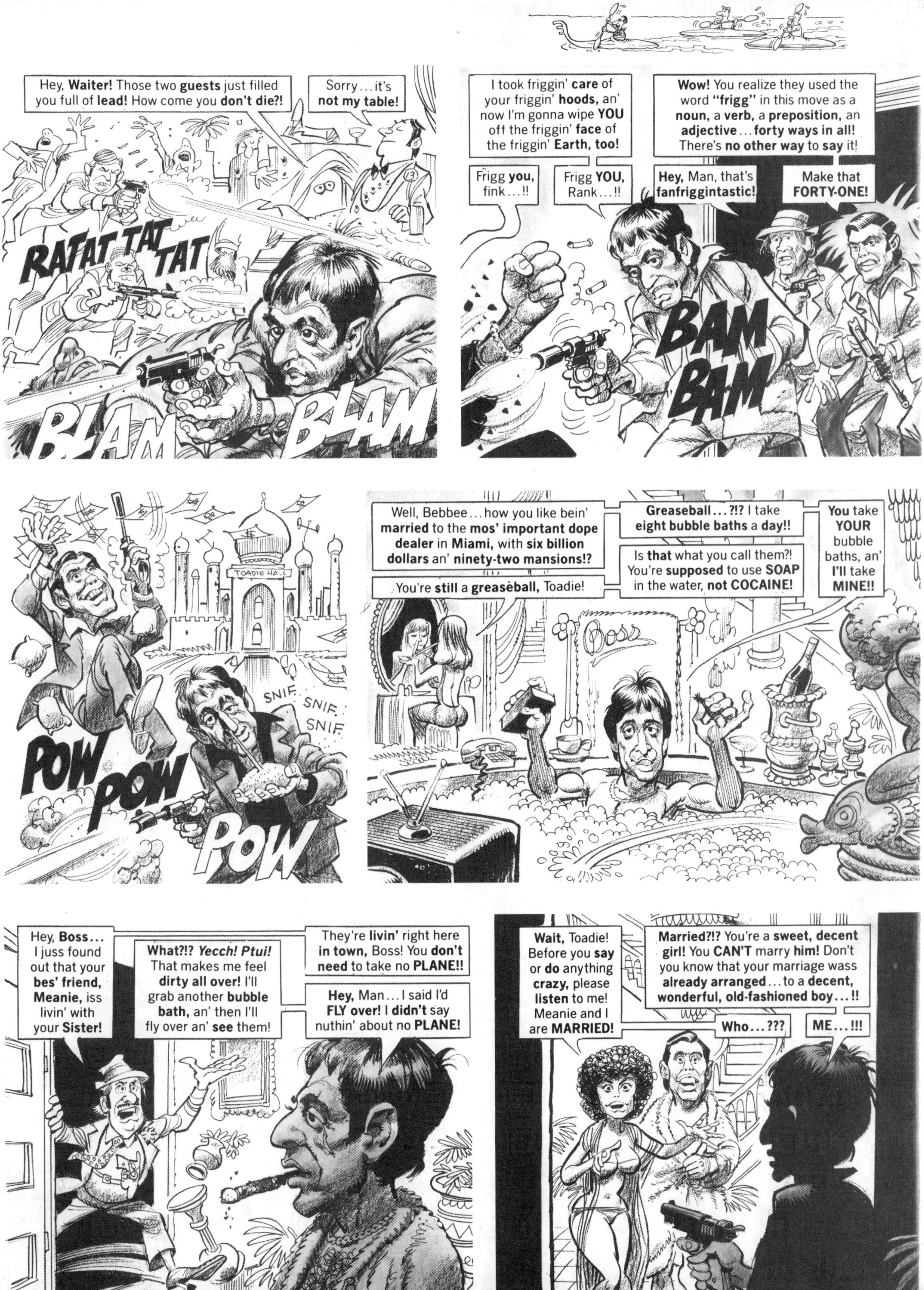

Hey, **Waiter!** Those two **guests** just filled you full of **lead!** How come you **don't die?!**
Sorry . . . it's **not my table!**
RATAT TAT TAT
BLAM BLAM
I took friggin' **care** of your friggin' **hoods,** an' now I'm gonna wipe **YOU** off the friggin' **face** of the friggin' **Earth, too!**
Frigg **you,** fink . . . !!
Frigg **YOU,** Rank . . . !!
Wow! You realize they used the word **"frigg"** in this move as a **noun,** a **verb,** a **preposition,** an **adjective . . . forty ways in all!** There's **no other way** to say **it**!
Hey, Man, that's **fanfriggintastic!**
Make that **FORTY-ONE!**
BAM BAM
TOADIE HALL
SNIF SNIF SNIF
POW POW POW
Well, Bebbee . . . how you like bein' **married** to the **mos' important dope dealer** in **Miami,** with **six billion dollars** an' **ninety-two mansions!?**
You're **still** a **greaseball,** Toadie!
Greaseball . . . ?!? I take **eight bubble baths** a **day!!**
Is **that** what you call them?! You're **supposed** to use **SOAP** in the water, **not COCAINE!**
You take **YOUR** bubble baths, an' **I'll** take **MINE!!**
Boss
Hey, **Boss . . .** I juss found out that your **bes' friend, Meanie,** iss livin' with your **Sister!**
What?!? *Yecch! Ptui!* That makes me feel **dirty all over!** I'll grab another **bubble bath,** an' then I'll fly over an' **see** them!
They're **livin'** right here **in town,** Boss! You **don't need** to take no **PLANE!!**
Hey, Man . . . I said I'd **FLY over! I didn't** say nuthin' about no **PLANE!**
Wait, Toadie! Before you **say** or **do** anything **crazy,** please **listen** to me! Meanie and I are **MARRIED!**
Married?!? You're a **sweet, decent girl!** You **CAN'T** marry **him!** Don't you know that your marriage wass **already arranged . . .** to a **decent, wonderful, old-fashioned boy . . . !!**
Who . . . ???
ME . . . !!!

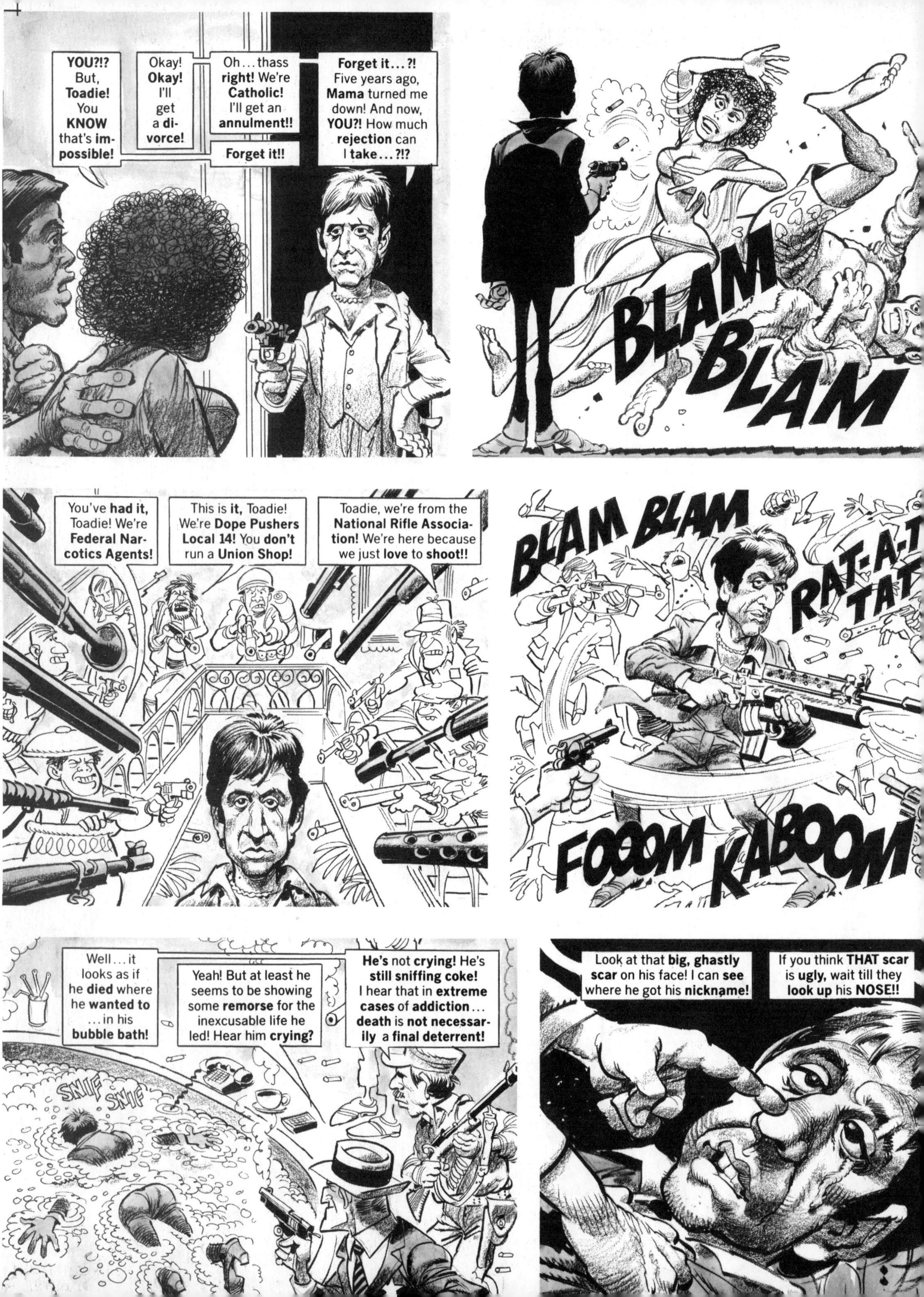
YOU?!? But, Toadie! You KNOW that's impossible!
Okay! Okay! I'll get a divorce!
Oh... thass right! We're Catholic! I'll get an annulment!!
Forget it!!
Forget it...?! Five years ago, Mama turned me down! And now, YOU?! How much rejection can I take...?!?
BLAM BLAM BLAM
You've had it, Toadie! We're Federal Narcotics Agents!
This is it, Toadie! We're Dope Pushers Local 14! You don't run a Union Shop!
Toadie, we're from the National Rifle Association! We're here because we just love to shoot!!
BLAM BLAM
RAT-A-TAT
FOOOM KABOOM
Well... it looks as if he died where he wanted to ...in his bubble bath!
Yeah! But at least he seems to be showing some remorse for the inexcusable life he led! Hear him crying?
He's not crying! He's still sniffing coke! I hear that in extreme cases of addiction... death is not necessarily a final deterrent!
SNIF SNIF
Look at that big, ghastly scar on his face! I can see where he got his nickname!
If you think THAT scar is ugly, wait till they look up his NOSE!!

WHAT DEDICATED GROUP DOES A LOT OF PLANTING, AND YET, NOTHING EVER COMES OF IT?

HERE WE GO WITH ANOTHER RIDICULOUS

MAD FOLD-IN

Spring is the time of year when our thoughts turn to the soil and "Spring Planting." And when it comes to planting, many people have "Green Thumbs." But there is one dedicated group of people who do a lot of planting, and yet nothing ever comes up. To find out who these people are, fold in the page as shown.

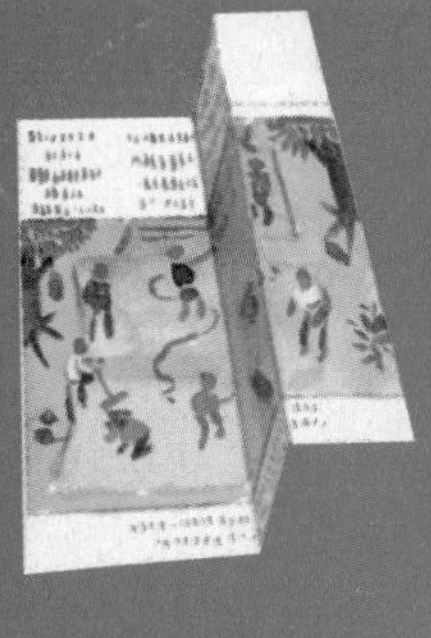

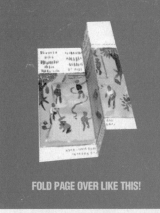

FOLD PAGE OVER LIKE THIS!

A▸ FOLD THIS SECTION OVER LEFT ◂B FOLD BACK SO "A" MEETS "B"

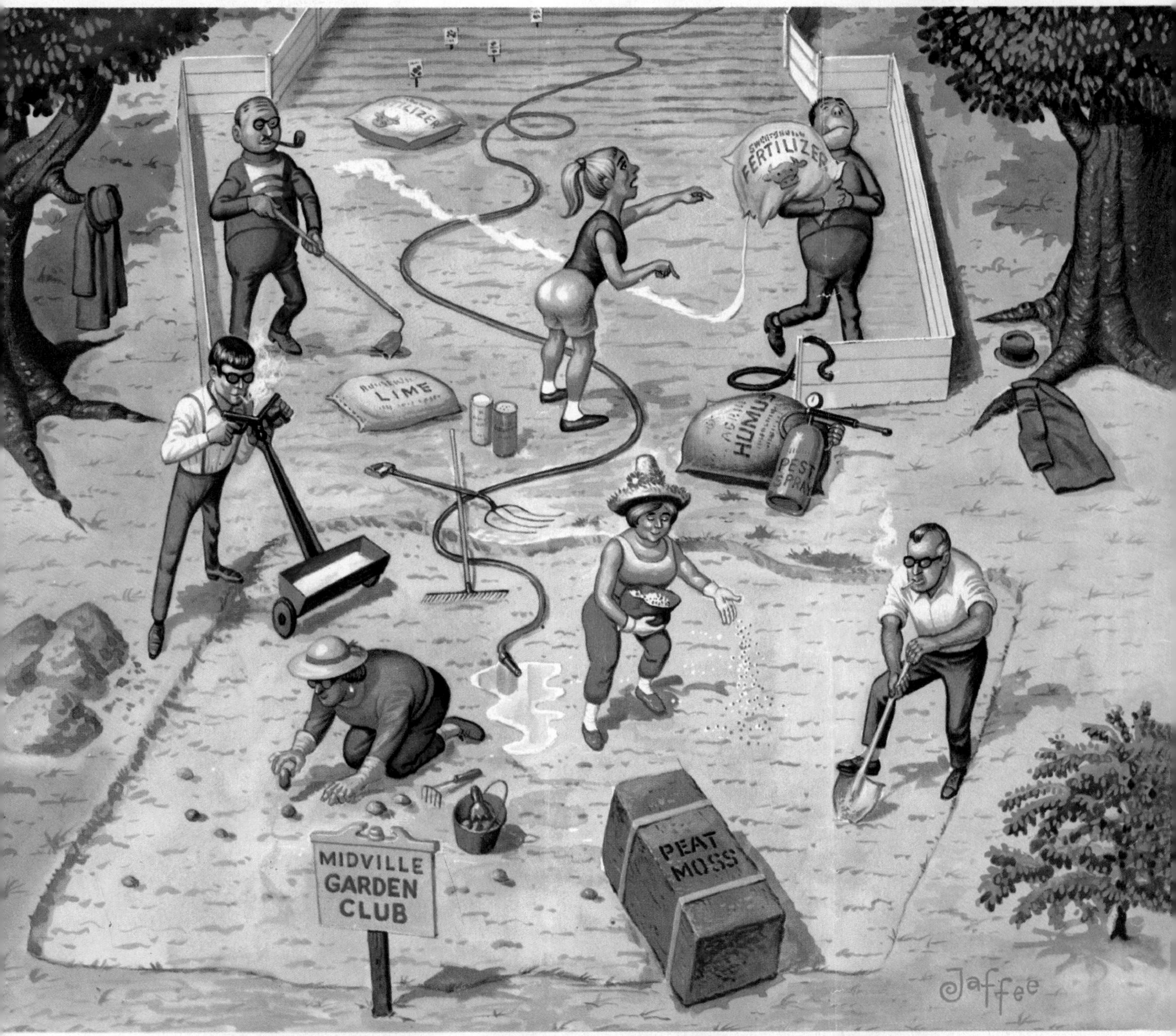

FERTILIZER
LIME
HUMUS
PEST SPRAY
MIDVILLE GARDEN CLUB
PEAT MOSS
Jaffee

THE UNSUCCESSFUL AMATEUR GARDENER, IN SO MANY CASES, IS THE ONE WHO FAILS TO FIND OUT ABOUT SOIL CONDITIONS BEFORE A VEGETABLE OR FLOWER SEED IS PLANTED.

A▸ ◂B

ARTIST & WRITER: AL JAFFEE

Not for nuttin', but ever since HBO first put dat dere show Da Sopranos on da air, everybody's freakin' actin' and talkin' like dey are wise guys. Alls we got to say is, "Hold your freakin' horses, Don Schmendrick!" To be a member in good standin' wit da boys, you foist gotta prove dat you're a tough guy and can handle yourself in certain "delicate" situations. Ya know, like cappin' a guy and cuttin' up his body and plantin' it all over the Joisey swamplands. Only then do you take da oath, swear your allegiance to da mafia and become what is known as a "made man." So, all you Paulie Walnuts Wannabes out dere, you think ya got what it takes? Don't make us freakin' laugh...

YOU CAN Fuhgeddabout BECOMING A Made Man IN THE Soprano MOB IF...

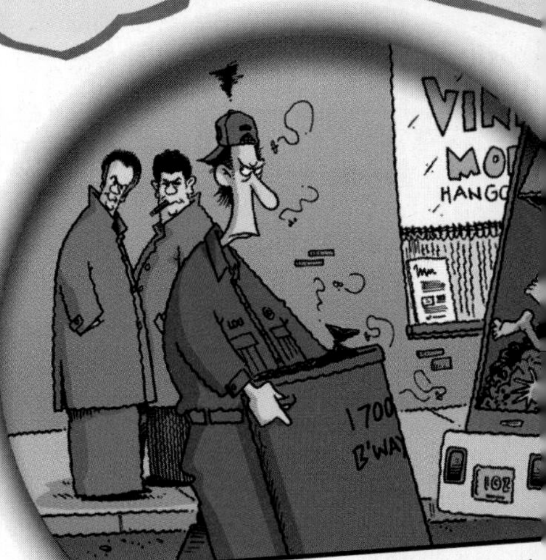
1700
B'WAY

You're the only "Waste Management Consultant" in your 12-man crew who actu wears coveralls and handles waste.

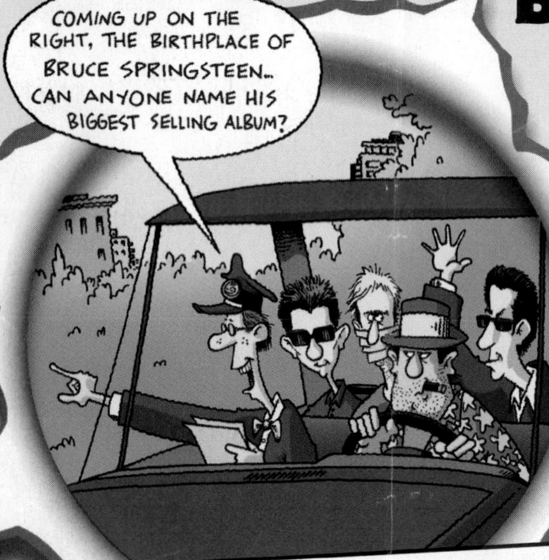
COMING UP ON THE RIGHT, THE BIRTHPLACE OF BRUCE SPRINGSTEEN... CAN ANYONE NAME HIS BIGGEST SELLING ALBUM?

When "taking a guy for a ride," your primary task is pointing out historical landmarks.

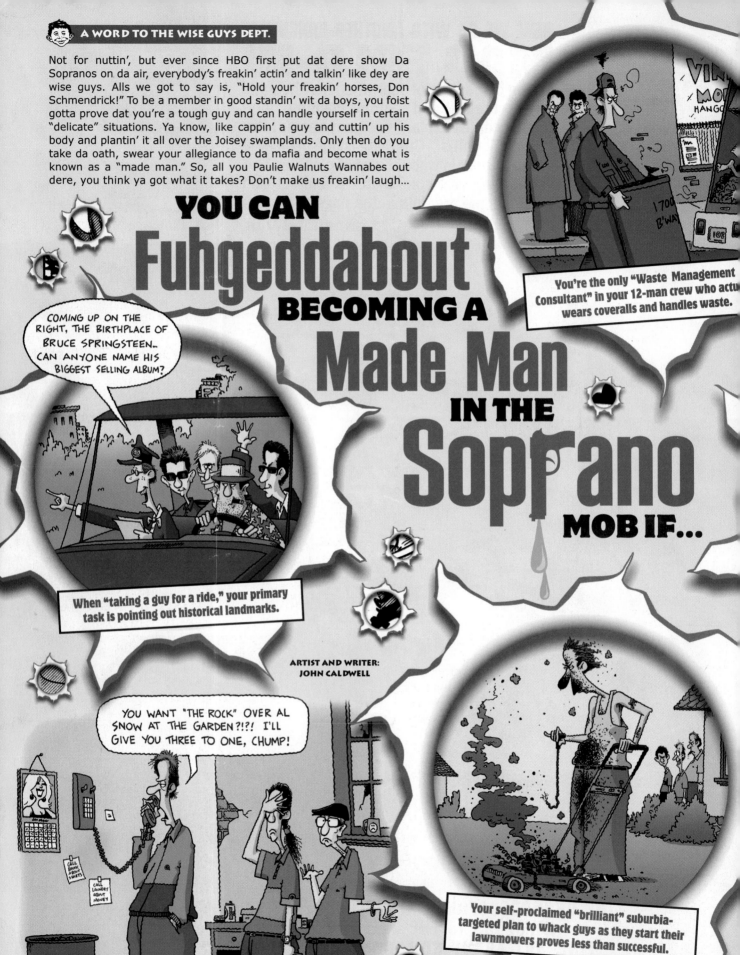

ARTIST AND WRITER:
JOHN CALDWELL

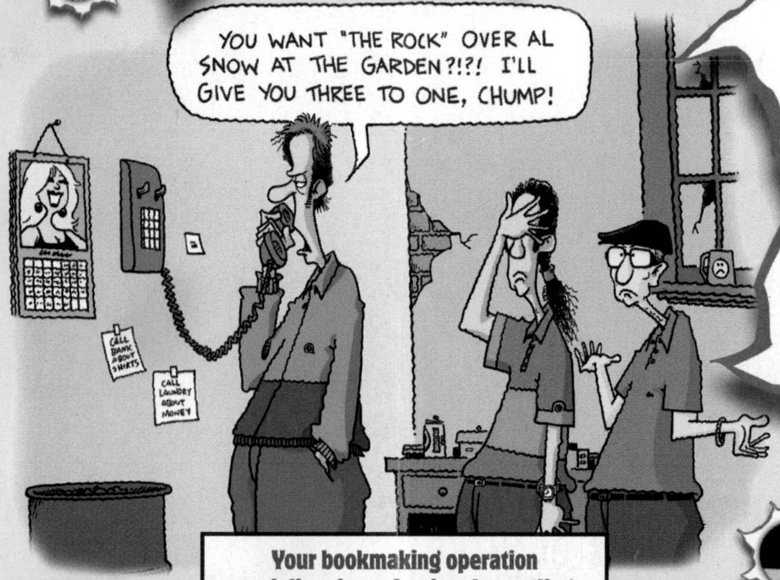
YOU WANT "THE ROCK" OVER AL SNOW AT THE GARDEN?!?! I'LL GIVE YOU THREE TO ONE, CHUMP!
CALL BANK ABOUT SHIRTS
CALL LAUNDRY ABOUT MONEY

Your bookmaking operation specializes in professional wrestling.

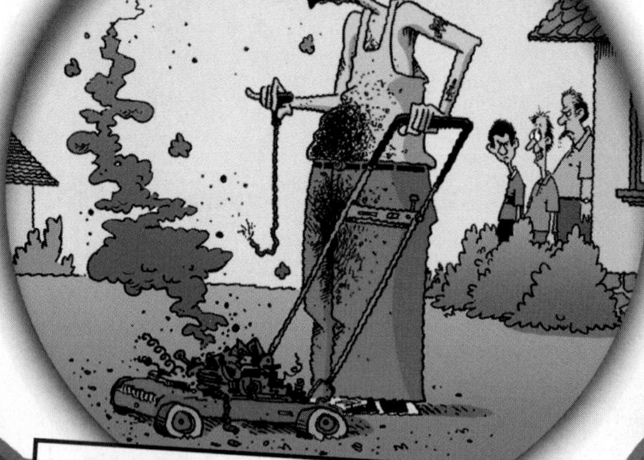

Your self-proclaimed "brilliant" suburbia-targeted plan to whack guys as they start their lawnmowers proves less than successful.

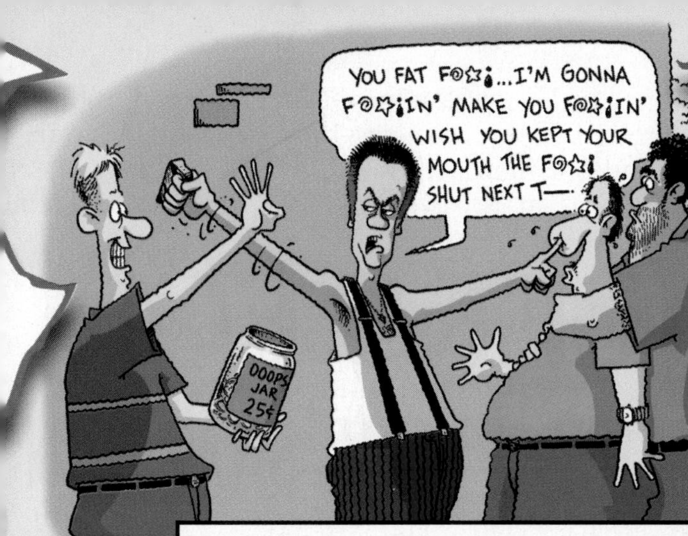
YOU FAT FO☆¡...I'M GONNA FO☆¡IN' MAKE YOU FO☆¡IN' WISH YOU KEPT YOUR MOUTH THE FO☆¡ SHUT NEXT T—.
OOOPS JAR 25¢

You continually pester guys with a stupid quarter jar every time somebody drops the F-word.

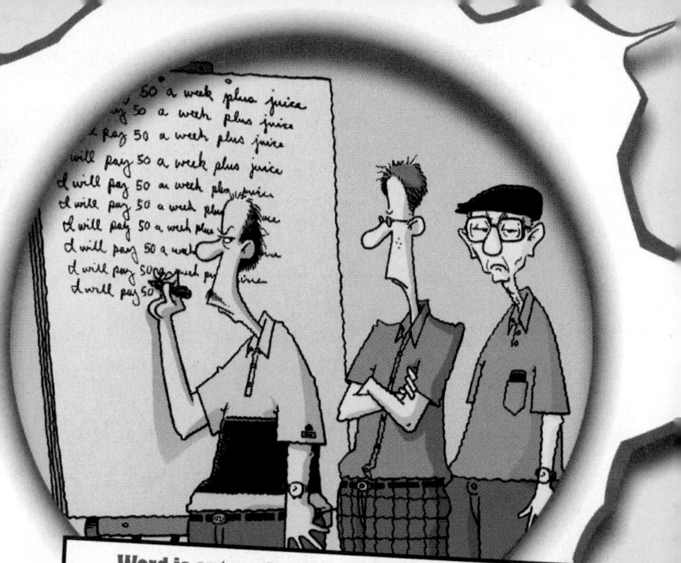
I will pay 50 a week plus juice

Word is out on the street that if someone's late paying off his gambling debts, there's a good chance you'll show up and give them a case of writer's cramp they'll never forget.

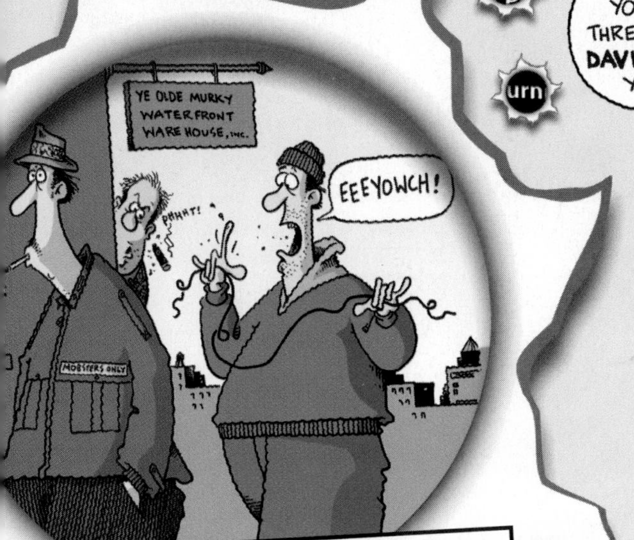
YE OLDE MURKY WATERFRONT WARE HOUSE, INC.
EEEYOWCH!
PHHHT!
MOBSTERS ONLY

You've never actually carried out a contract hit due to your propensity for piano wire cuts.

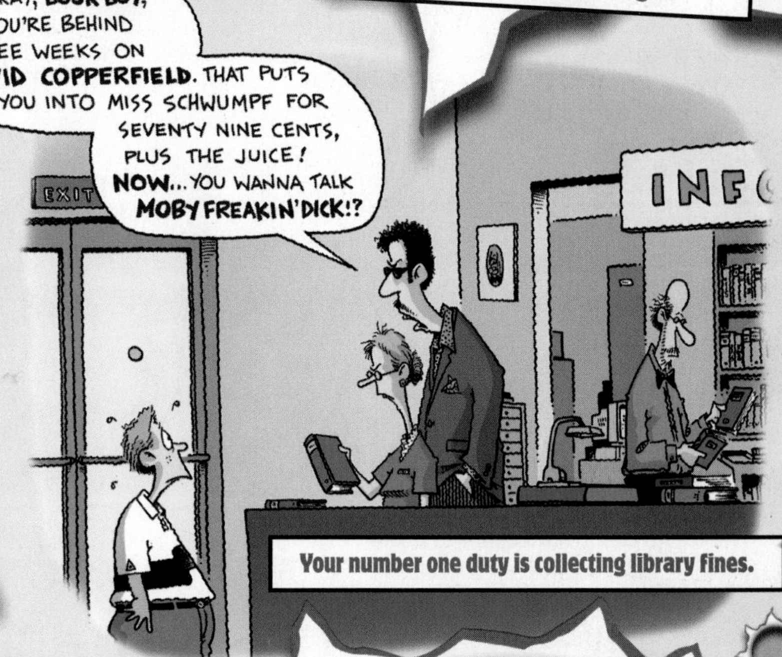
OKAY, BOOK BOY, YOU'RE BEHIND THREE WEEKS ON DAVID COPPERFIELD. THAT PUTS YOU INTO MISS SCHWUMPF FOR SEVENTY NINE CENTS, PLUS THE JUICE! NOW...YOU WANNA TALK MOBY FREAKIN' DICK!?
EXIT
INF

Your number one duty is collecting library fines.

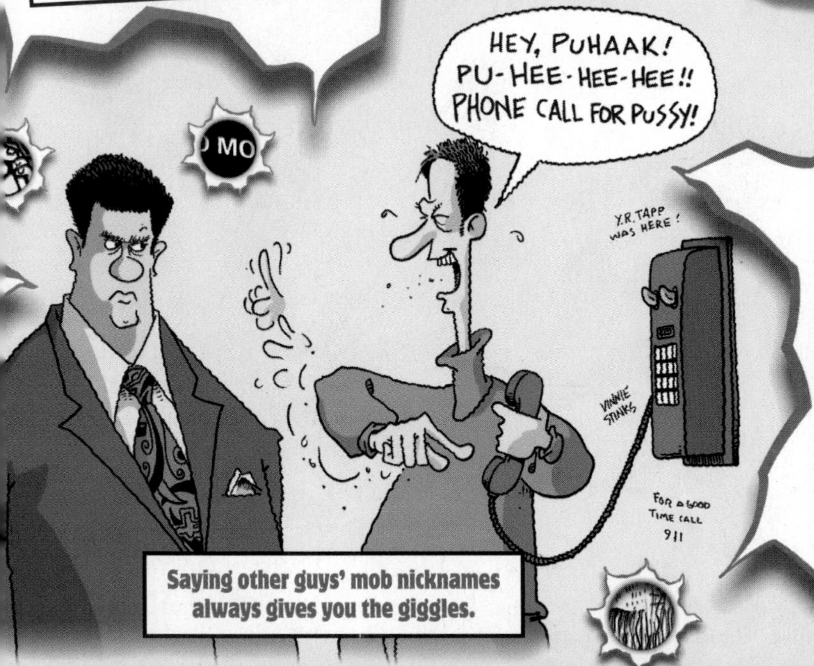
HEY, PUHAAK! PU-HEE-HEE-HEE!! PHONE CALL FOR PUSSY!
Y.R. TAPP WAS HERE!
VINNIE STINKS
FOR A GOOD TIME CALL 911

Saying other guys' mob nicknames always gives you the giggles.

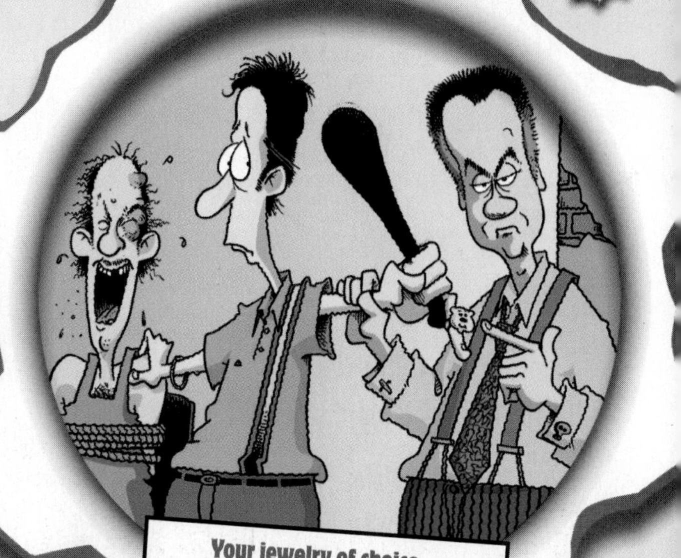

Your jewelry of choice — a Winnie the Pooh pinkie ring.

PROPS AND ROBBERS DEPT.

Street crime is rising at an alarming rate. Every day, people are mugged, robbed a beaten. The police would like to help, but Heaven knows they have their hands f with gamblers, illegal parkers and Sunday Blue Law violators. Nor can anyone exp help from his neighbor. Nobody wants to get involved. Alarms, whistles and sunc

CRIME FOILERS FOR T

MUGGINGS, HOLD-UPS, PURSE-SNATCHING

THE PHONY FRONT

BUS STOP
WANTED

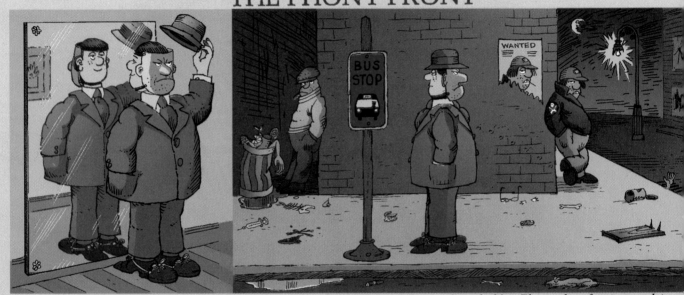

Almost all muggers count on the element of surprise. They attack from behind to avoid tangling with anyone who can fight back. This costume prevents all that. It consists of a two-way suit and shirt. Phony shoe fronts complete the ensemble. No matter which way mugger approaches, he always thinks he's facing you, and you're watching him.

THE SPINY ATTACHE CASE

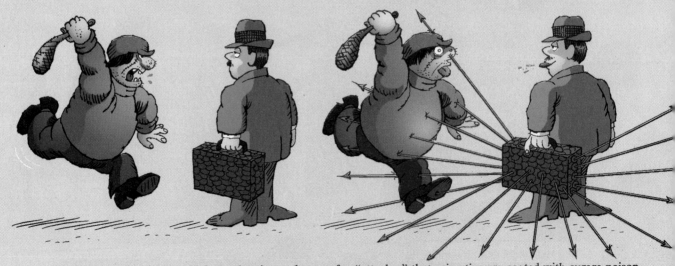

Pushbutton trigger in handle instantly releases dozens of porcupine-like telescoping barbed steel spines. Warning "attacker" that spine tips are coated with curare poison guarantees safety . . . if he hasn't run into them already.

oise-makers are useless. And carrying a weapon is even worse. With surprise on his de, the mugger can quickly disarm the average person and turn the weapon against m. So what we need are devices that even crippled old ladies can rely upon with nfidence as they walk the lonely city streets at night. Mainly, we need these MAD

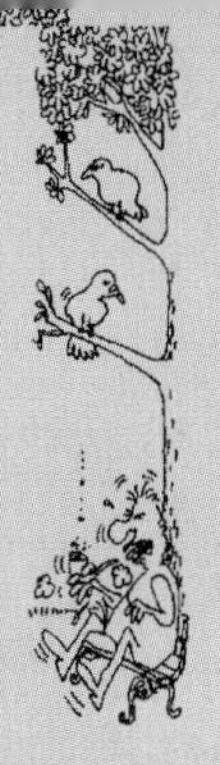

IE AVERAGE CITIZEN

ND OTHER STREET ATTACK FOILERS

RTIST & WRITER: AL JAFFEE

THE BALL-BEARING POCKET BOOK

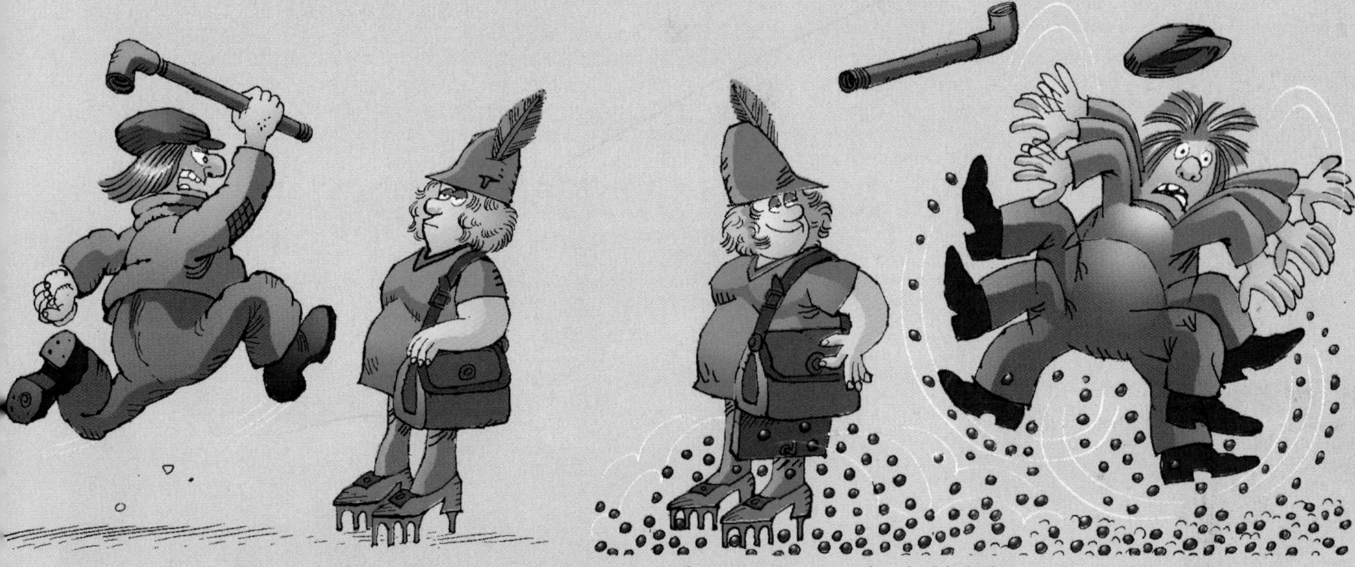

As "attacker" appears, pocketbook-wearer presses trigger and thousands of tiny lightweight plastic ball-bearings are released. "Attacker" is suddenly rendered helpless as he struggles to maintain his balance. Meanwhile, "victim" walks safely away over treacherous ball-bearings with the aid of the specially-designed spiked shoes she is wearing.

THE AIR BAG STRETCH SUIT (OR DRESS)

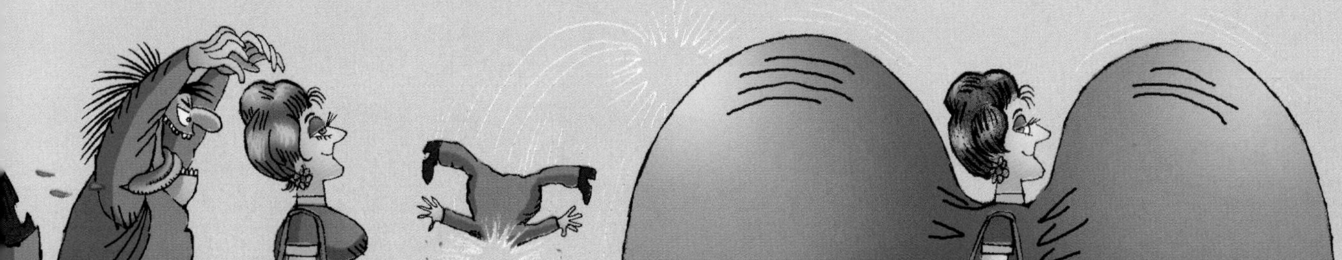

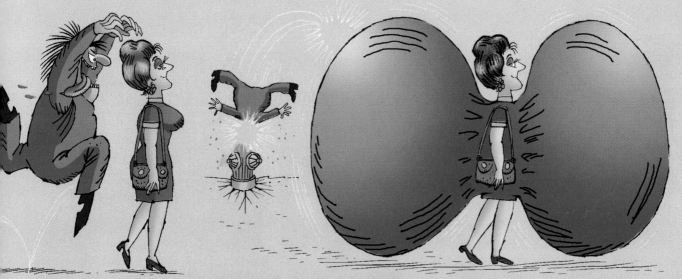

The idea for this protective device came from auto safety experiments. When "victim" is attacked, air bags instantly inflate and fling mugger violently away. However, caution must be exercised to avoid sudden embraces of loved ones.

BURGLARIES, BREAK-INS, THEFTS, ROB

THE TRAP DOOR WELCOME MAT

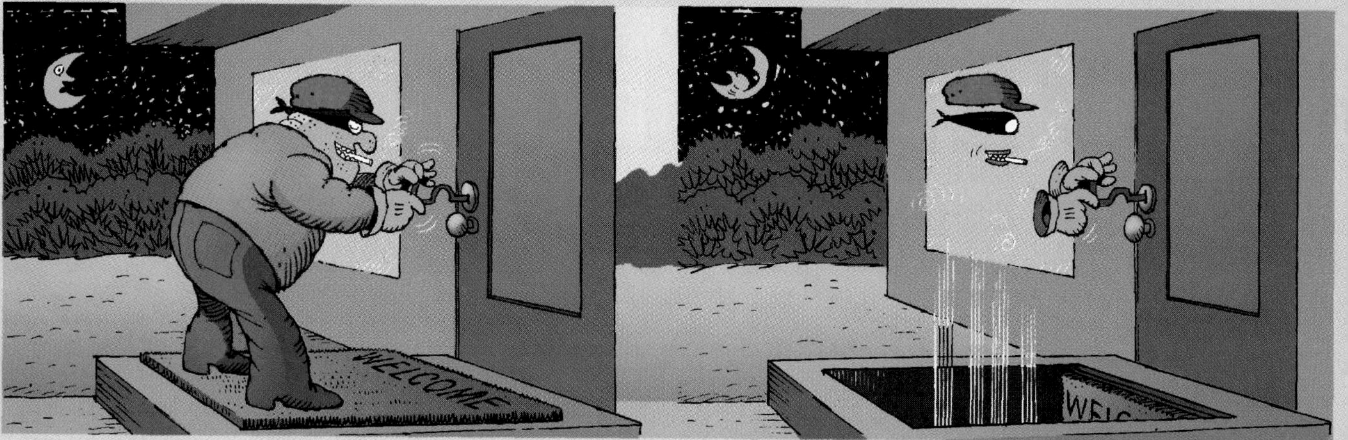
WELCOME

Special lock on door is calibrated to accept special key. Any other device such as a jimmy, screwdriver, hairpin or foreign key sets off mechanism that opens trap door. If homeowner intends to be away for an extended period, it is advisable to leave some food and water in the trap. Otherwise, disgusting sight will greet him on his return.

THE SPRING LOADED WINDOW

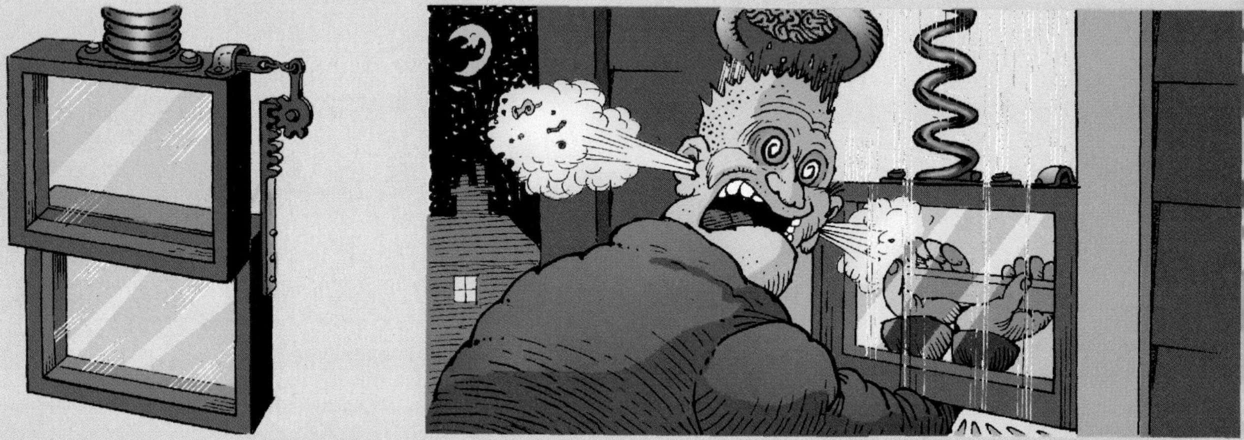

When burglar lifts lower (inner) sash, it hits mechanism (A) which releases spring (B). Upper (outer) sash comes down with thrust equal to two tons of weight, trapping thief in the act. Too bad if he's a moonlighting pianist.

THE FEROCIOUS ANIMAL

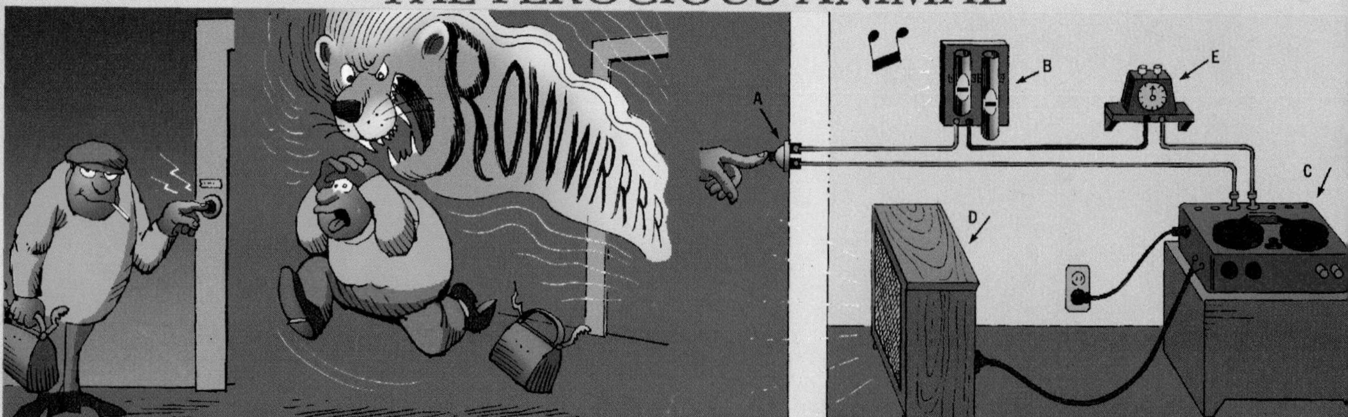
ROWWRRRR
A
B
E
C
D

Since burglar always rings doorbell first to make sure no one is home, this simple set-up effectively discourages him. When bell-button (A) is pressed, it rings chimes (B) and starts tape (C) which emits thunderous animal roars through loudspeaker (D). Timer switch (E) stops the tape after 5 minutes. If another burglar comes, it starts all over again. Set-up can accommodate 6 or 7 burglars, which should just about cover one night's supply in most cities.

ES AND OTHER HOUSE CRIME FOILERS

THE AUTOMATIC WINDOW BARS

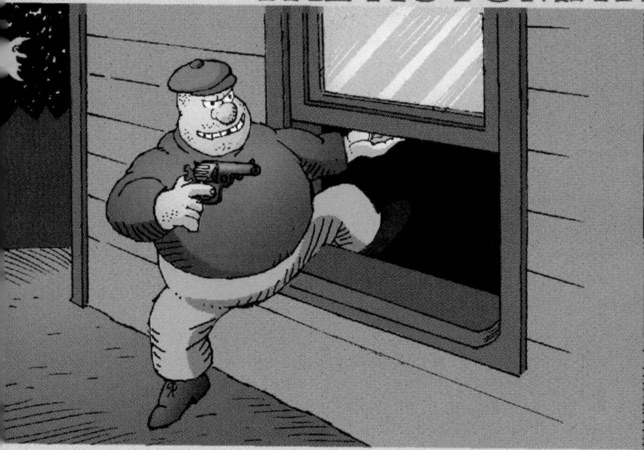

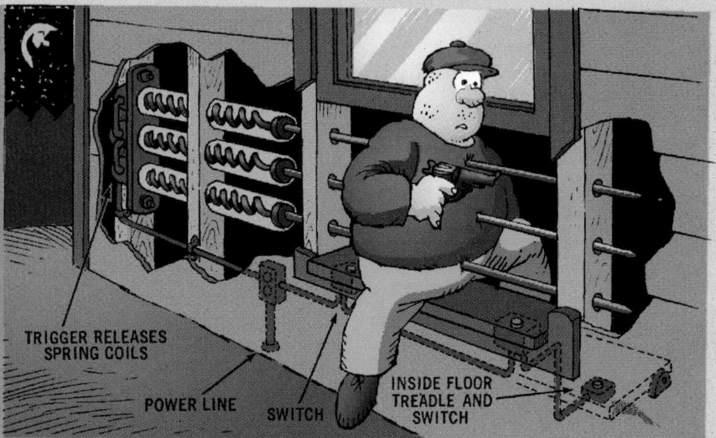

TRIGGER RELEASES SPRING COILS
POWER LINE
SWITCH
INSIDE FLOOR TREADLE AND SWITCH

Spears are hidden in window frame. When burglar puts his weight on window sill, switch is activated and spears are released which effectively bar entry to thief. Too bad—*heh-heh*—if he's caught in the middle! Note: floor treadle safety feature (A) which cuts current to spring switch so that a person opening window from the inside is protected.

THE SLAMMING SHUTTERS

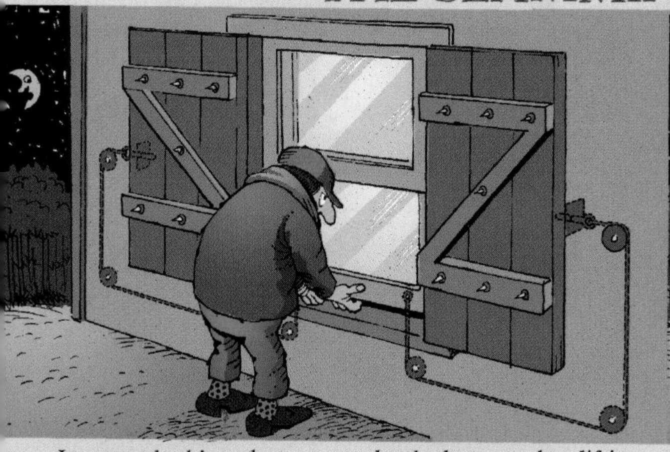

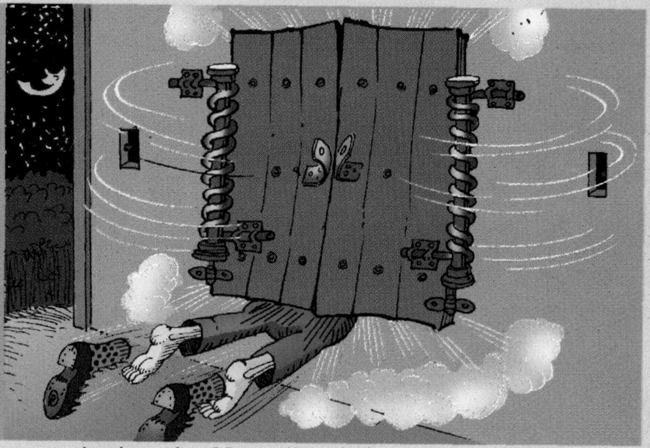

Innocent-looking shutters are hooked up so that lifting window releases spring-hinges and they crash on unsuspecting intruder. Naturally, window panes are made of shatterproof glass to avoid cuts and bloodshed and—ecch.

THE GUILLOTINE WINDOW

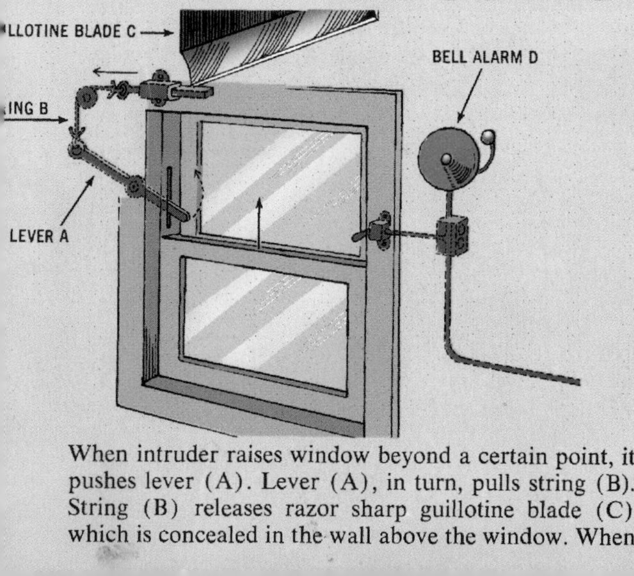

LLOTINE BLADE C
BELL ALARM D
ING B
LEVER A

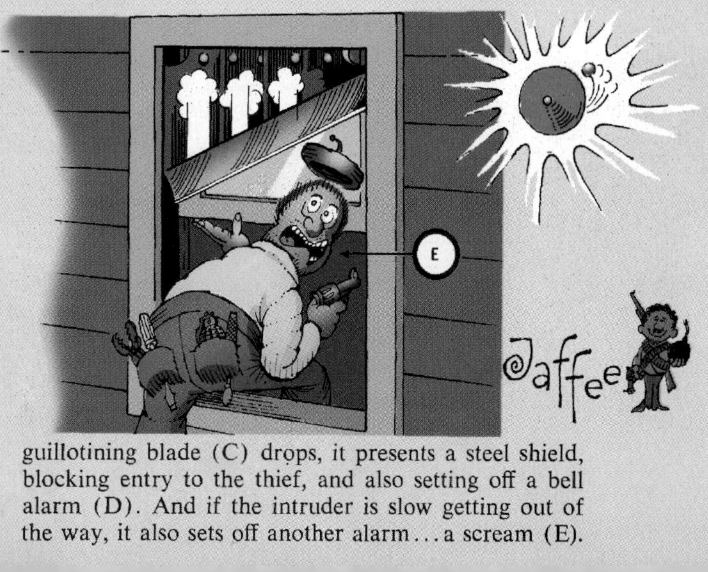

E
Jaffee

When intruder raises window beyond a certain point, it pushes lever (A). Lever (A), in turn, pulls string (B). String (B) releases razor sharp guillotine blade (C) which is concealed in the wall above the window. When guillotining blade (C) drops, it presents a steel shield, blocking entry to the thief, and also setting off a bell alarm (D). And if the intruder is slow getting out of the way, it also sets off another alarm . . . a scream (E).

OPENED SESAME DEPT.

IF SESAME STREET BRANCHED OUT INTO SPECIALIZED AVENUES OF EDUCATION

MAFIA STREET

ARTIST: JACK DAVIS WRITER: FRANK JACOBS

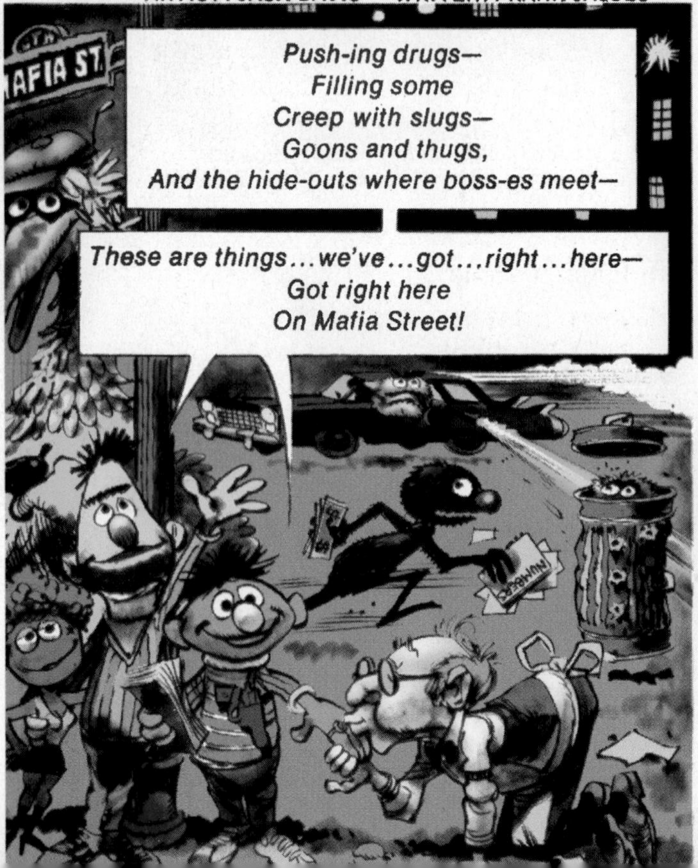

MAFIA ST.
Push-ing drugs— Filling some Creep with slugs— Goons and thugs, And the hide-outs where boss-es meet—
These are things...we've...got...right...here— Got right here On Mafia Street!

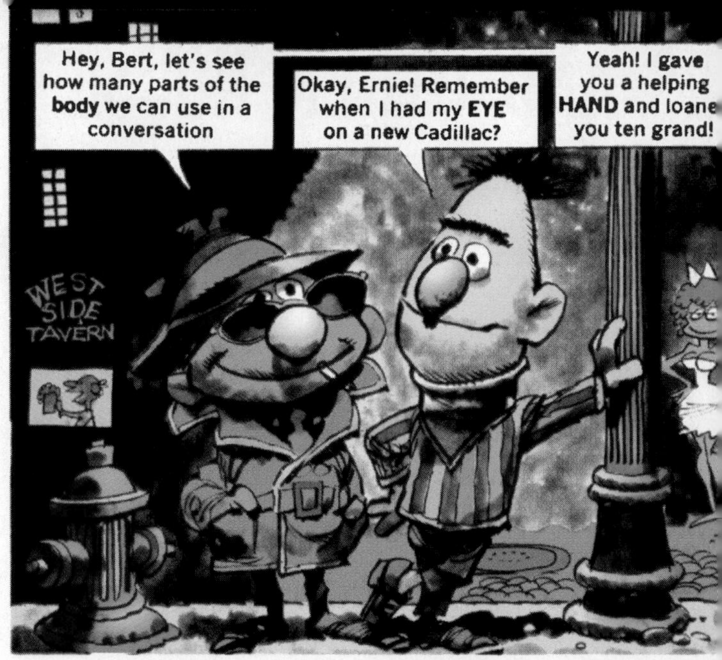

Hey, Bert, let's see how many parts of the body we can use in a conversation
Okay, Ernie! Remember when I had my EYE on a new Cadillac?
Yeah! I gave you a helping HAND and loane you ten grand!
WEST SIDE TAVERN

ABCDEFGHIJKLMNOPQRSTUVWXYZ0123

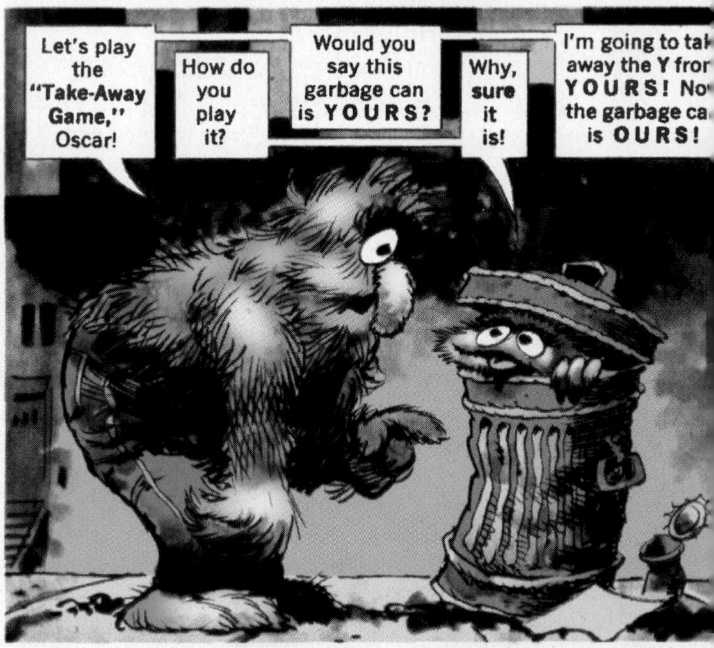

Let's play the "Take-Away Game," Oscar!
How do you play it?
Would you say this garbage can is YOURS?
Why, sure it is!
I'm going to tak away the Y fror YOURS! No the garbage ca is OURS!

ABCDEFGHIJKLMNOPQRSTUVWXYZ0123

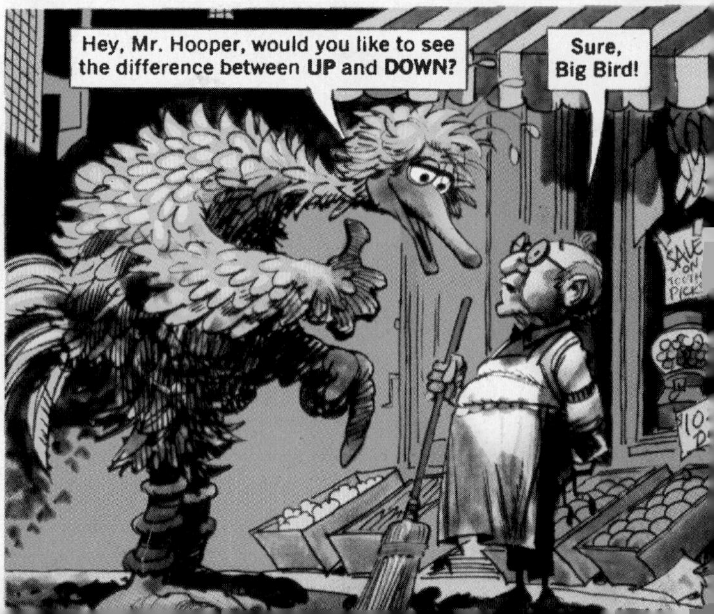

Hey, Mr. Hooper, would you like to see the difference between UP and DOWN?
Sure, Big Bird!
SALE ON TOOTH PICKS

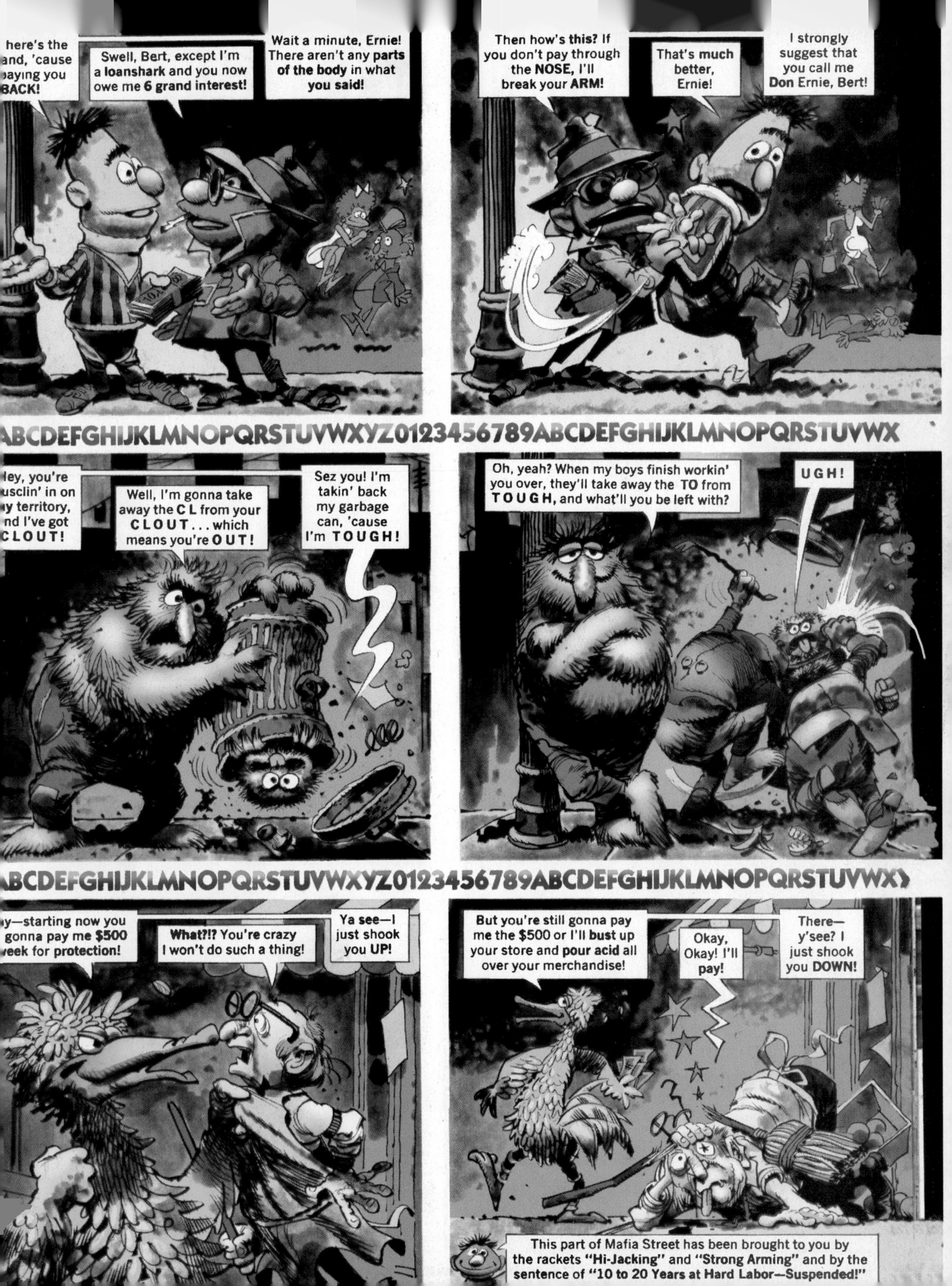

here's the and, 'cause aying you BACK!
Swell, Bert, except I'm a loanshark and you now owe me 6 grand interest!
Wait a minute, Ernie! There aren't any parts of the body in what you said!
Then how's this? If you don't pay through the NOSE, I'll break your ARM!
That's much better, Ernie!
I strongly suggest that you call me Don Ernie, Bert!
ABCDEFGHIJKLMNOPQRSTUVWXYZ0123456789ABCDEFGHIJKLMNOPQRSTUVWX
ley, you're usclin' in on y territory, nd I've got CLOUT!
Well, I'm gonna take away the C L from your CLOUT . . . which means you're OUT!
Sez you! I'm takin' back my garbage can, 'cause I'm TOUGH!
Oh, yeah? When my boys finish workin' you over, they'll take away the TO from TOUGH, and what'll you be left with?
UGH!
ABCDEFGHIJKLMNOPQRSTUVWXYZ0123456789ABCDEFGHIJKLMNOPQRSTUVWX
y—starting now you gonna pay me $500 week for protection!
What?!? You're crazy I won't do such a thing!
Ya see—I just shook you UP!
But you're still gonna pay me the $500 or I'll bust up your store and pour acid all over your merchandise!
Okay, Okay! I'll pay!
There—y'see? I just shook you DOWN!
This part of Mafia Street has been brought to you by the rackets "Hi-Jacking" and "Strong Arming" and by the sentence of "10 to 20 Years at Hard Labor—Suspended!"

DON MARTIN DEPT.

LATE ONE NIGHT IN A BANK

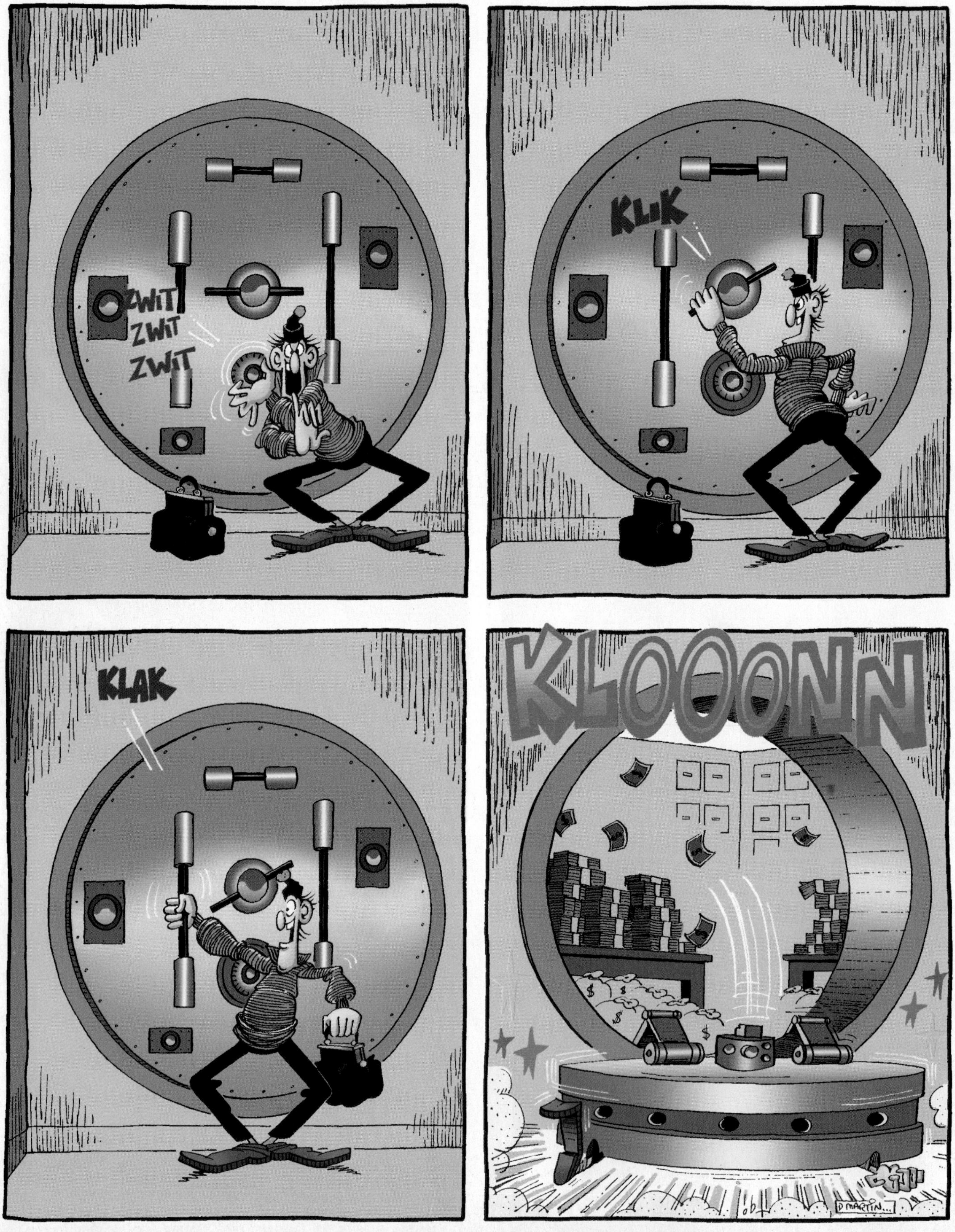
ZWIT
ZWIT
ZWIT
KLIK
KLAK
KLOOONN

ARTIST: DON MARTIN WRITER: DUCK EDWING

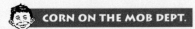

Can you name America's First Family? If your answer was Bush, you're dead wrong. The first family of the USA is the Sopranos — Tony, Carmela, A.J., Meadow, Silvio, Uncle Junior, Paulie — all of them. This noted, let us see them at work and at play as we present…

THE Sopranos FAMILY CIRCUS

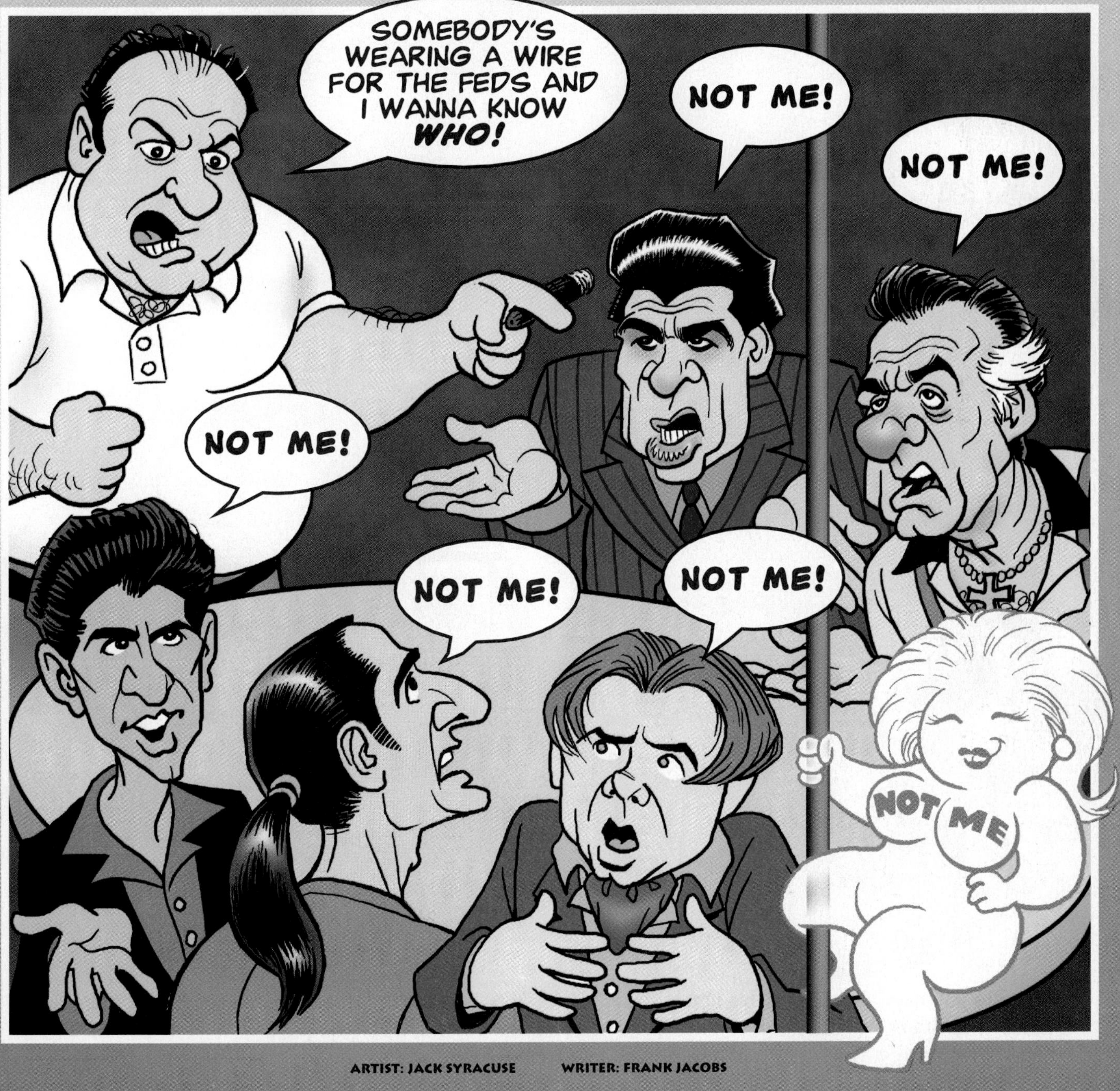
SOMEBODY'S WEARING A WIRE FOR THE FEDS AND I WANNA KNOW WHO!
NOT ME!
NOT ME!
NOT ME!
NOT ME!
NOT ME!
NOT ME

ARTIST: JACK SYRACUSE WRITER: FRANK JACOBS

THE Sopranos FAMILY CIRCUS

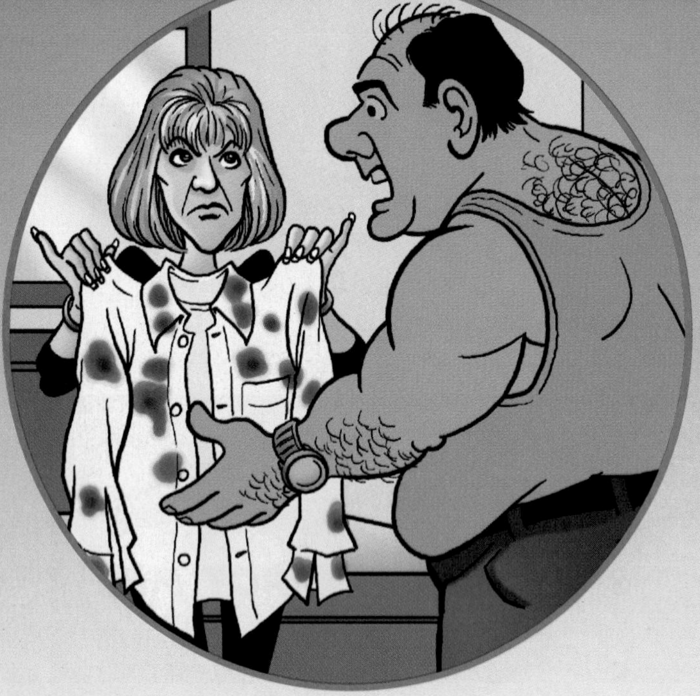

"I swear it's not lipstick—it's BLOOD!"

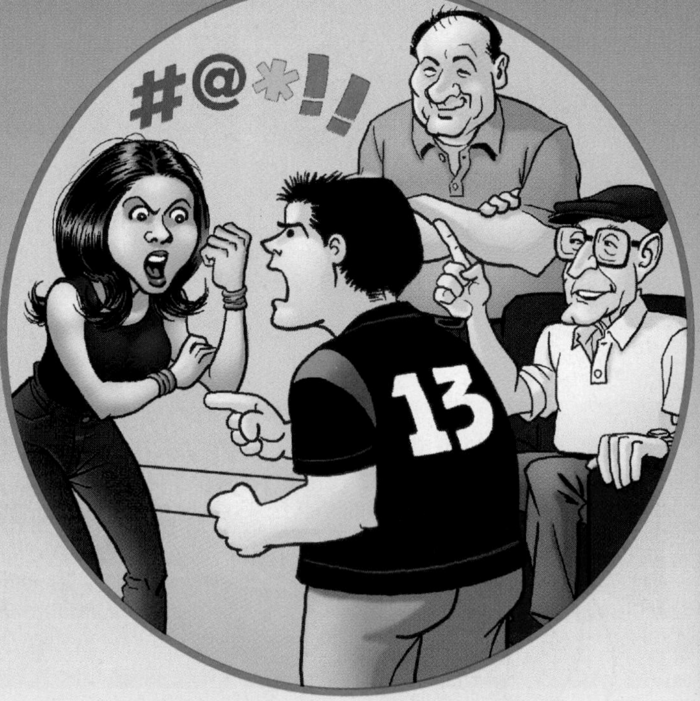
#@*!!
13

"I remember when you were a baby and you said your first F-word!"

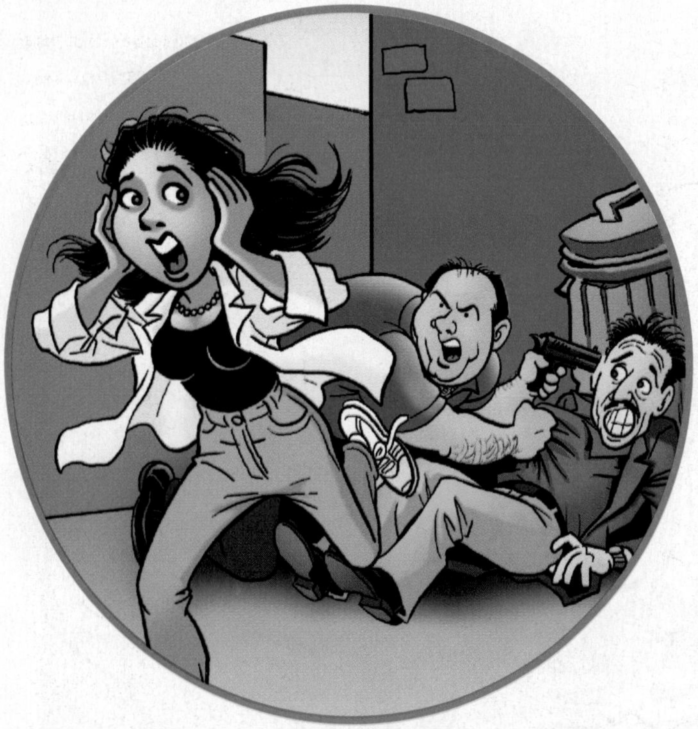

"What are you mad at me for? This whole 'take your daughter to work day' was your idea!"

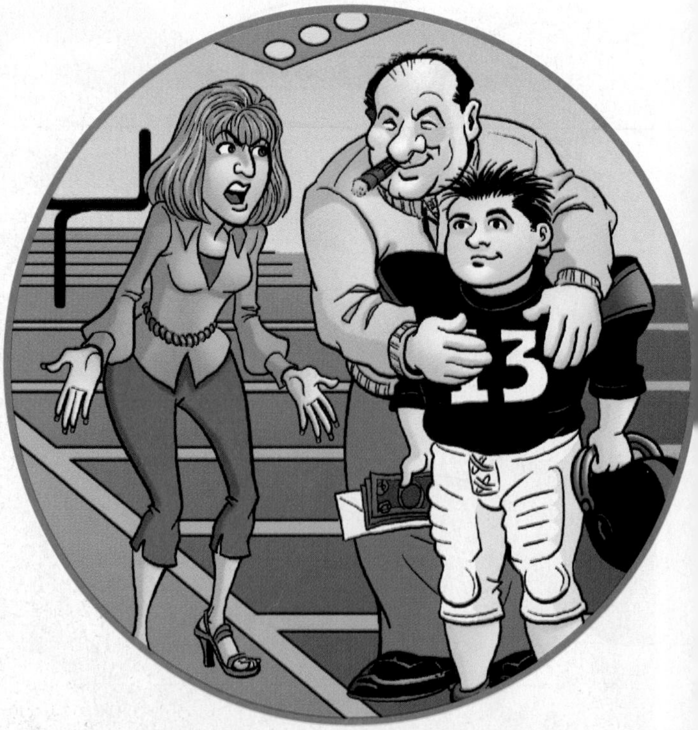
13

"When I said 'father and son bonding' I didn't mean having him shave points off his first varsity game!"

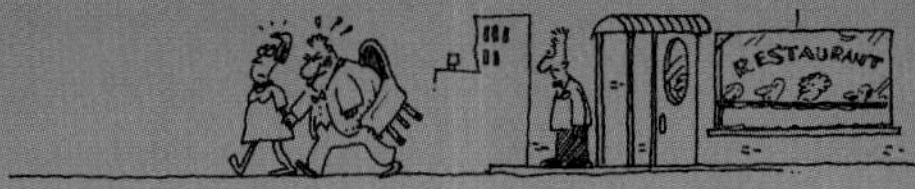
RESTAURANT

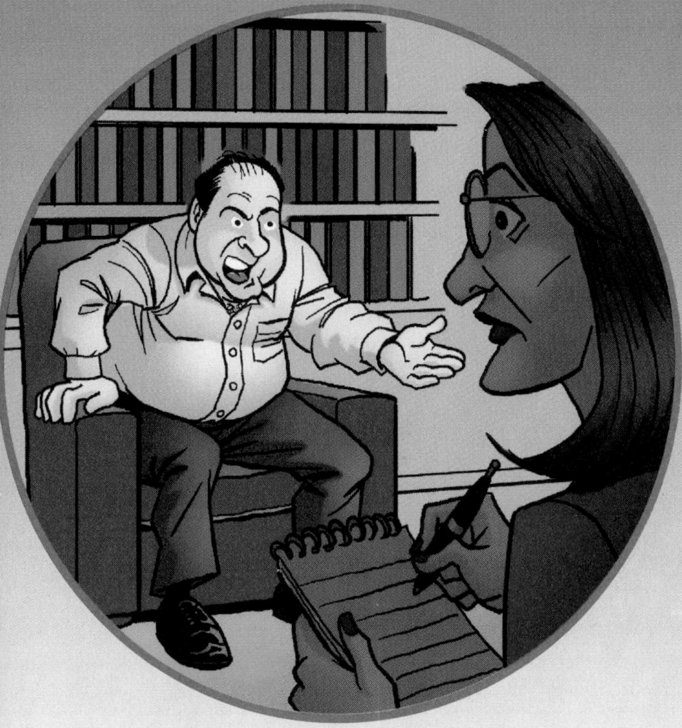

"No progress?!? I've made a fortune re-selling those little pills you've been giving me!"

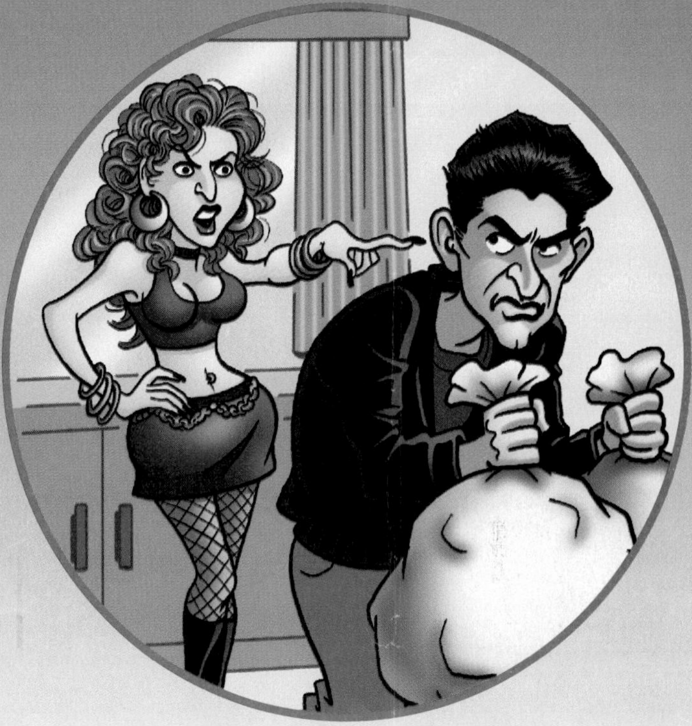

"Made man or not, you still have to take out the garbage!"

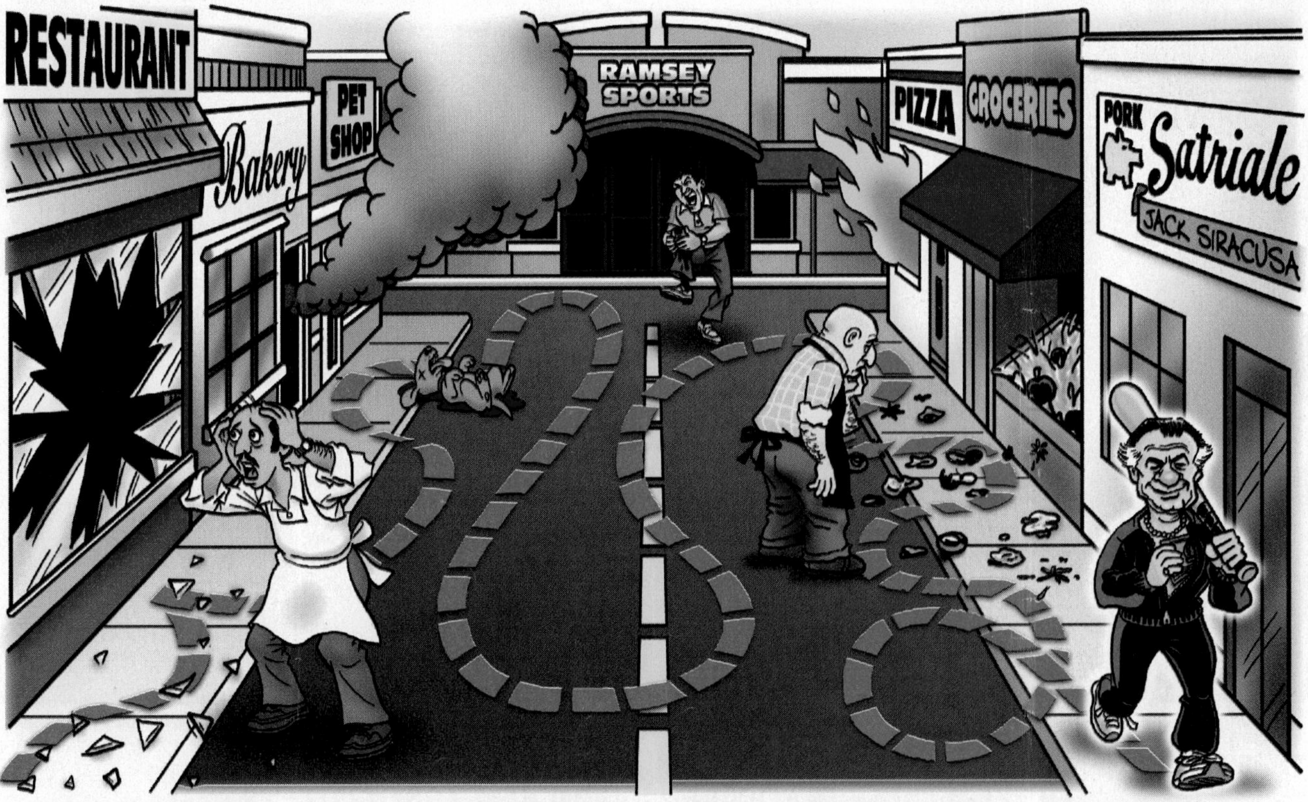
RESTAURANT
Bakery
PET SHOP
RAMSEY SPORTS
PIZZA
GROCERIES
PORK
Satriale
JACK SIRACUSA

PAULIE WALNUTS' COLLECTION ROUTE

WHAT FREQUENTLY PROSECUTED CRIME FAMILY IS TRYING TO MUSCLE IN ON NEW YORK?

HERE WE GO WITH ANOTHER RIDICULOUS

MAD FOLD-IN

Historically, organized crime figures like the Gottis, Castellanos and Gambinos have always looked upon New York as a haven for their illegal activity. To find out who the newest family to move into the neighborhood is, fold page in as shown.

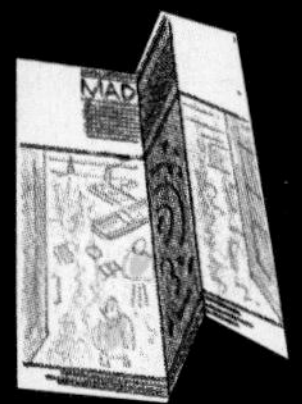

FOLD PAGE OVER LIKE THIS!

A ▶ FOLD PAGE OVER LEFT ◀ B FOLD BACK SO THAT "A" MEETS "B"

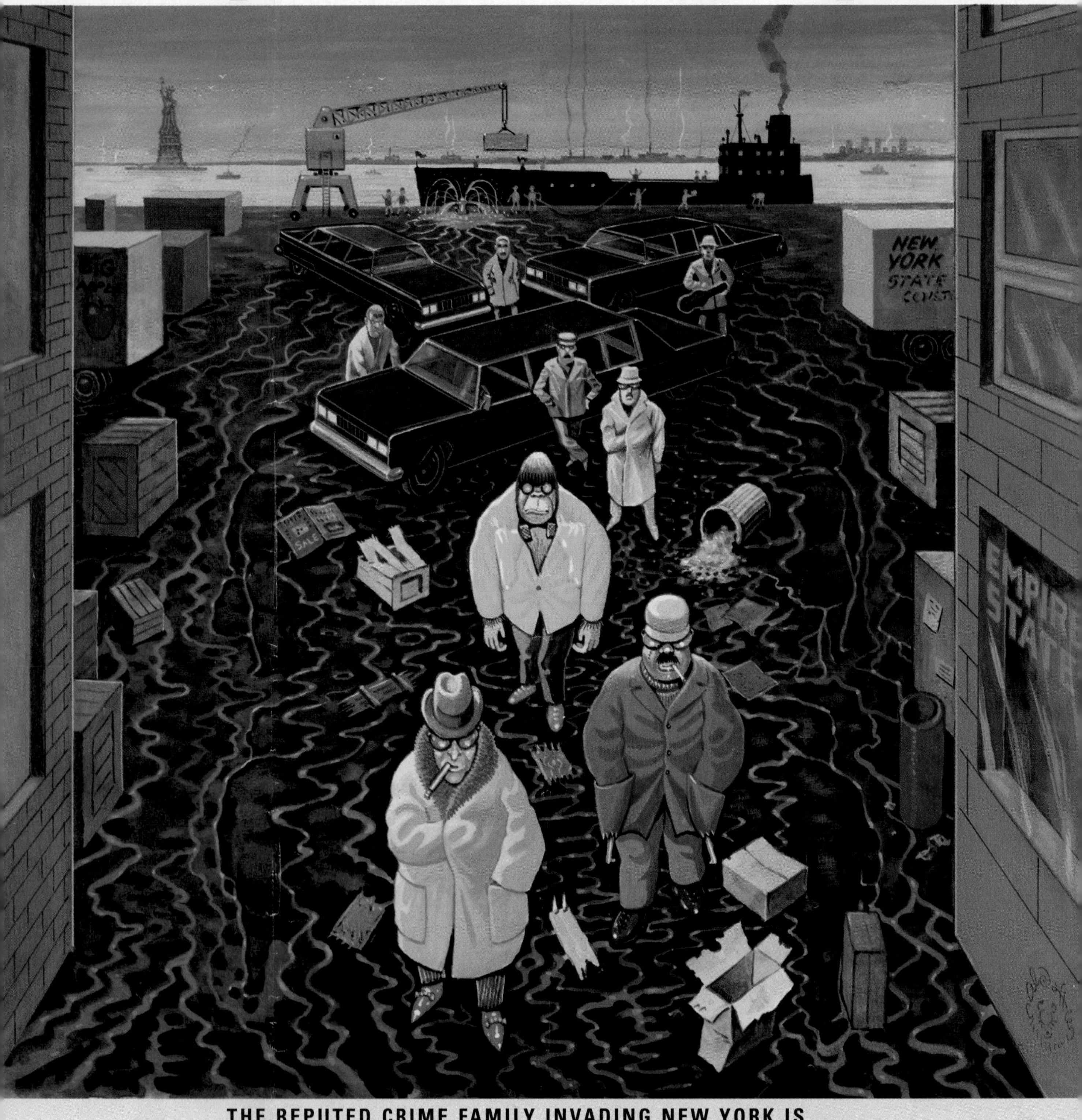
NEW YORK STATE

THE REPUTED CRIME FAMILY INVADING NEW YORK IS CLEARLY OUT TO TAKE OVER. IT IS ANXIOUS TO GET IN-TO EVERYTHING THAT IS CRUCIAL TO NEW YORK CITIZENS

A ▶ ARTIST AND WRITER: AL JAFFEE ◀ B

SAFE ON SECOND DEPT.

THE HEIST

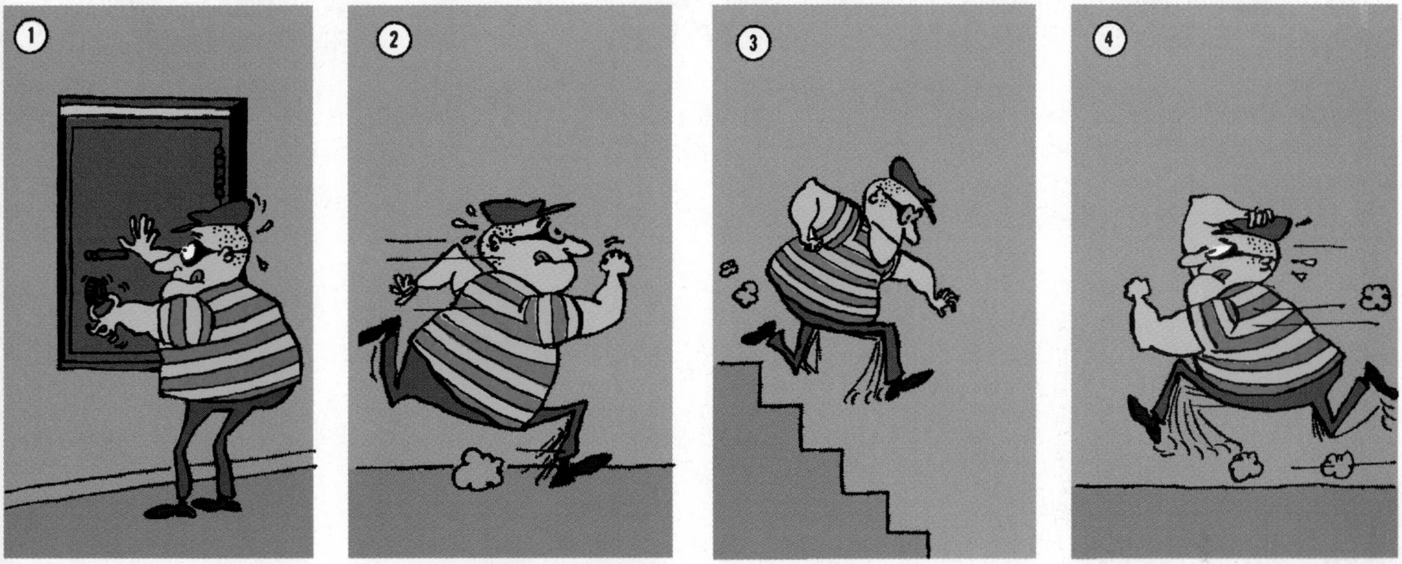

ARTIST & WRITER: SERGIO RAGONES

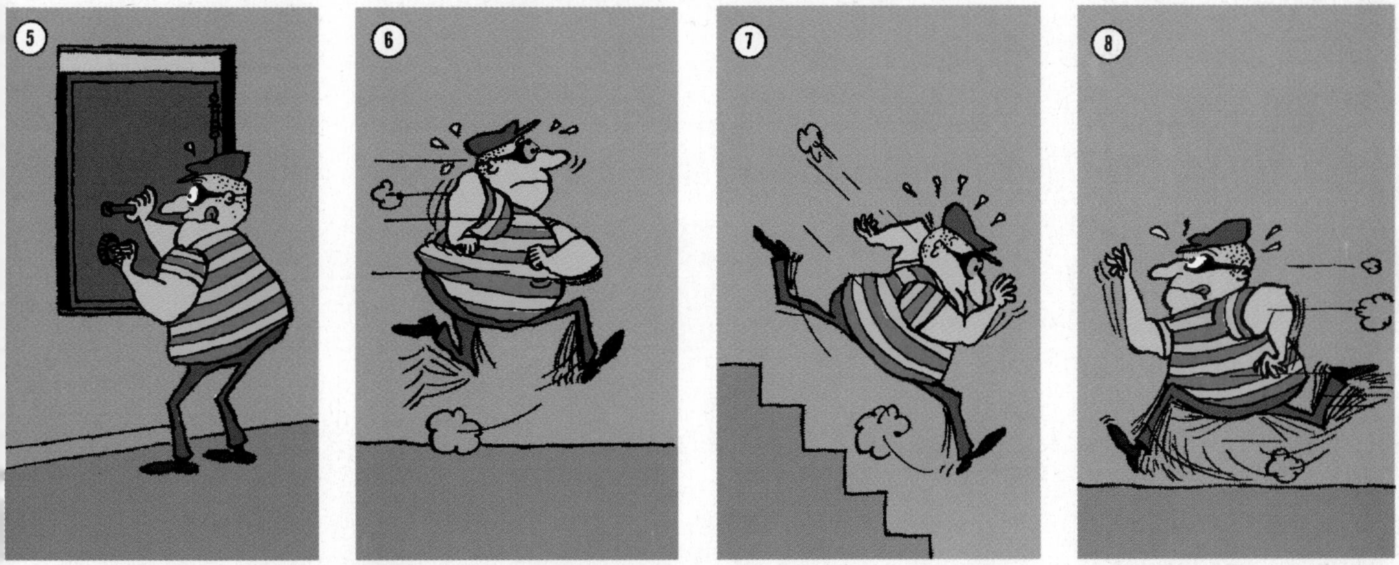

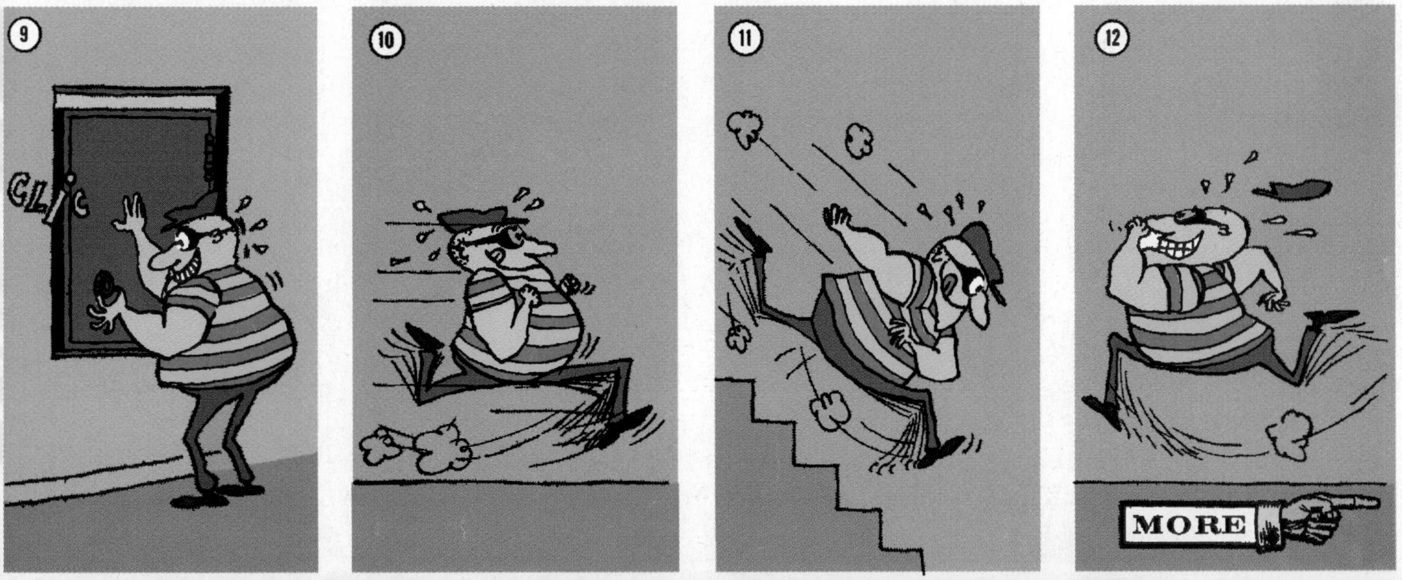
CLIC
MORE

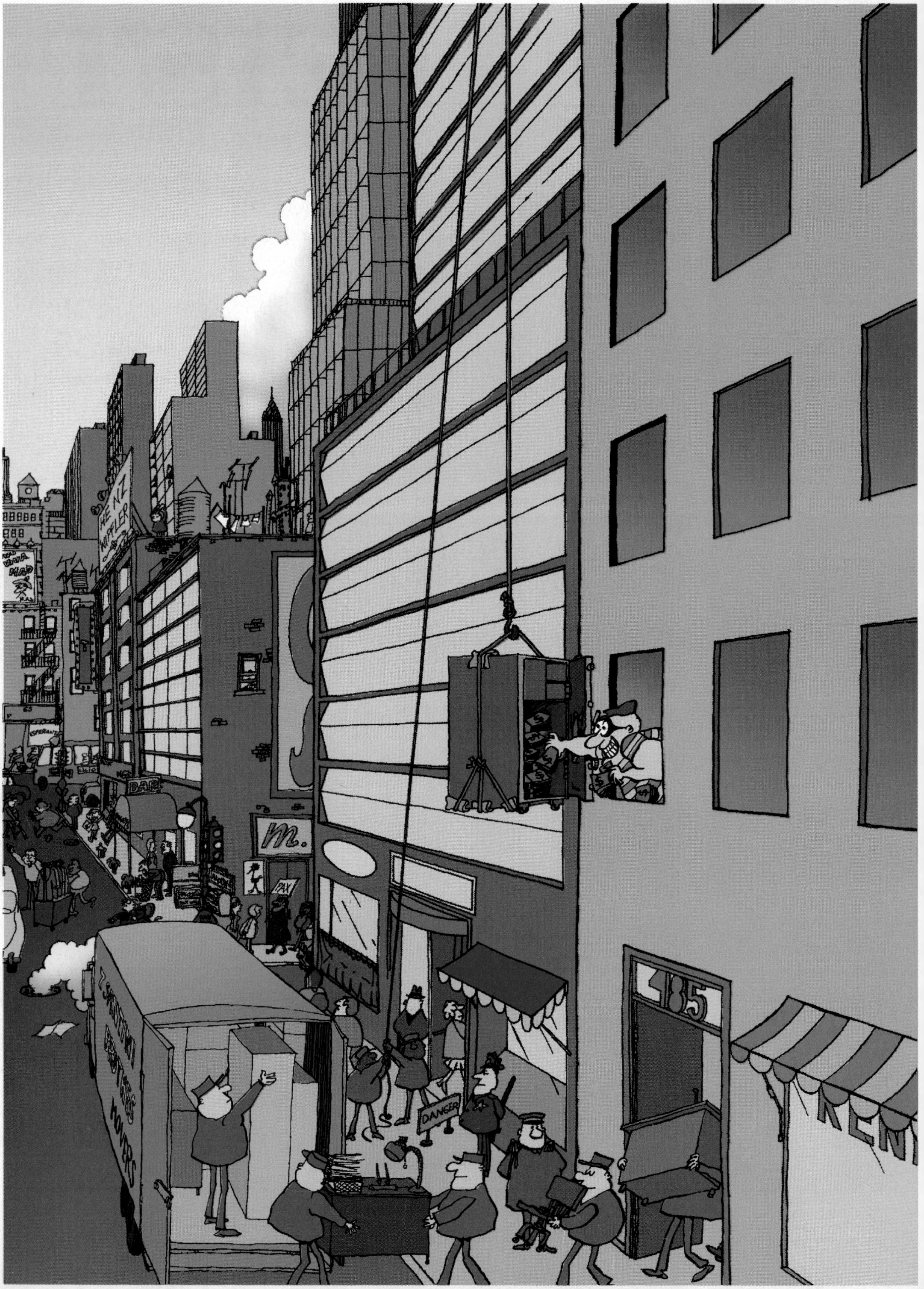
HEINZ KIPPLER
BAR
m.
PAX
DANGER
485
MOVERS

TALES FROM THE DOCK SIDE DEPT.

ONE FINE MORNING IN MIAMI

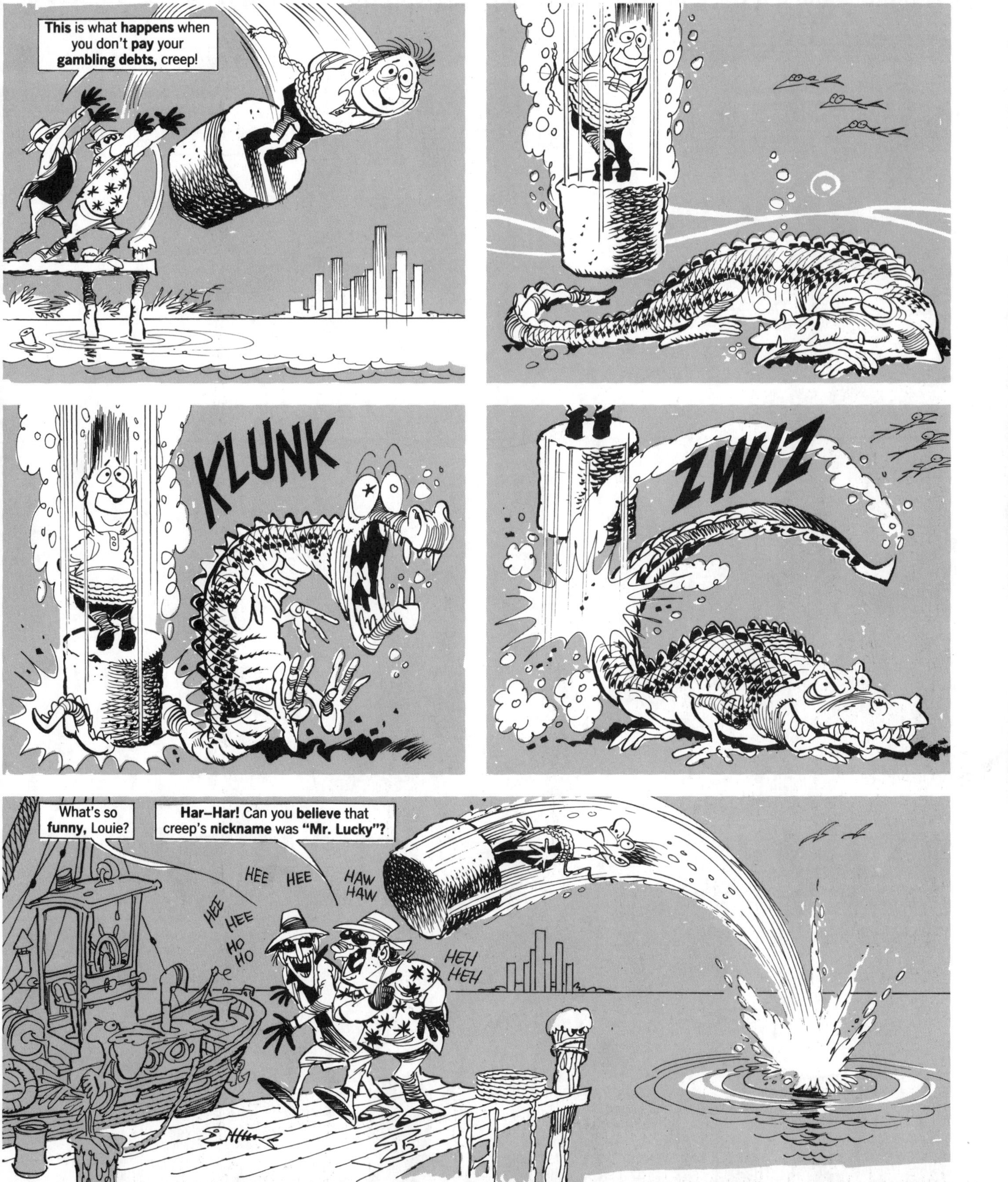

This is what happens when you don't pay your gambling debts, creep!
KLUNK
ZWIZ
What's so funny, Louie?
Har–Har! Can you believe that creep's nickname was "Mr. Lucky"?
HEE HEE
HAW HAW
HEE HEE
HO HO
HEH HEH

ARTIST: JACK DAVIS WRITER: DUCK EDWING

GUNS 'N' NEUROSIS DEPT.

This is a series about a lovable family man — a "Godfather Knows Best" if you will! This show is on HBO! It's best viewed if you get cable — illegally! So get comfortable, sit back in your undershirt and watch...

The

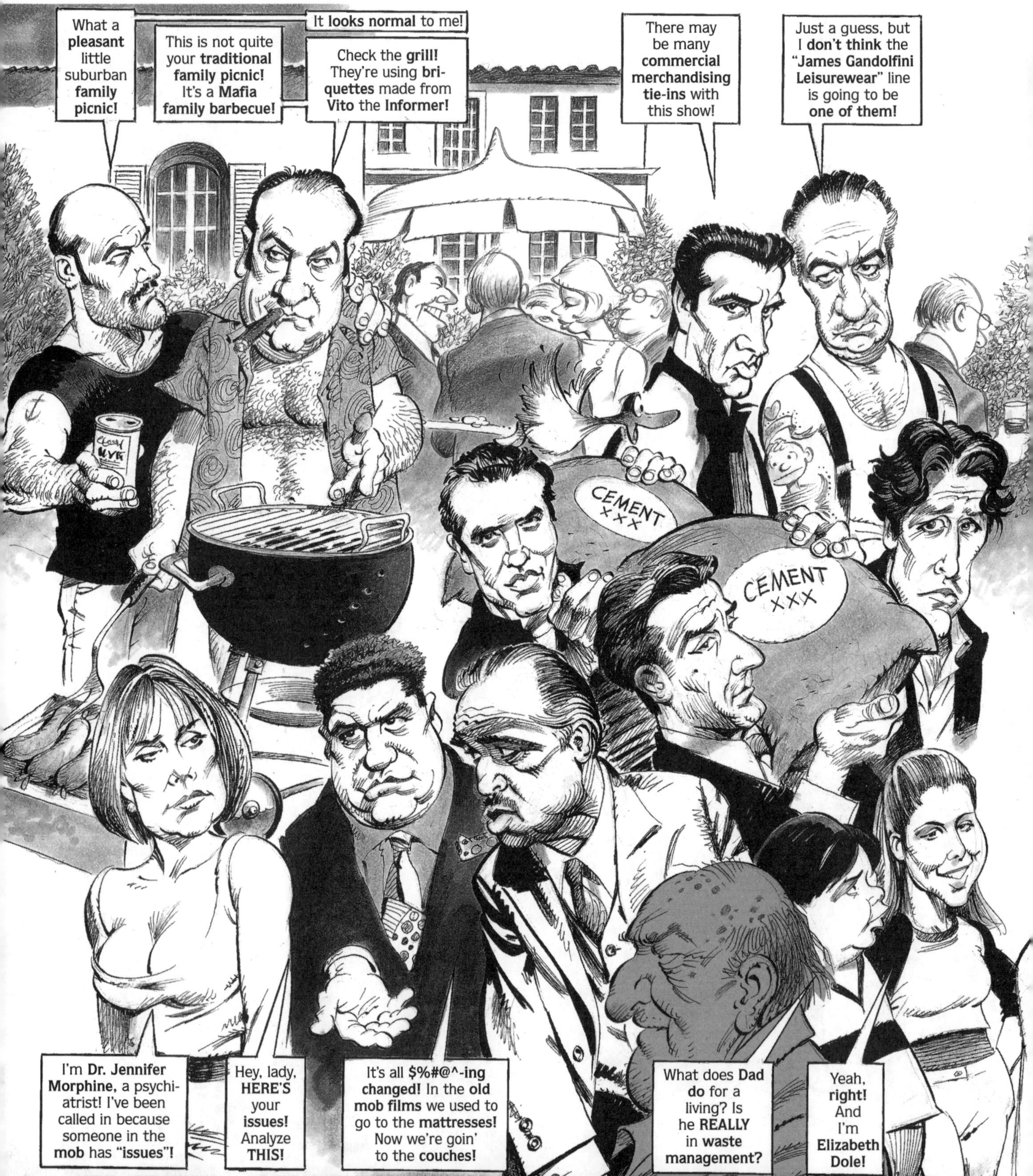

What a pleasant little suburban family picnic!
This is not quite your traditional family picnic! It's a Mafia family barbecue!
It looks normal to me!
Check the grill! They're using briquettes made from Vito the Informer!
There may be many commercial merchandising tie-ins with this show!
Just a guess, but I don't think the "James Gandolfini Leisurewear" line is going to be one of them!
CEMENT XXX
CEMENT XXX
I'm Dr. Jennifer Morphine, a psychiatrist! I've been called in because someone in the mob has "issues"!
Hey, lady, HERE'S your issues! Analyze THIS!
It's all $%#@^-ing changed! In the old mob films we used to go to the mattresses! Now we're goin' to the couches!
What does Dad do for a living? Is he REALLY in waste management?
Yeah, right! And I'm Elizabeth Dole!

ARTIST: MORT DRUCKER WRITER: ARNIE KOGEN

Supremos

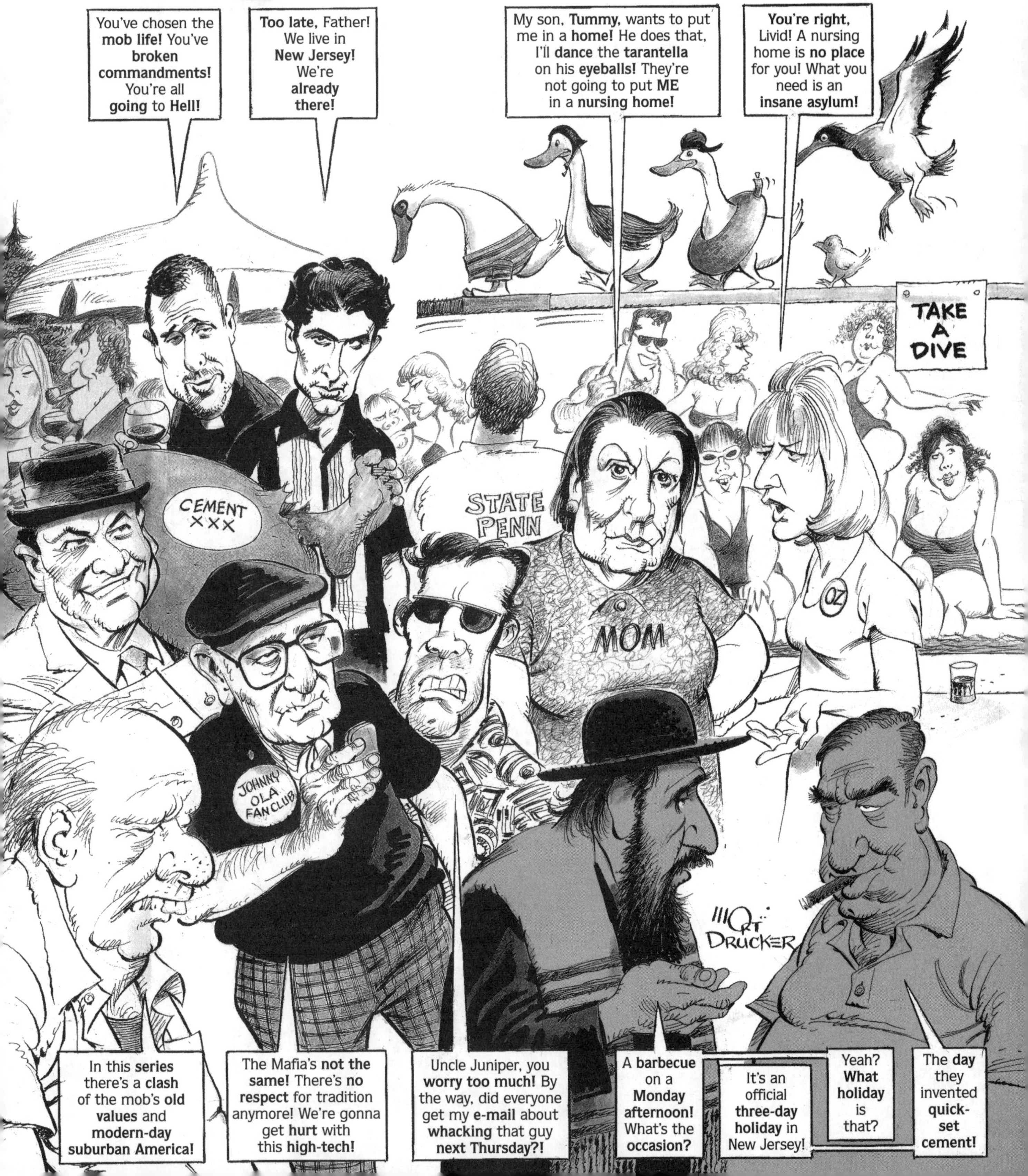

You've chosen the mob life! You've broken commandments! You're all going to Hell!
Too late, Father! We live in New Jersey! We're already there!
My son, Tummy, wants to put me in a home! He does that, I'll dance the tarantella on his eyeballs! They're not going to put ME in a nursing home!
You're right, Livid! A nursing home is no place for you! What you need is an insane asylum!
TAKE A DIVE
CEMENT XXX
STATE PENN
MOM
OZ
JOHNNY OLA FAN CLUB
MORT DRUCKER
In this series there's a clash of the mob's old values and modern-day suburban America!
The Mafia's not the same! There's no respect for tradition anymore! We're gonna get hurt with this high-tech!
Uncle Juniper, you worry too much! By the way, did everyone get my e-mail about whacking that guy next Thursday?!
A barbecue on a Monday afternoon! What's the occasion?
It's an official three-day holiday in New Jersey!
Yeah? What holiday is that?
The day they invented quick-set cement!

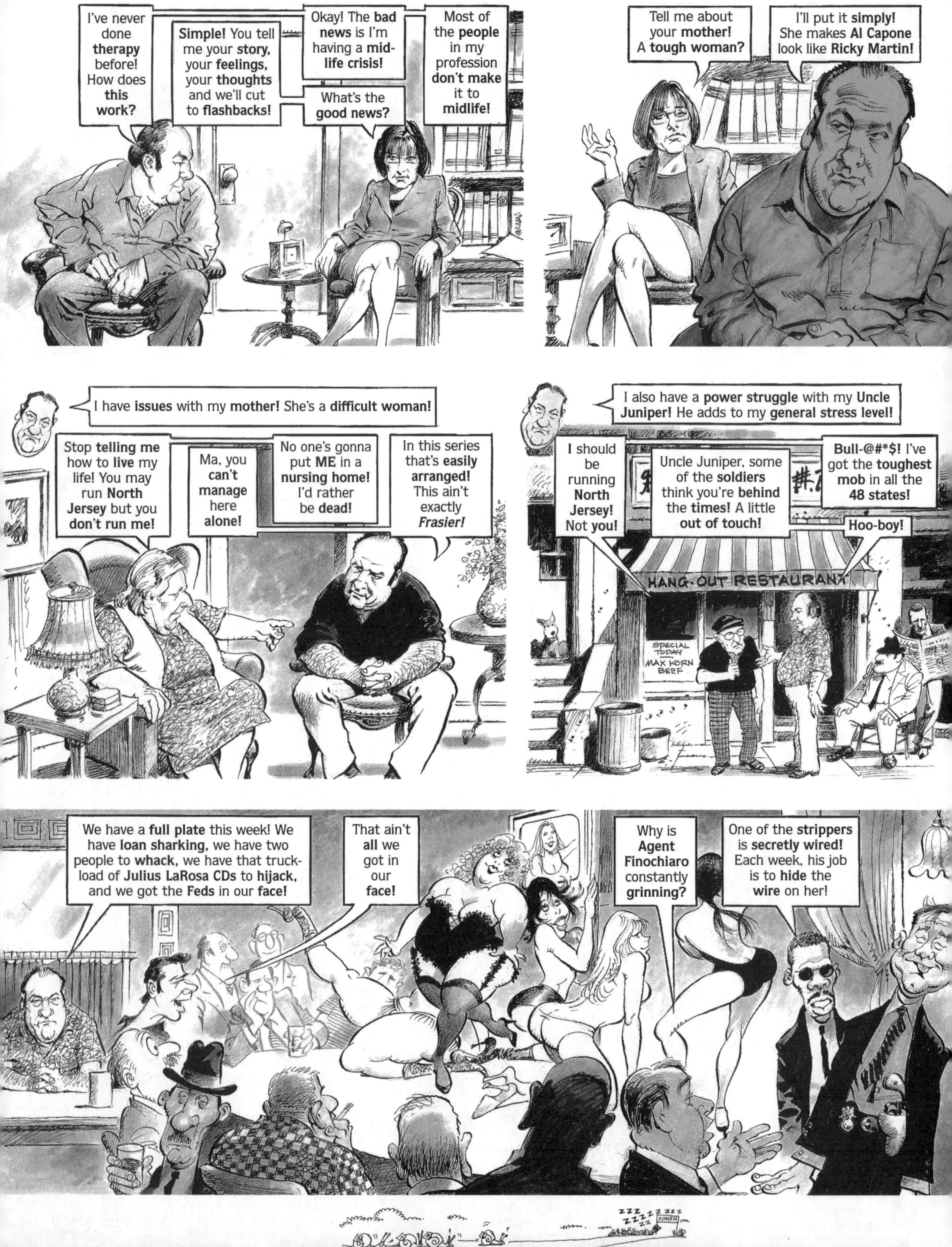

I've never done therapy before! How does this work?
Simple! You tell me your story, your feelings, your thoughts and we'll cut to flashbacks!
Okay! The bad news is I'm having a mid-life crisis!
What's the good news?
Most of the people in my profession don't make it to midlife!
Tell me about your mother! A tough woman?
I'll put it simply! She makes Al Capone look like Ricky Martin!
I have issues with my mother! She's a difficult woman!
Stop telling me how to live my life! You may run North Jersey but you don't run me!
Ma, you can't manage here alone!
No one's gonna put ME in a nursing home! I'd rather be dead!
In this series that's easily arranged! This ain't exactly Frasier!
I also have a power struggle with my Uncle Juniper! He adds to my general stress level!
I should be running North Jersey! Not you!
Uncle Juniper, some of the soldiers think you're behind the times! A little out of touch!
Bull-@#*$! I've got the toughest mob in all the 48 states!
Hoo-boy!
HANG-OUT RESTAURANT
SPECIAL TODAY MAX KORN BEEF
We have a full plate this week! We have loan sharking, we have two people to whack, we have that truck-load of Julius LaRosa CDs to hijack, and we got the Feds in our face!
That ain't all we got in our face!
Why is Agent Finochiaro constantly grinning?
One of the strippers is secretly wired! Each week, his job is to hide the wire on her!
ZZZ ZZZZ ZZZ
FINISH

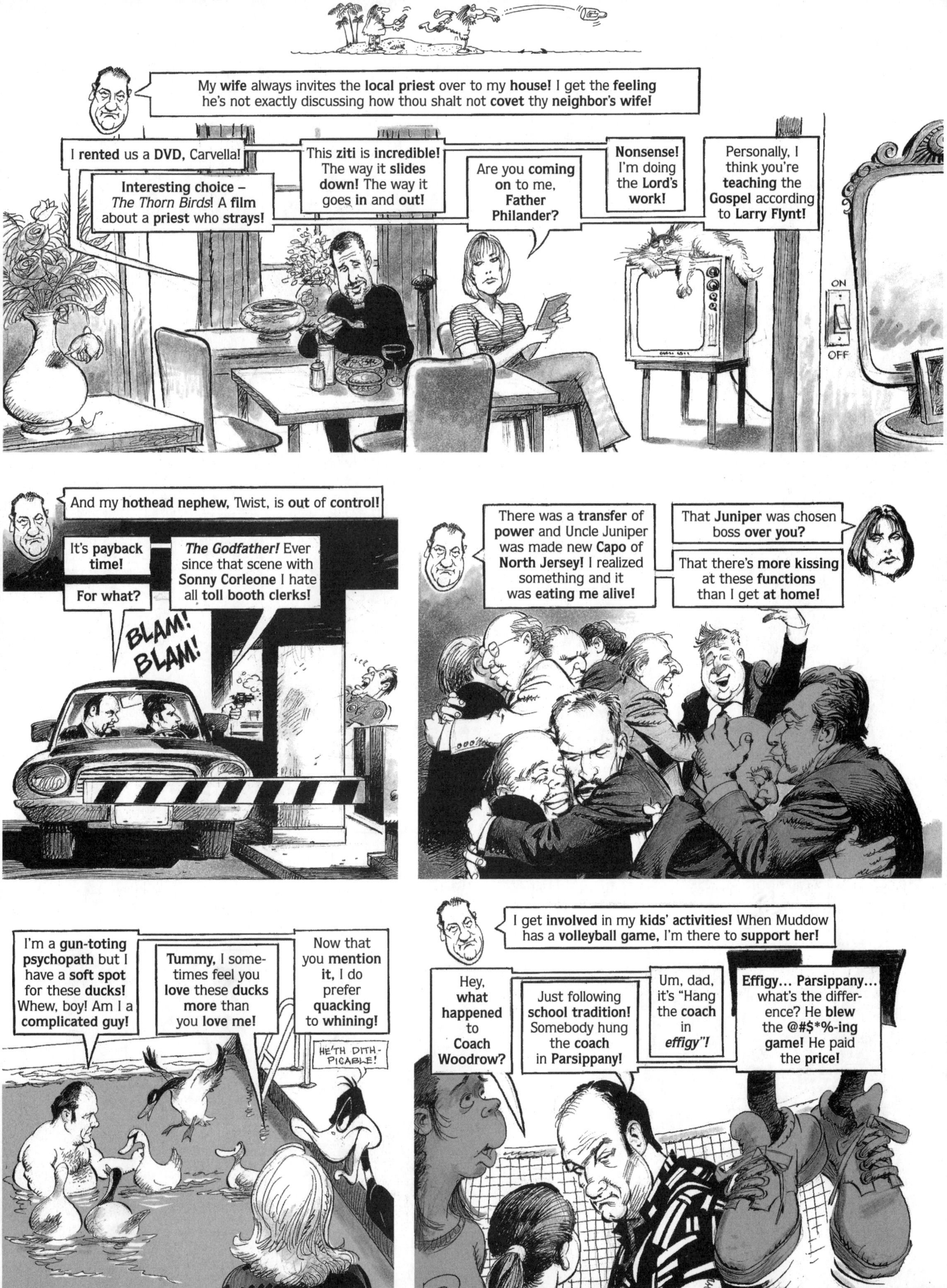

My wife always invites the local priest over to my house! I get the feeling he's not exactly discussing how thou shalt not covet thy neighbor's wife!
I rented us a DVD, Carvella!
Interesting choice – The Thorn Birds! A film about a priest who strays!
This ziti is incredible! The way it slides down! The way it goes in and out!
Are you coming on to me, Father Philander?
Nonsense! I'm doing the Lord's work!
Personally, I think you're teaching the Gospel according to Larry Flynt!
ON
OFF
And my hothead nephew, Twist, is out of control!
It's payback time!
For what?
The Godfather! Ever since that scene with Sonny Corleone I hate all toll booth clerks!
BLAM! BLAM!
There was a transfer of power and Uncle Juniper was made new Capo of North Jersey! I realized something and it was eating me alive!
That Juniper was chosen boss over you?
That there's more kissing at these functions than I get at home!
I'm a gun-toting psychopath but I have a soft spot for these ducks! Whew, boy! Am I a complicated guy!
Tummy, I sometimes feel you love these ducks more than you love me!
Now that you mention it, I do prefer quacking to whining!
HE'TH DITH-PICABLE!
I get involved in my kids' activities! When Muddow has a volleyball game, I'm there to support her!
Hey, what happened to Coach Woodrow?
Just following school tradition! Somebody hung the coach in Parsippany!
Um, dad, it's "Hang the coach in effigy"!
Effigy... Parsippany... what's the difference? He blew the @#$*%-ing game! He paid the price!

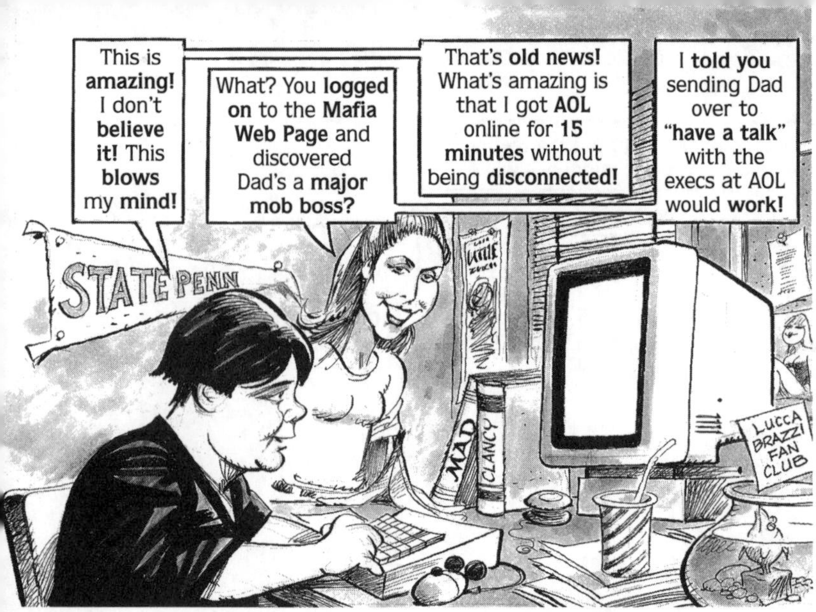
This is amazing! I don't believe it! This blows my mind!
What? You logged on to the Mafia Web Page and discovered Dad's a major mob boss?
That's old news! What's amazing is that I got AOL online for 15 minutes without being disconnected!
I told you sending Dad over to "have a talk" with the execs at AOL would work!
STATE PENN
MAD
CLANCY
LUCCA BRAZZI FAN CLUB

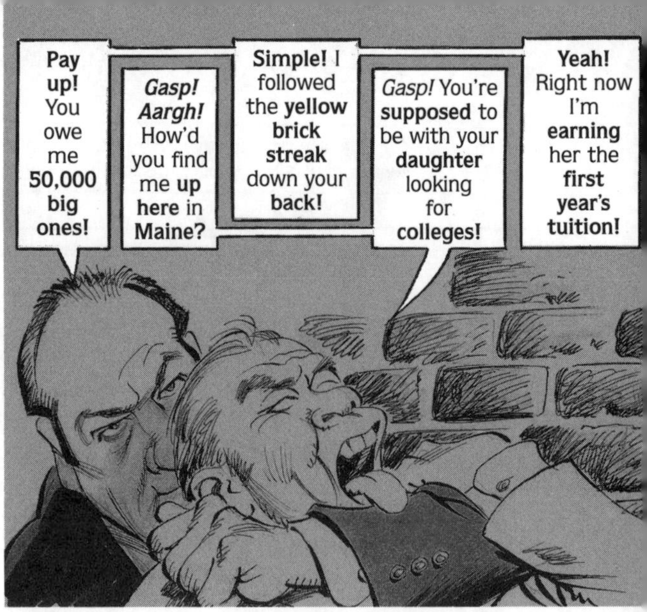
Pay up! You owe me 50,000 big ones!
Gasp! Aargh! How'd you find me up here in Maine?
Simple! I followed the yellow brick streak down your back!
Gasp! You're supposed to be with your daughter looking for colleges!
Yeah! Right now I'm earning her the first year's tuition!

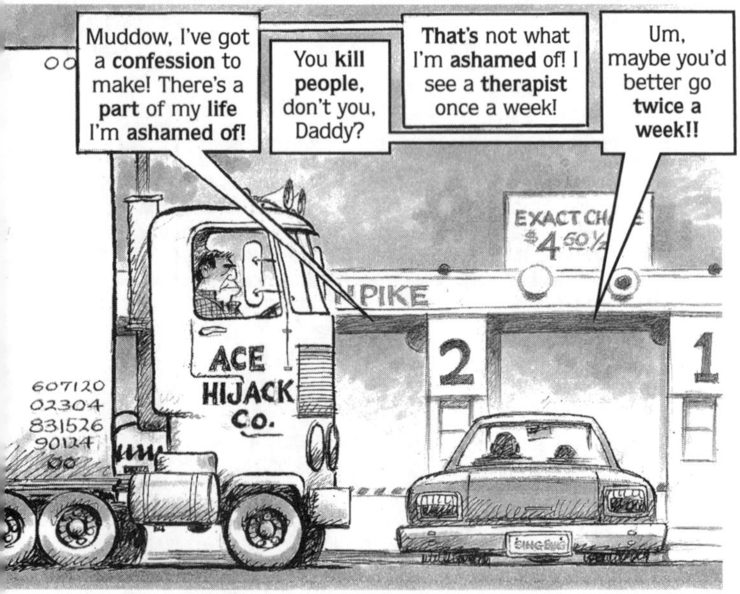
Muddow, I've got a confession to make! There's a part of my life I'm ashamed of!
You kill people, don't you, Daddy?
That's not what I'm ashamed of! I see a therapist once a week!
Um, maybe you'd better go twice a week!!
ACE HIJACK Co.
607120
02304
831526
90124

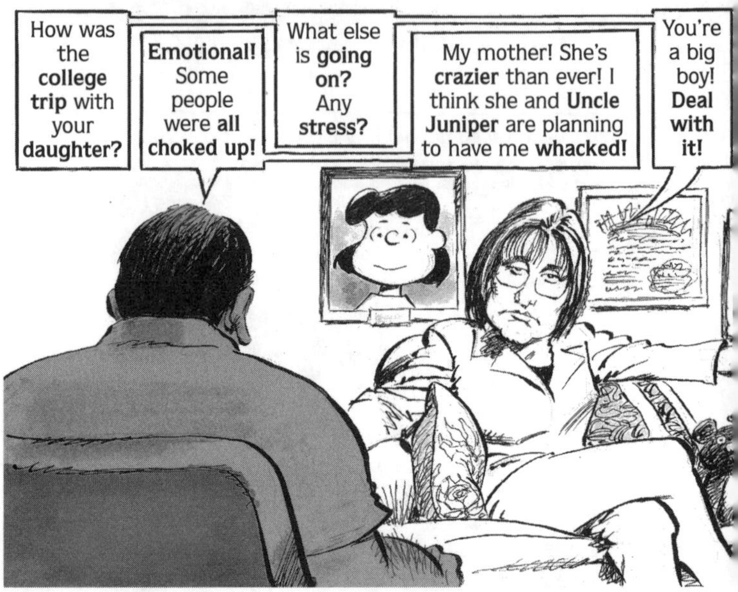
How was the college trip with your daughter?
Emotional! Some people were all choked up!
What else is going on? Any stress?
My mother! She's crazier than ever! I think she and Uncle Juniper are planning to have me whacked!
You're a big boy! Deal with it!

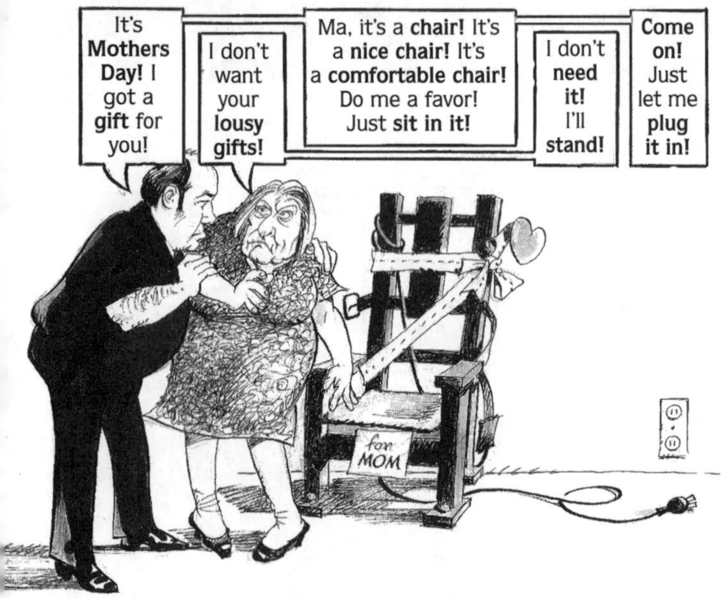
It's Mothers Day! I got a gift for you!
I don't want your lousy gifts!
Ma, it's a chair! It's a nice chair! It's a comfortable chair! Do me a favor! Just sit in it!
I don't need it! I'll stand!
Come on! Just let me plug it in!
for MOM

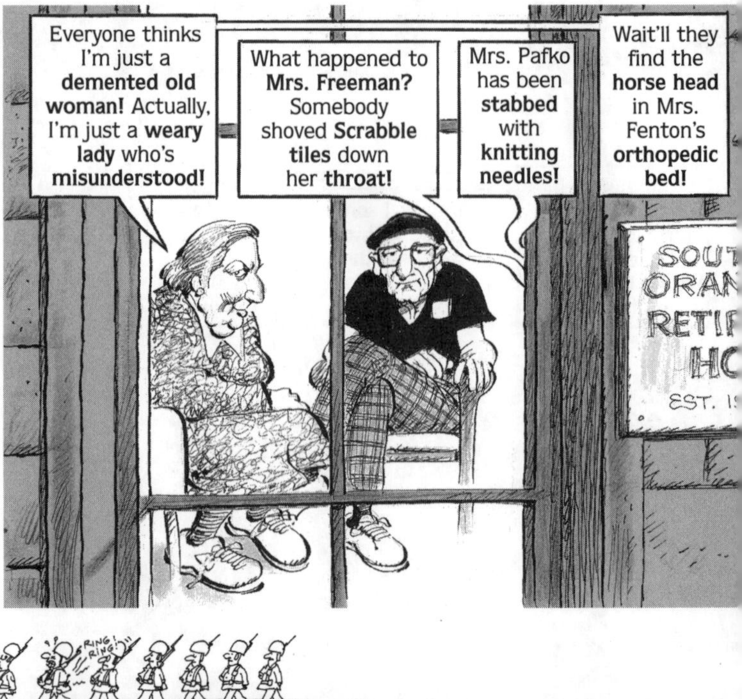
Everyone thinks I'm just a demented old woman! Actually, I'm just a weary lady who's misunderstood!
What happened to Mrs. Freeman? Somebody shoved Scrabble tiles down her throat!
Mrs. Pafko has been stabbed with knitting needles!
Wait'll they find the horse head in Mrs. Fenton's orthopedic bed!

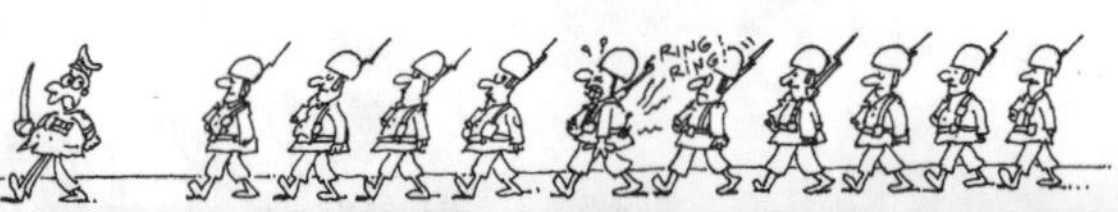
RING! RING!

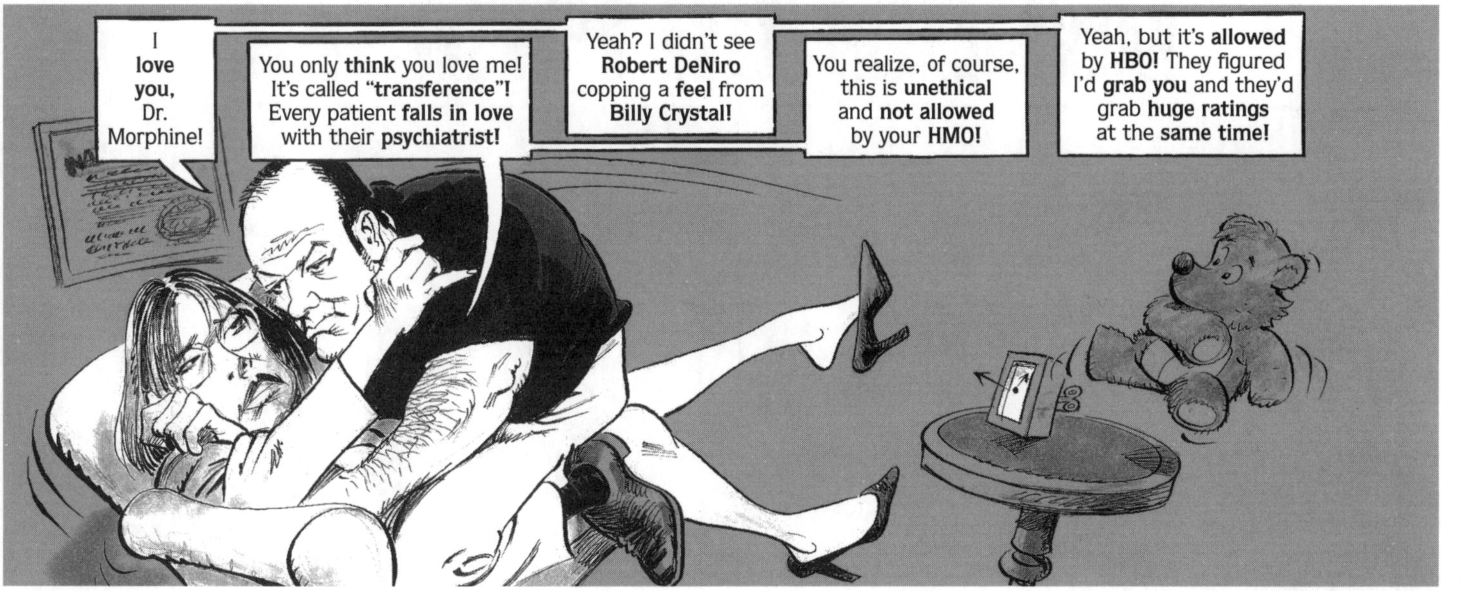
I love you, Dr. Morphine!
You only think you love me! It's called "transference"! Every patient falls in love with their psychiatrist!
Yeah? I didn't see Robert DeNiro copping a feel from Billy Crystal!
You realize, of course, this is unethical and not allowed by your HMO!
Yeah, but it's allowed by HBO! They figured I'd grab you and they'd grab huge ratings at the same time!

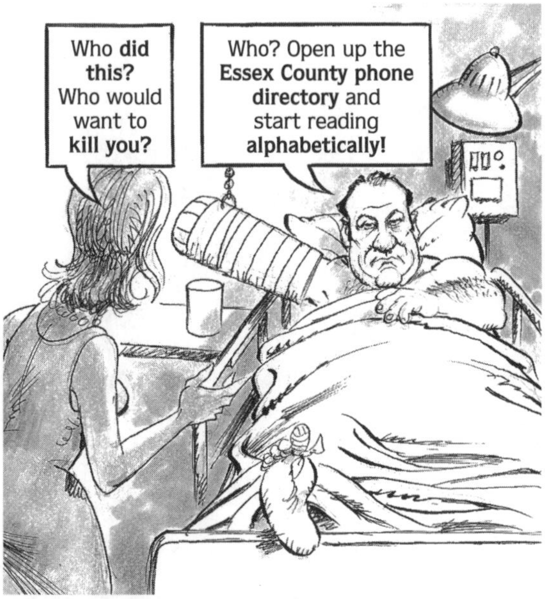
Who did this? Who would want to kill you?
Who? Open up the Essex County phone directory and start reading alphabetically!

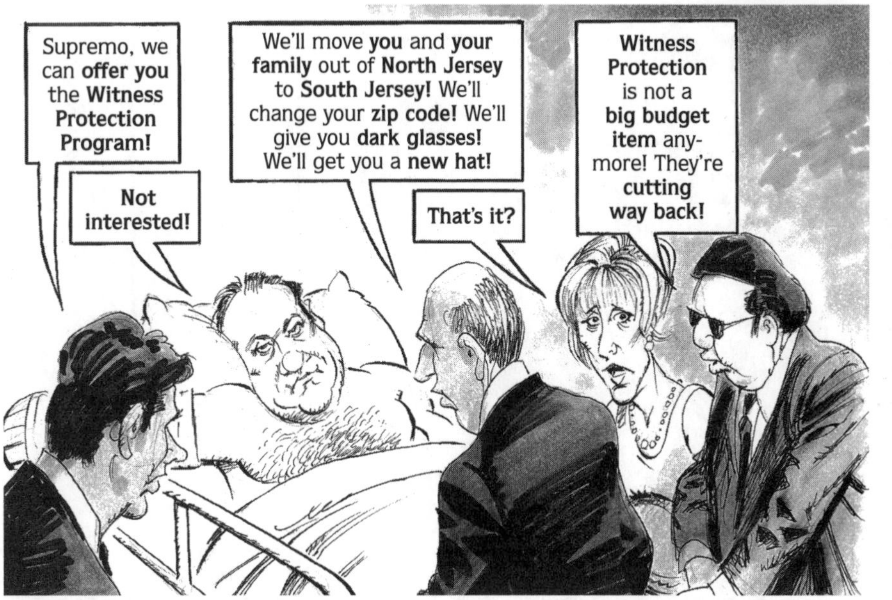
Supremo, we can offer you the Witness Protection Program!
Not interested!
We'll move you and your family out of North Jersey to South Jersey! We'll change your zip code! We'll give you dark glasses! We'll get you a new hat!
That's it?
Witness Protection is not a big budget item any-more! They're cutting way back!

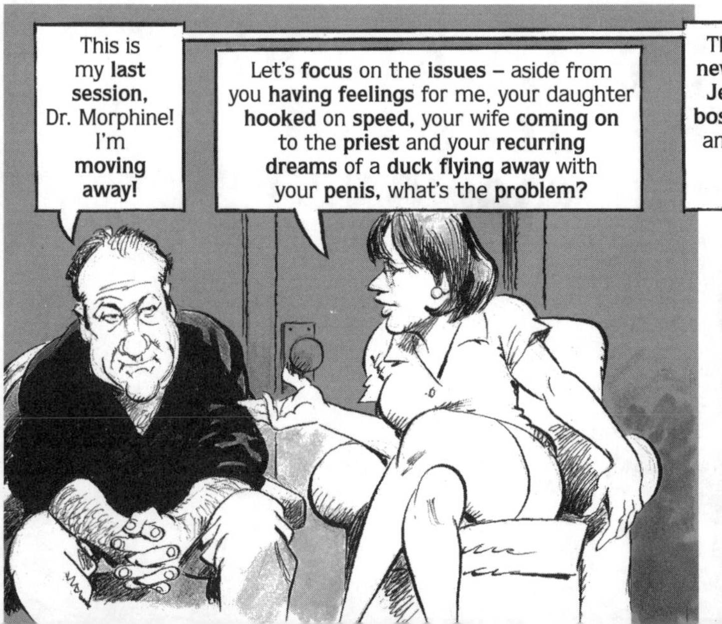
This is my last session, Dr. Morphine! I'm moving away!
Let's focus on the issues – aside from you having feelings for me, your daughter hooked on speed, your wife coming on to the priest and your recurring dreams of a duck flying away with your penis, what's the problem?

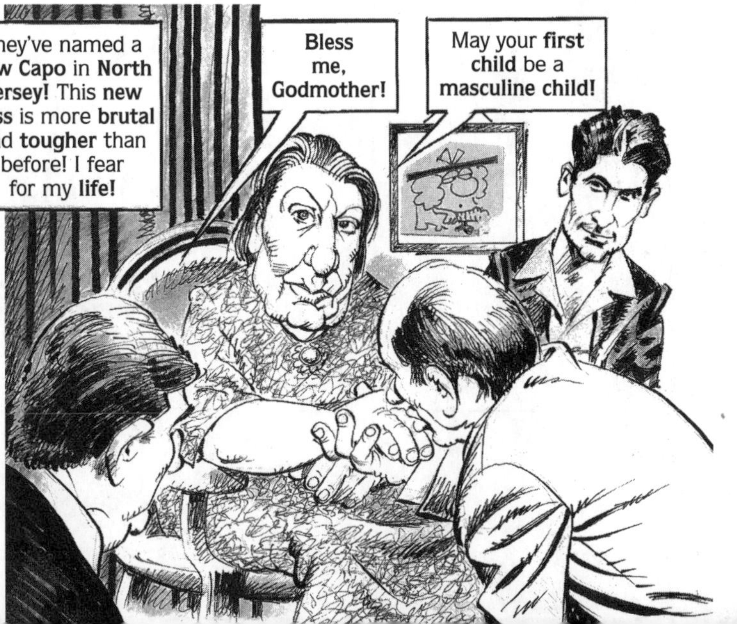
They've named a new Capo in North Jersey! This new boss is more brutal and tougher than before! I fear for my life!
Bless me, Godmother!
May your first child be a masculine child!

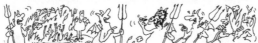

ALLEY OOPS! DEPT.

DRAMA ON PAGE 72

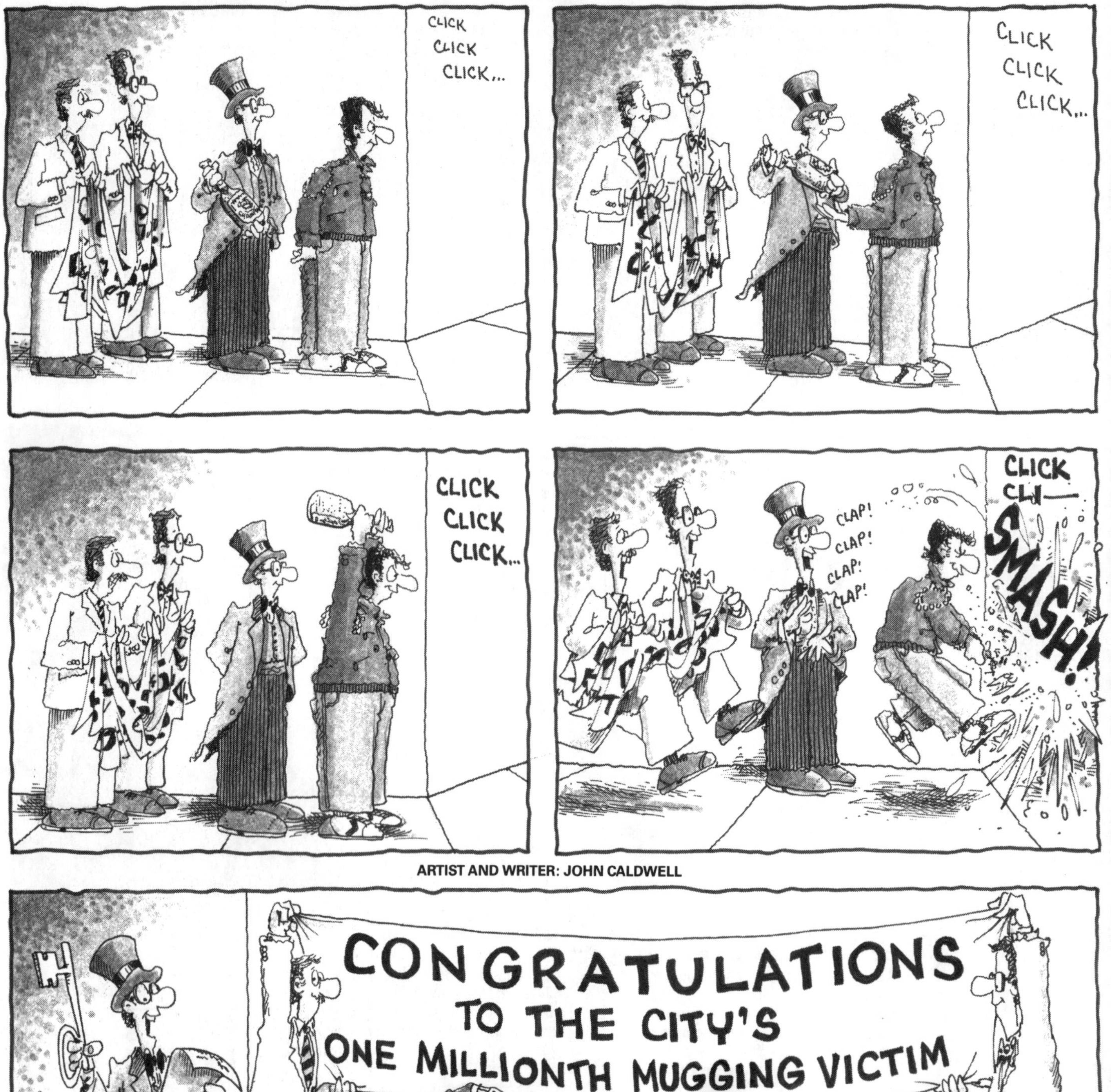
CLICK
CLICK
CLICK...
CLICK
CLICK
CLICK...
CLICK
CLICK
CLICK...
CLAP!
CLAP!
CLAP!
CLAP!
CLICK
CLI—
SMASH!!

ARTIST AND WRITER: JOHN CALDWELL

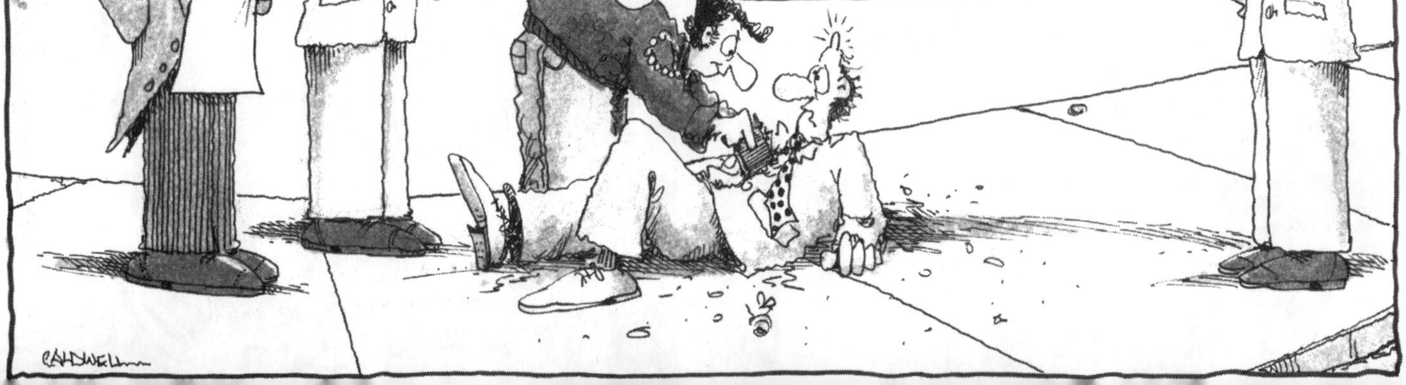
CONGRATULATIONS
TO THE CITY'S
ONE MILLIONTH MUGGING VICTIM
CALDWELL

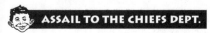

These days it's common wisdom that "all politicians are crooks." But there are big differences! And if you don't believe us, just take a look as we compare the most powerful man on television, Tony Soprano, to the second most powerful man in the White House (next to Dick Cheney), George W. Bush! As we see them, here are...

THE SUBTLE DIFFERENCES BETWEEN TONY SOPRANO & GEORGE W. BUSH

ARTIST: SAM SISCO WRITER: STAN SINBERG

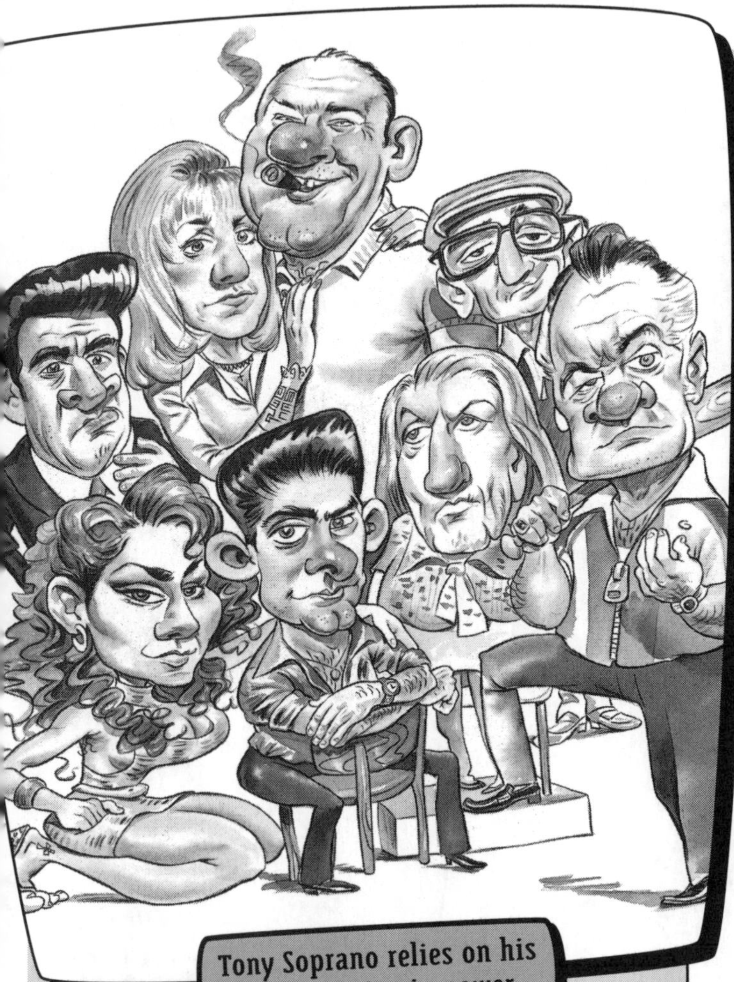

Tony Soprano relies on his family to stay in power.

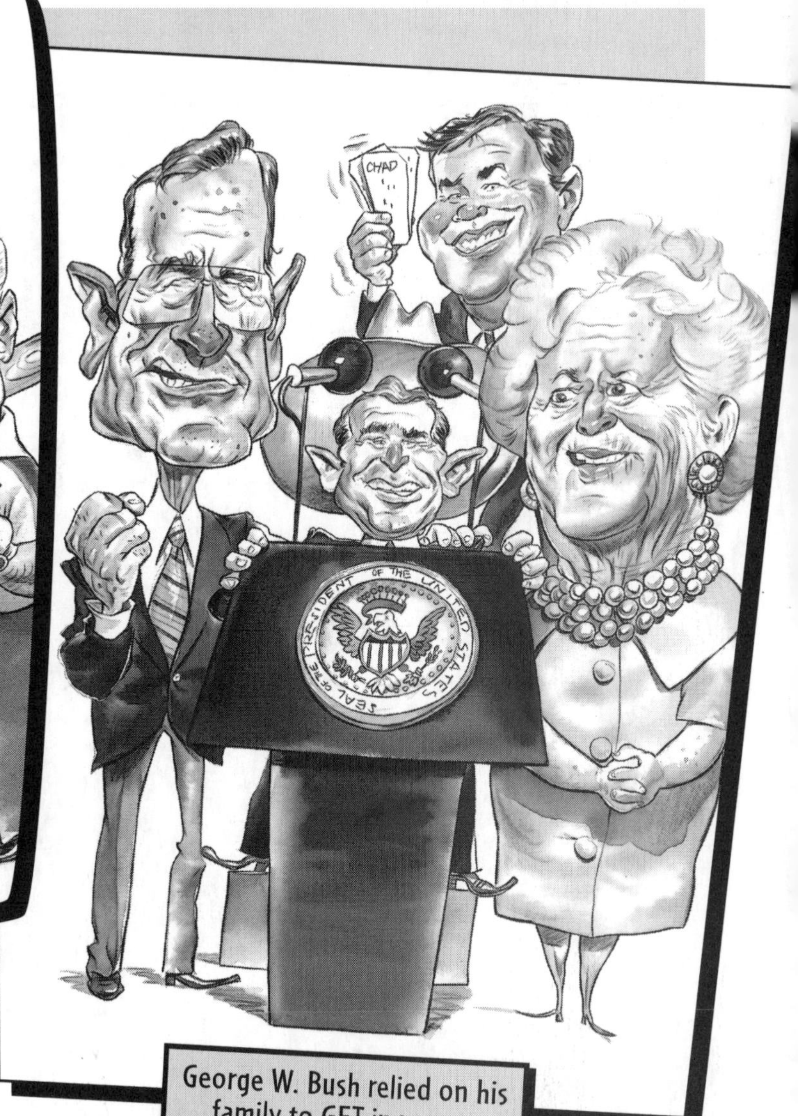
CHAD

George W. Bush relied on his family to GET in power.

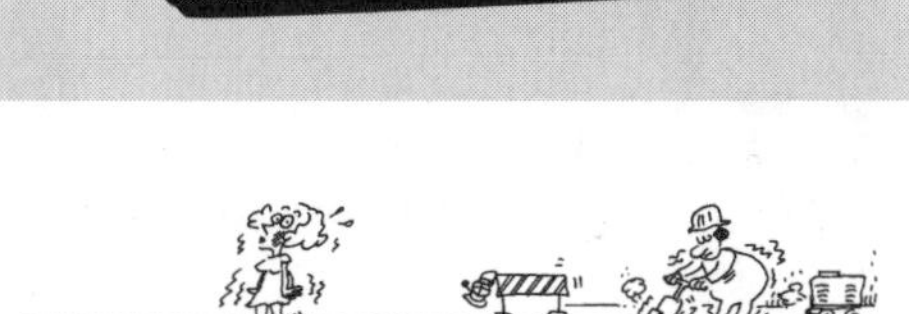

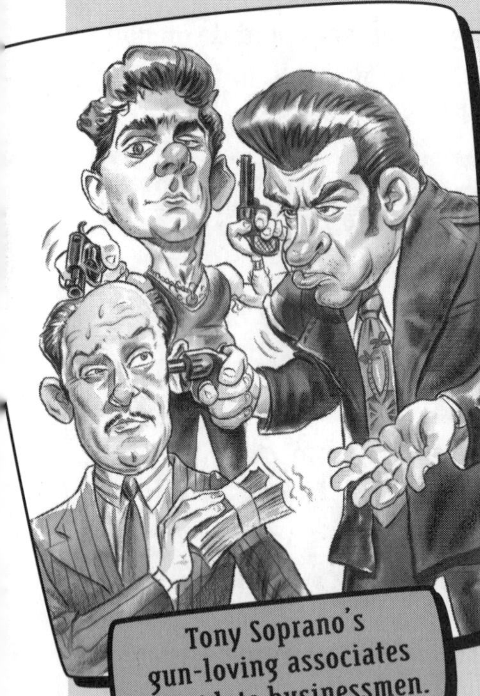
Tony Soprano's gun-loving associates intimidate businessmen.

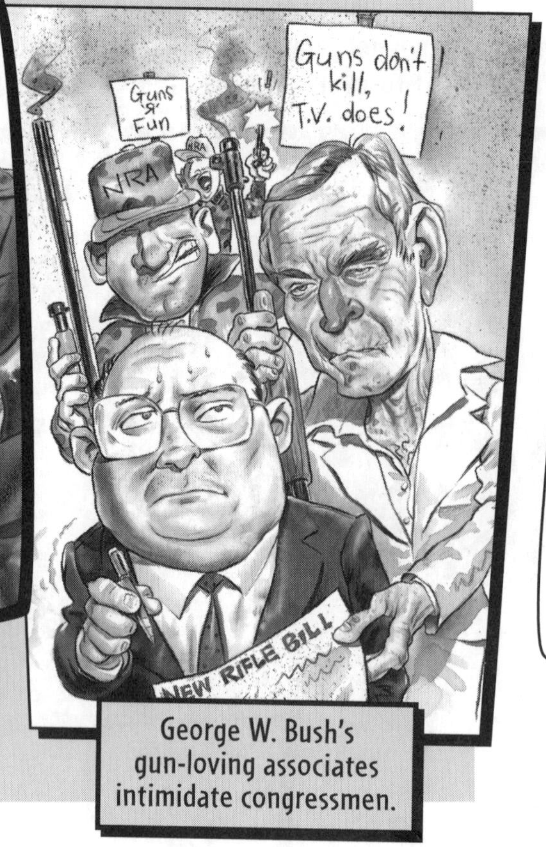
'Guns 'R' Fun
NRA
Guns don't kill, T.V. does!
NEW RIFLE BILL
George W. Bush's gun-loving associates intimidate congressmen.

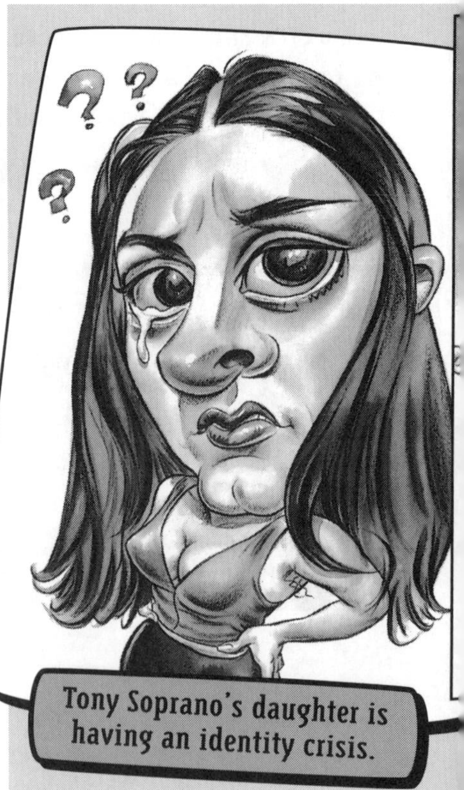
Tony Soprano's daughter is having an identity crisis.

THE SUBTLE DIFFERENCES BETWEEN

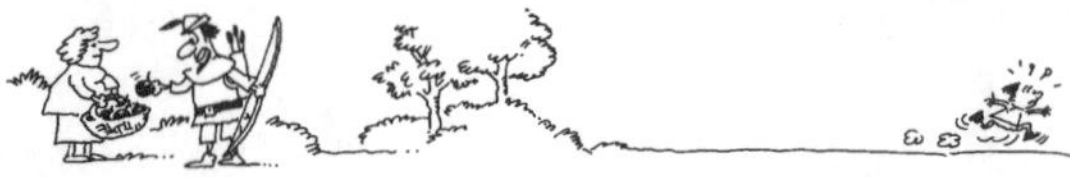

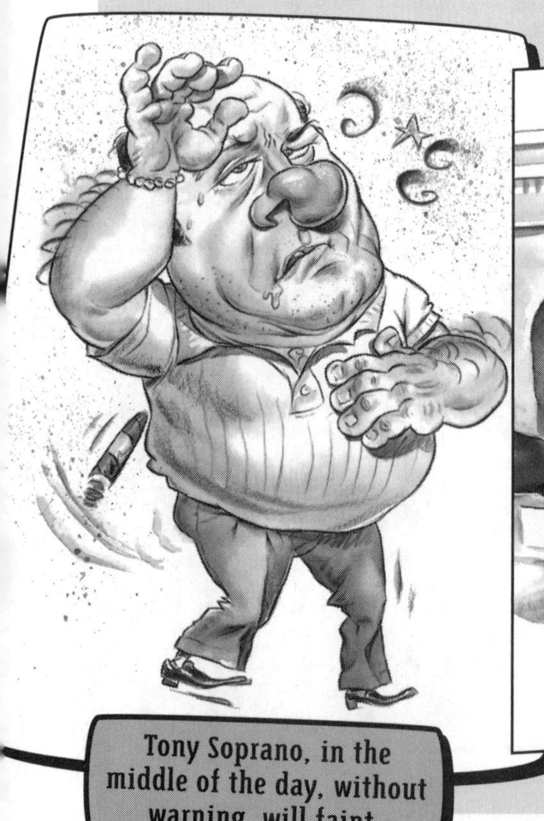
Tony Soprano, in the middle of the day, without warning, will faint.

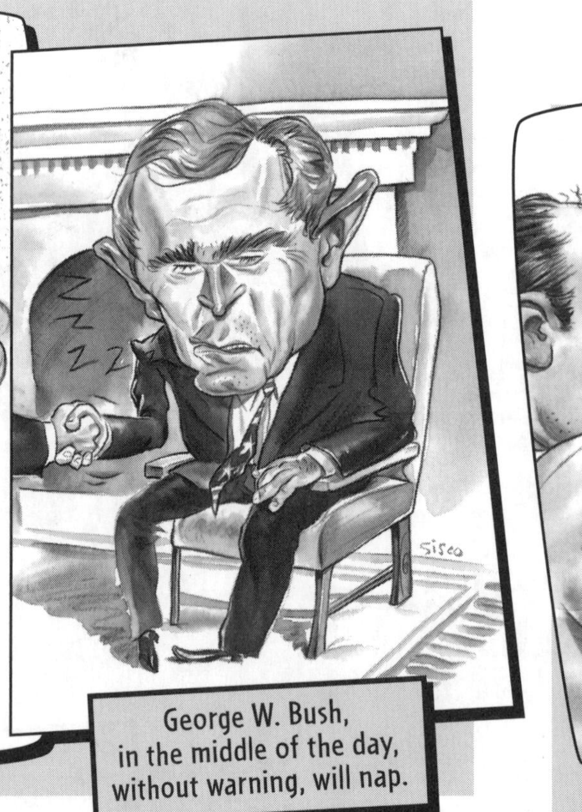
Sisco
George W. Bush, in the middle of the day, without warning, will nap.

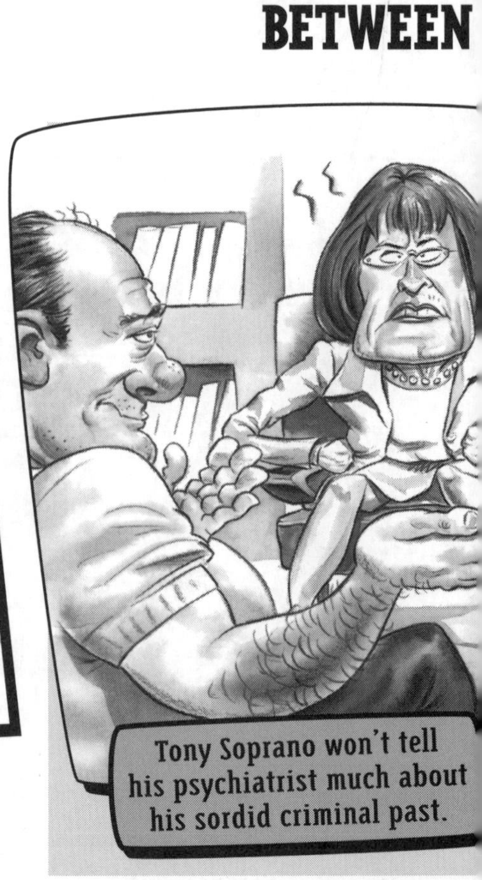
Tony Soprano won't tell his psychiatrist much about his sordid criminal past.

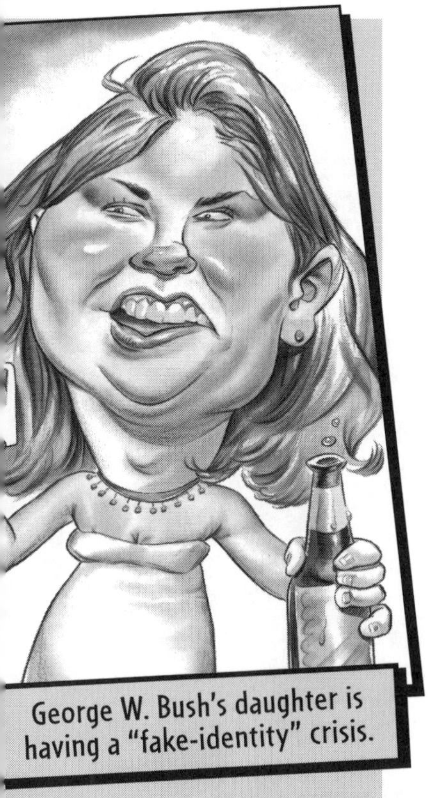
George W. Bush's daughter is having a "fake-identity" crisis.

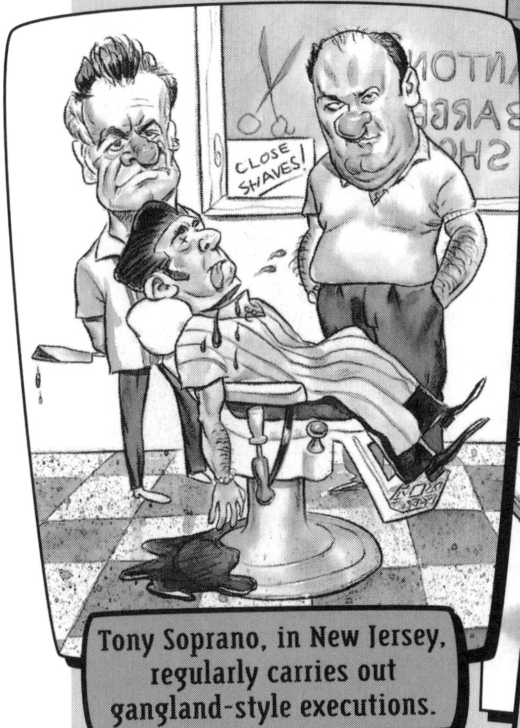
CLOSE SHAVES!
Tony Soprano, in New Jersey, regularly carries out gangland-style executions.

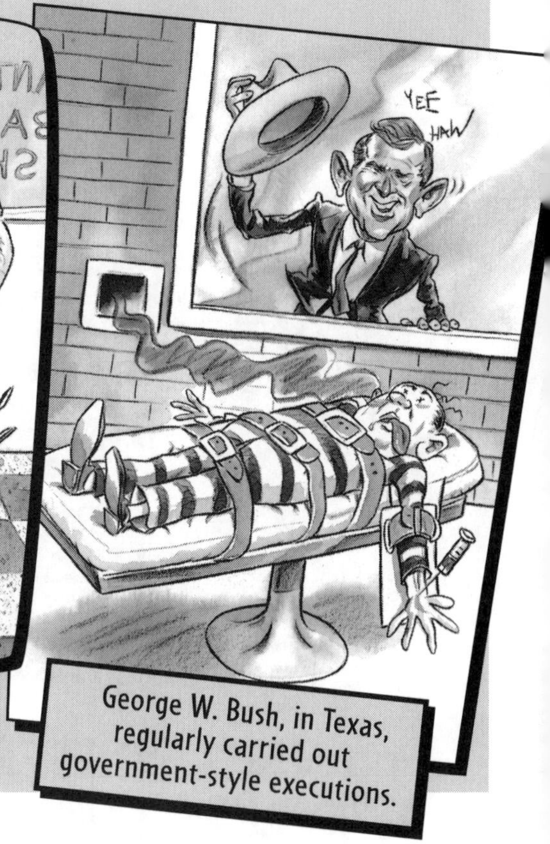
YEE HAW
George W. Bush, in Texas, regularly carried out government-style executions.

ONY SOPRANO & EORGE W. BUSH

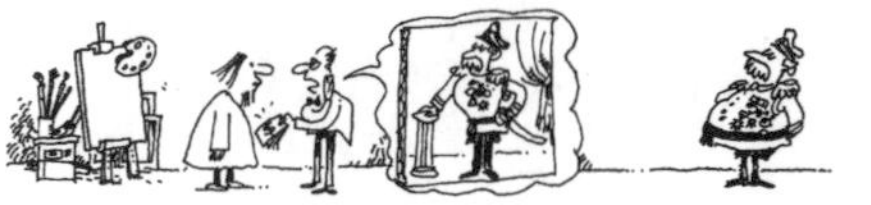

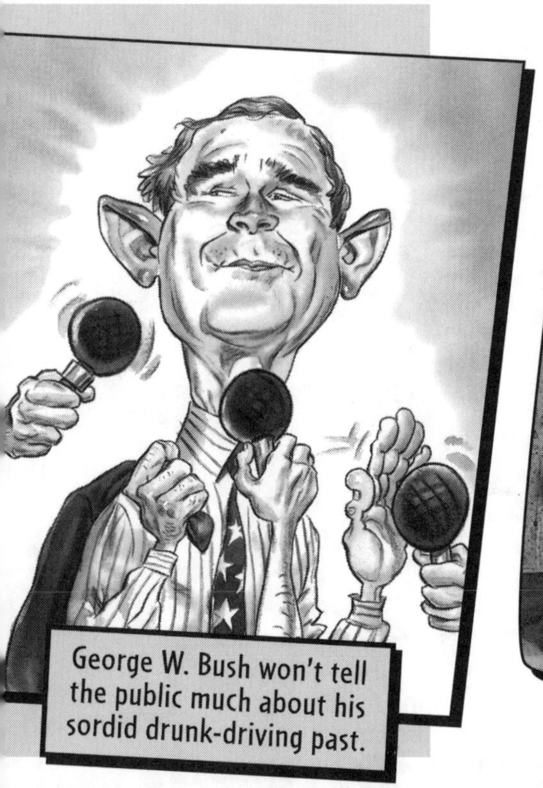
George W. Bush won't tell the public much about his sordid drunk-driving past.

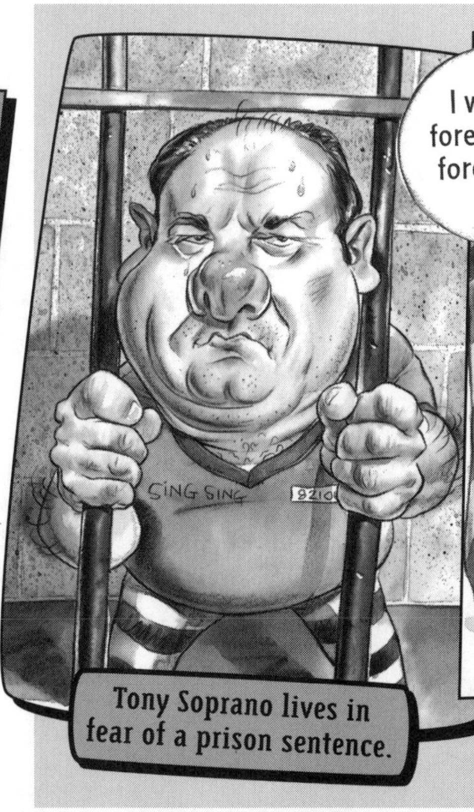
SING SING
Tony Soprano lives in fear of a prison sentence.

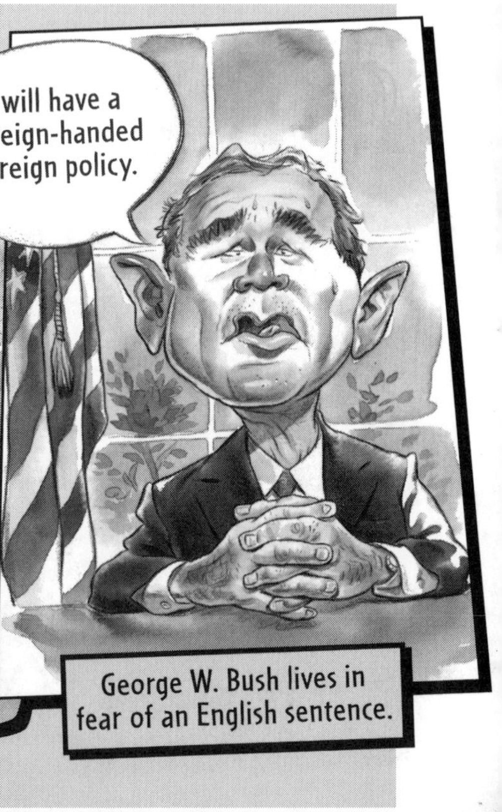
I will have a foreign-handed foreign policy.
George W. Bush lives in fear of an English sentence.

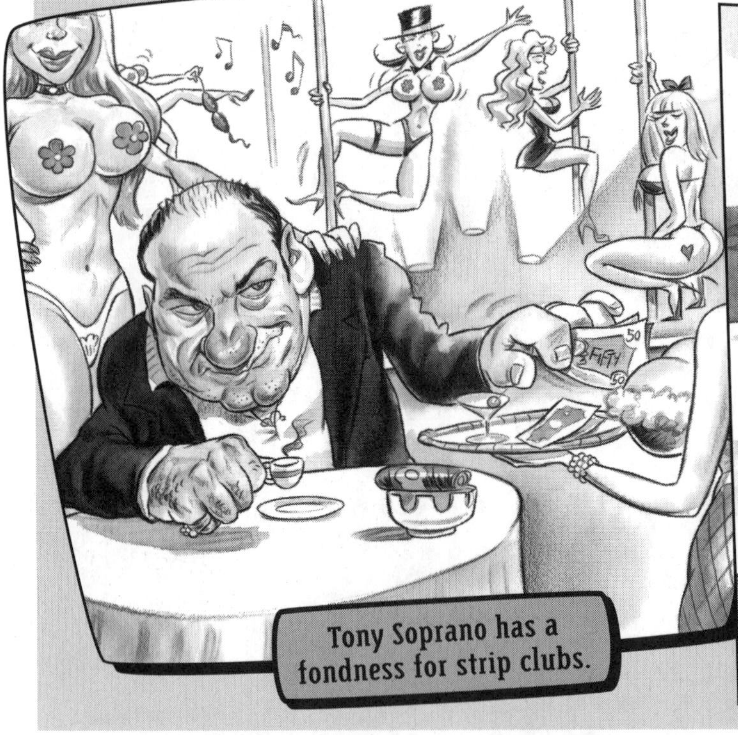
Tony Soprano has a fondness for strip clubs.

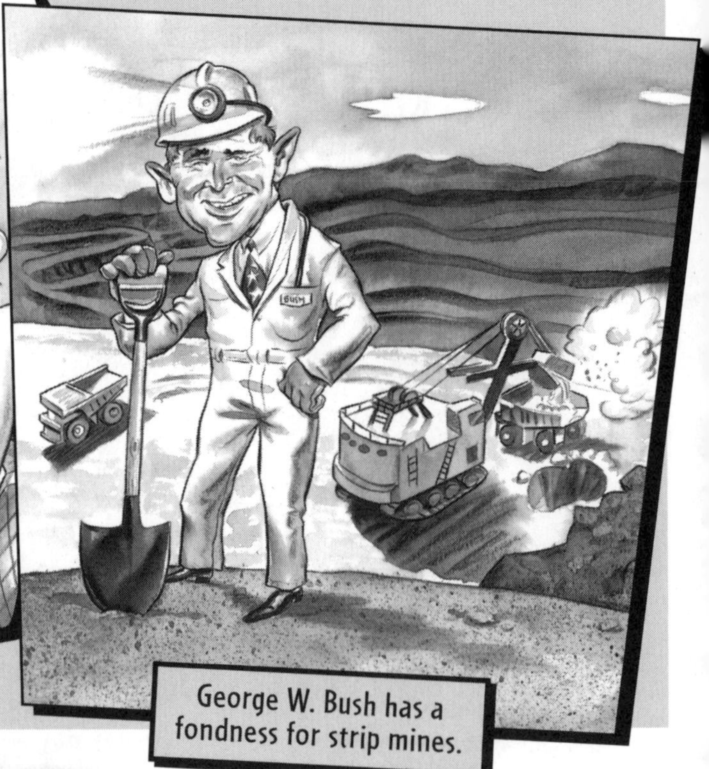
George W. Bush has a fondness for strip mines.

THE SUBTLE DIFFERENCES BETWEEN TONY SOPRANO & GEORGE W. BUSH

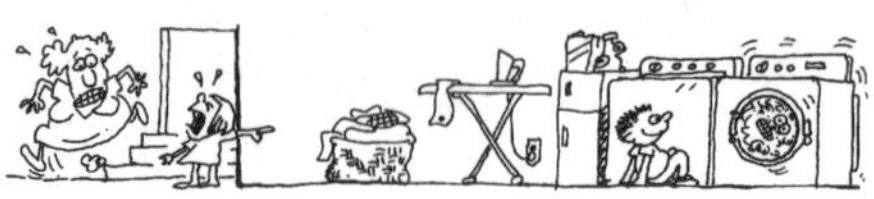

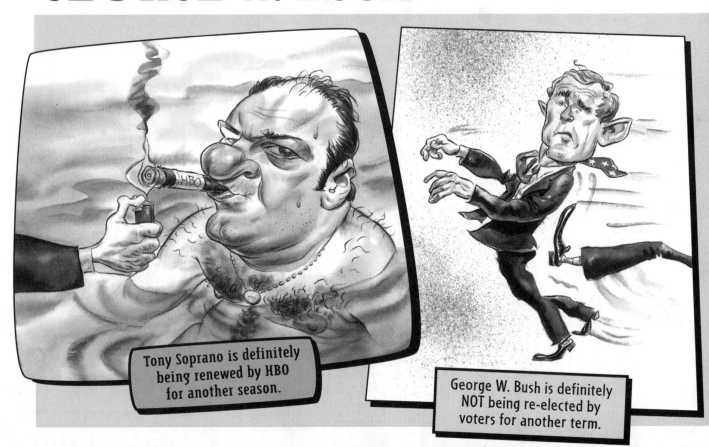

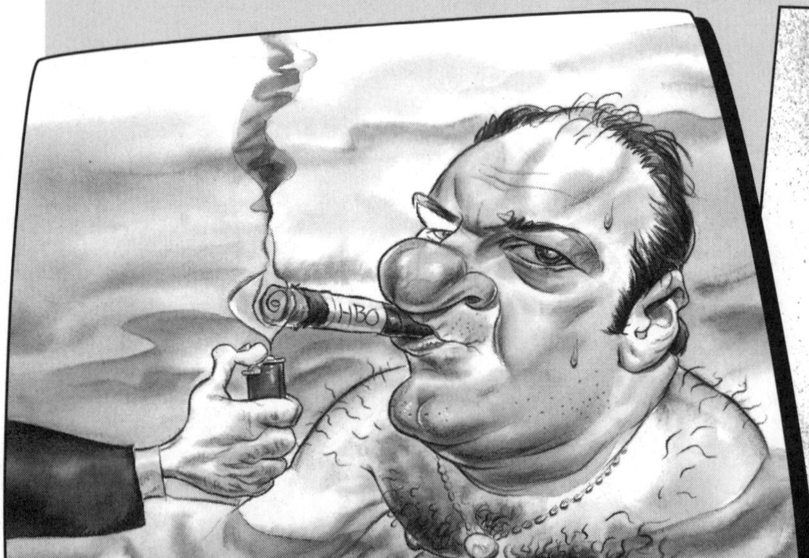
HBO
Tony Soprano is definitely being renewed by HBO for another season.

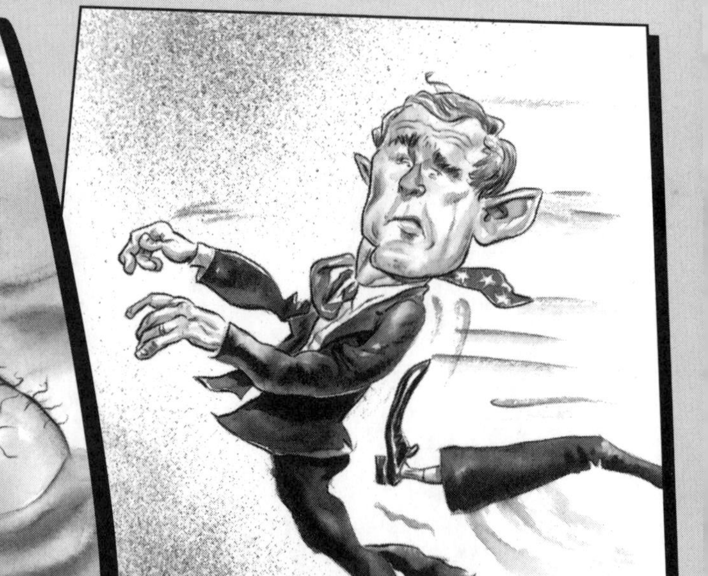
George W. Bush is definitely NOT being re-elected by voters for another term.

There was once a classic television show called "The Untouchables." It had powerful characters and crisp dialogue, and it entertainingly chronicled a feeling of what Chicago was like during the time of Prohibition. It became a cult favorite! Wouldn't you think Hollywood execs would leave well enough alone and keep a classic "untouchable"? Hoo-Hah! Get real! Not when there's mega-bucks to be made! They went ahead and made a feature film version of that popular series! For those who fondly remember the TV show, this new cast isn't the "Untouchables." They're more like...

THE UNWATCHABLES

ARTIST: ANGELO TORRES WRITER: ARNIE KOGEN

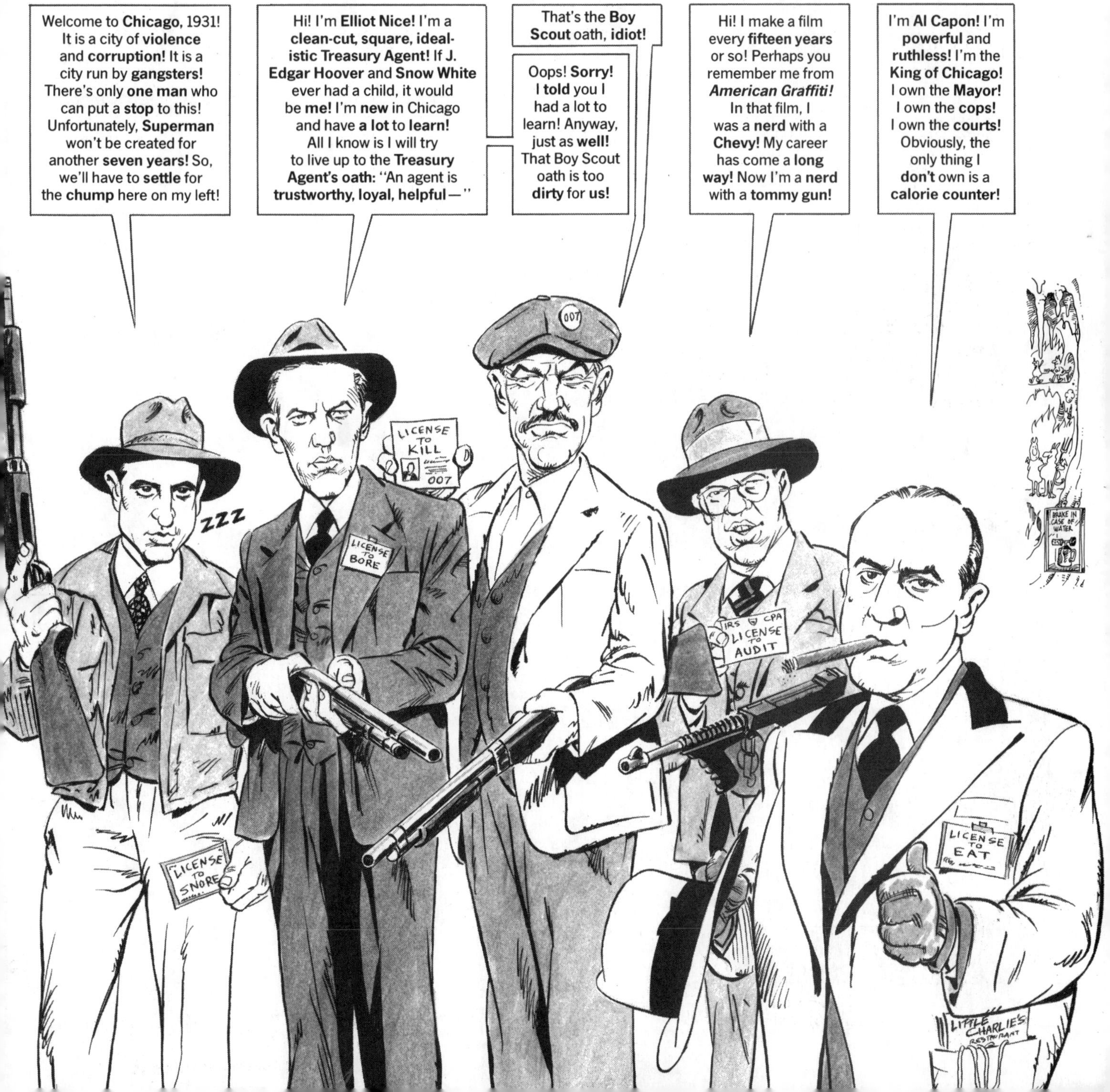
Welcome to Chicago, 1931! It is a city of violence and corruption! It is a city run by gangsters! There's only one man who can put a stop to this! Unfortunately, Superman won't be created for another seven years! So, we'll have to settle for the chump here on my left!
Hi! I'm Elliot Nice! I'm a clean-cut, square, idealistic Treasury Agent! If J. Edgar Hoover and Snow White ever had a child, it would be me! I'm new in Chicago and have a lot to learn! All I know is I will try to live up to the Treasury Agent's oath: "An agent is trustworthy, loyal, helpful—"
That's the Boy Scout oath, idiot!
Oops! Sorry! I told you I had a lot to learn! Anyway, just as well! That Boy Scout oath is too dirty for us!
Hi! I make a film every fifteen years or so! Perhaps you remember me from American Graffiti! In that film, I was a nerd with a Chevy! My career has come a long way! Now I'm a nerd with a tommy gun!
I'm Al Capon! I'm powerful and ruthless! I'm the King of Chicago! I own the Mayor! I own the cops! I own the courts! Obviously, the only thing I don't own is a calorie counter!
007
LICENSE TO KILL
007
ZZZ
LICENSE TO BORE
IRS CPA LICENSE TO AUDIT
LICENSE TO SNORE
LICENSE TO EAT
LITTLE CHARLIE'S RESTAURANT

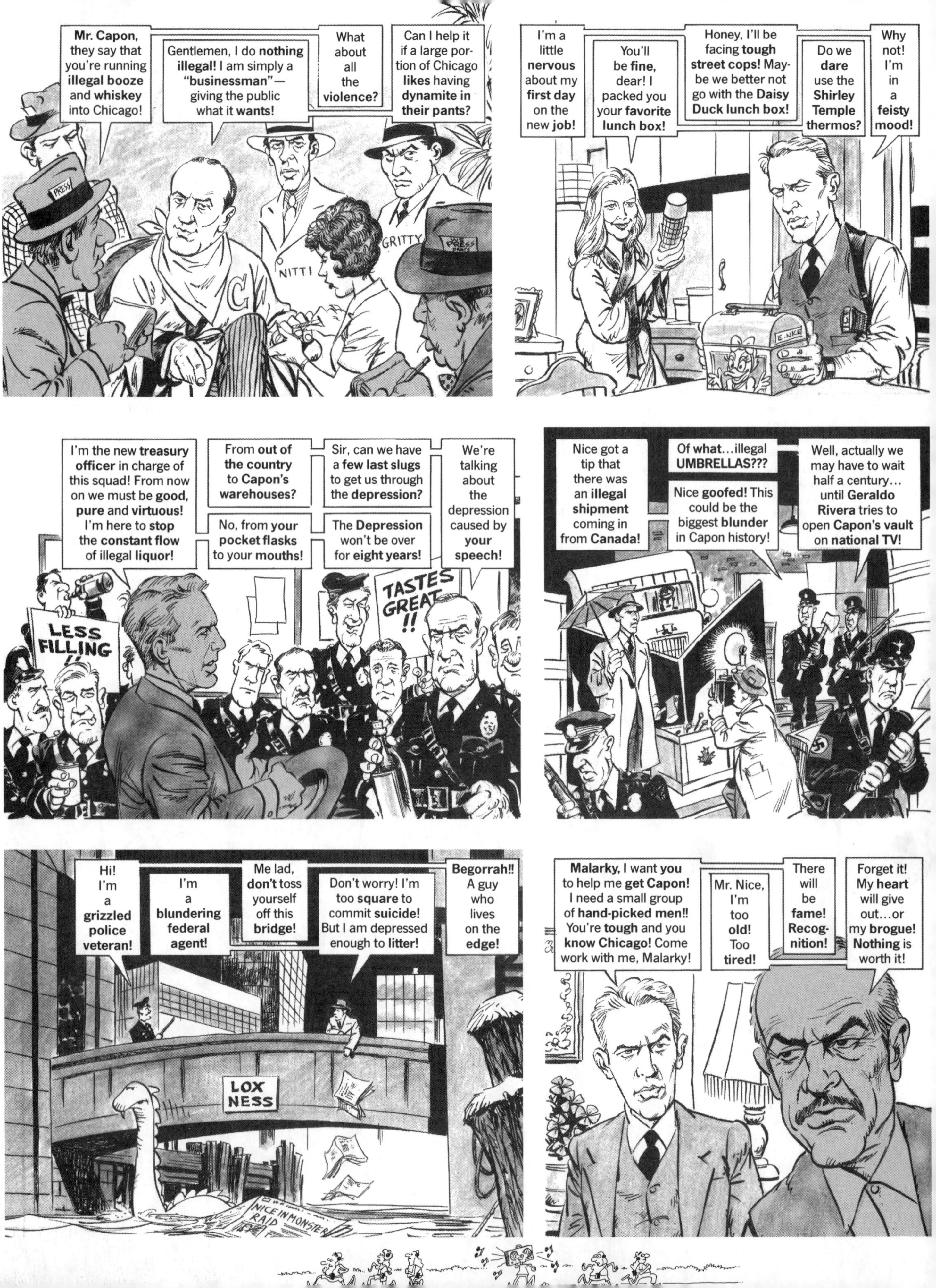
Mr. Capon, they say that you're running illegal booze and whiskey into Chicago!
Gentlemen, I do nothing illegal! I am simply a "businessman"—giving the public what it wants!
What about all the violence?
Can I help it if a large portion of Chicago likes having dynamite in their pants?
PRESS
NITTI
GRITTY
I'm a little nervous about my first day on the new job!
You'll be fine, dear! I packed you your favorite lunch box!
Honey, I'll be facing tough street cops! Maybe we better not go with the Daisy Duck lunch box!
Do we dare use the Shirley Temple thermos?
Why not! I'm in a feisty mood!
E.NICE
I'm the new treasury officer in charge of this squad! From now on we must be good, pure and virtuous! I'm here to stop the constant flow of illegal liquor!
From out of the country to Capon's warehouses?
No, from your pocket flasks to your mouths!
Sir, can we have a few last slugs to get us through the depression?
The Depression won't be over for eight years!
We're talking about the depression caused by your speech!
LESS FILLING !!
TASTES GREAT !!
Nice got a tip that there was an illegal shipment coming in from Canada!
Of what…illegal UMBRELLAS???
Nice goofed! This could be the biggest blunder in Capon history!
Well, actually we may have to wait half a century… until Geraldo Rivera tries to open Capon's vault on national TV!
Hi! I'm a grizzled police veteran!
I'm a blundering federal agent!
Me lad, don't toss yourself off this bridge!
Don't worry! I'm too square to commit suicide! But I am depressed enough to litter!
Begorrah!! A guy who lives on the edge!
LOX NESS
NICE IN MONSTER RAID
Malarky, I want you to help me get Capon! I need a small group of hand-picked men!! You're tough and you know Chicago! Come work with me, Malarky!
Mr. Nice, I'm too old! Too tired!
There will be fame! Recognition!
Forget it! My heart will give out…or my brogue! Nothing is worth it!

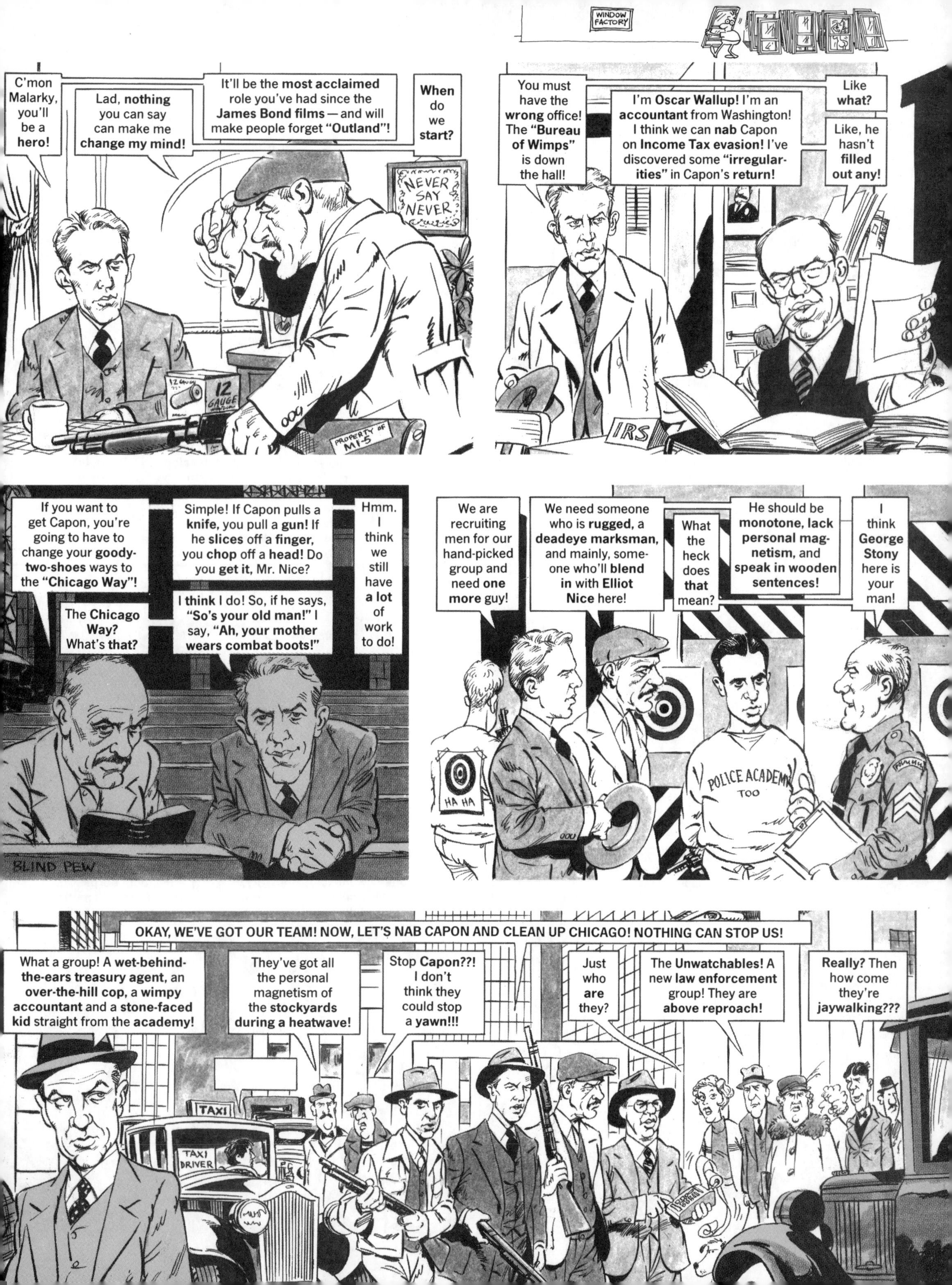

WINDOW FACTORY
C'mon Malarky, you'll be a hero!
Lad, nothing you can say can make me change my mind!
It'll be the most acclaimed role you've had since the James Bond films — and will make people forget "Outland"!
When do we start?
NEVER SAY NEVER
12 GAUGE
PROPERTY OF MI-5
You must have the wrong office! The "Bureau of Wimps" is down the hall!
I'm Oscar Wallup! I'm an accountant from Washington! I think we can nab Capon on Income Tax evasion! I've discovered some "irregularities" in Capon's return!
Like what?
Like, he hasn't filled out any!
IRS
If you want to get Capon, you're going to have to change your goody-two-shoes ways to the "Chicago Way"!
The Chicago Way? What's that?
Simple! If Capon pulls a knife, you pull a gun! If he slices off a finger, you chop off a head! Do you get it, Mr. Nice?
I think I do! So, if he says, "So's your old man!" I say, "Ah, your mother wears combat boots!"
Hmm. I think we still have a lot of work to do!
BLIND PEW
We are recruiting men for our hand-picked group and need one more guy!
We need someone who is rugged, a deadeye marksman, and mainly, someone who'll blend in with Elliot Nice here!
What the heck does that mean?
He should be monotone, lack personal magnetism, and speak in wooden sentences!
I think George Stony here is your man!
HA HA
POLICE ACADEMY TOO
OKAY, WE'VE GOT OUR TEAM! NOW, LET'S NAB CAPON AND CLEAN UP CHICAGO! NOTHING CAN STOP US!
What a group! A wet-behind-the-ears treasury agent, an over-the-hill cop, a wimpy accountant and a stone-faced kid straight from the academy!
They've got all the personal magnetism of the stockyards during a heatwave!
Stop Capon??! I don't think they could stop a yawn!!!
Just who are they?
The Unwatchables! A new law enforcement group! They are above reproach!
Really? Then how come they're jaywalking???
TAXI
TAXI DRIVER

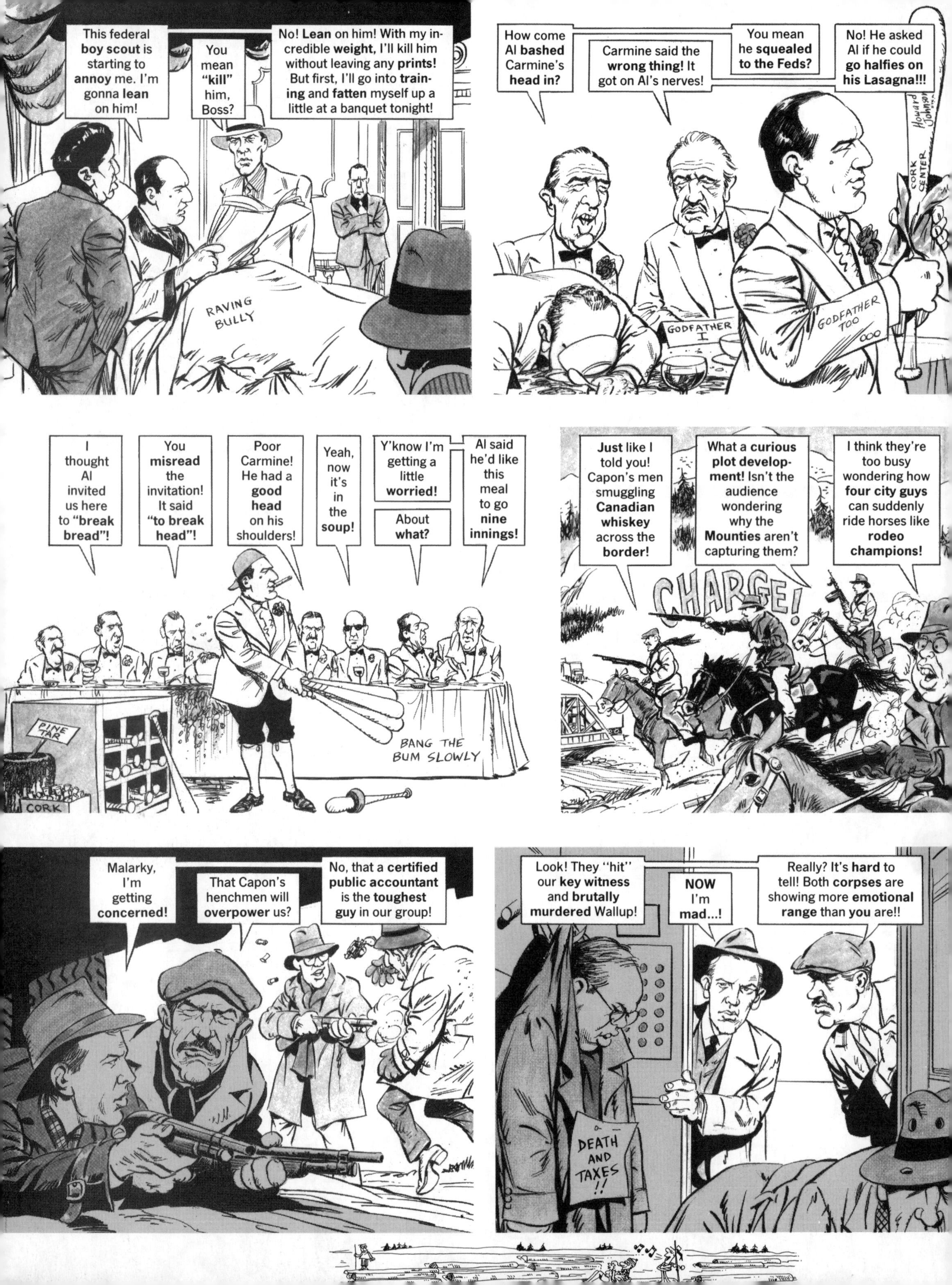

This federal **boy scout** is starting to **annoy** me. I'm gonna **lean** on him!
You mean **"kill"** him, Boss?
No! **Lean** on him! With my incredible **weight,** I'll kill him without leaving any **prints!** But first, I'll go into **training** and **fatten** myself up a little at a banquet tonight!
RAVING BULLY
How come Al **bashed** Carmine's **head in?**
Carmine said the **wrong thing!** It got on Al's nerves!
You mean he **squealed to the Feds?**
No! He asked Al if he could **go halfies on his Lasagna!!!**
Howard Johnson
CORK CENTER
GODFATHER I
GODFATHER TOO
I thought Al invited us here to **"break bread"!**
You **misread** the invitation! It said **"to break head"!**
Poor Carmine! He had a **good head** on his shoulders!
Yeah, now it's in the **soup!**
Y'know I'm getting a little **worried!**
About **what?**
Al said he'd like this meal to go **nine innings!**
PINE TAR
CORK
BANG THE BUM SLOWLY
Just like I told you! Capon's men smuggling **Canadian whiskey** across the **border!**
What a **curious plot development!** Isn't the audience wondering why the **Mounties** aren't capturing them?
I think they're too busy wondering how **four city guys** can suddenly ride horses like **rodeo champions!**
CHARGE!
Malarky, I'm getting **concerned!**
That Capon's henchmen will **overpower** us?
No, that a **certified public accountant** is the **toughest guy** in our group!
Look! They "hit" our **key witness** and **brutally murdered** Wallup!
NOW I'm **mad...!**
Really? It's **hard** to tell! Both **corpses** are showing more **emotional range** than **you** are!!
DEATH AND TAXES!!

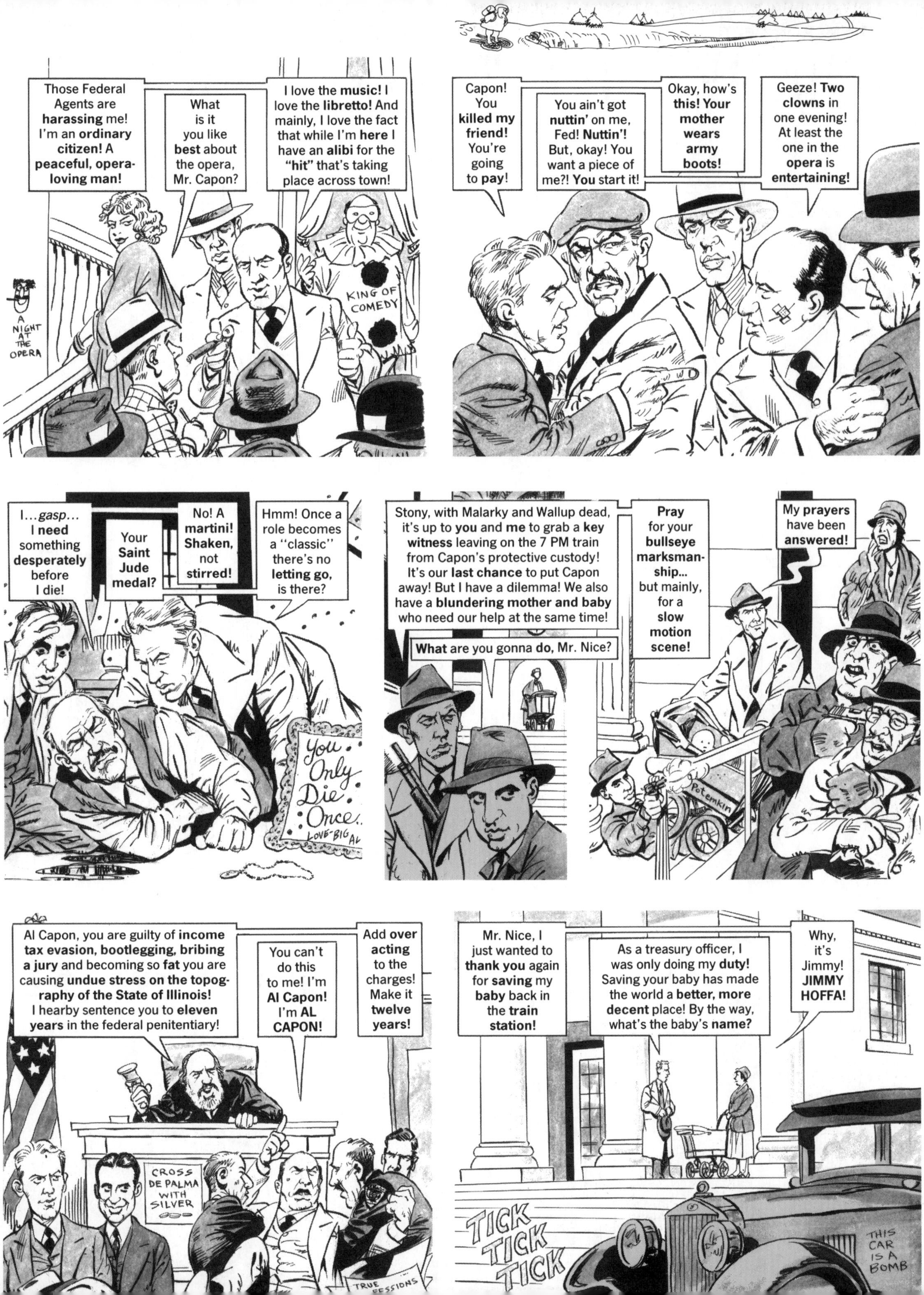
Those Federal Agents are harassing me! I'm an ordinary citizen! A peaceful, opera-loving man!
What is it you like best about the opera, Mr. Capon?
I love the music! I love the libretto! And mainly, I love the fact that while I'm here I have an alibi for the "hit" that's taking place across town!
KING OF COMEDY
A NIGHT AT THE OPERA
Capon! You killed my friend! You're going to pay!
You ain't got nuttin' on me, Fed! Nuttin'! But, okay! You want a piece of me?! You start it!
Okay, how's this! Your mother wears army boots!
Geeze! Two clowns in one evening! At least the one in the opera is entertaining!
I…gasp… I need something desperately before I die!
Your Saint Jude medal?
No! A martini! Shaken, not stirred!
Hmm! Once a role becomes a "classic" there's no letting go, is there?
You Only Die Once.. LOVE-BIG AL
Stony, with Malarky and Wallup dead, it's up to you and me to grab a key witness leaving on the 7 PM train from Capon's protective custody! It's our last chance to put Capon away! But I have a dilemma! We also have a blundering mother and baby who need our help at the same time!
What are you gonna do, Mr. Nice?
Pray for your bullseye marksmanship… but mainly, for a slow motion scene!
My prayers have been answered!
Potemkin
Al Capon, you are guilty of income tax evasion, bootlegging, bribing a jury and becoming so fat you are causing undue stress on the topography of the State of Illinois! I hearby sentence you to eleven years in the federal penitentiary!
You can't do this to me! I'm Al Capon! I'm AL CAPON!
Add over acting to the charges! Make it twelve years!
CROSS DE PALMA WITH SILVER
TRUE ESSIONS
Mr. Nice, I just wanted to thank you again for saving my baby back in the train station!
As a treasury officer, I was only doing my duty! Saving your baby has made the world a better, more decent place! By the way, what's the baby's name?
Why, it's Jimmy! JIMMY HOFFA!
TICK TICK TICK
THIS CAR IS A BOMB

DON MARTIN DEPT.

ANOTHER GREAT BANK ROBBERY

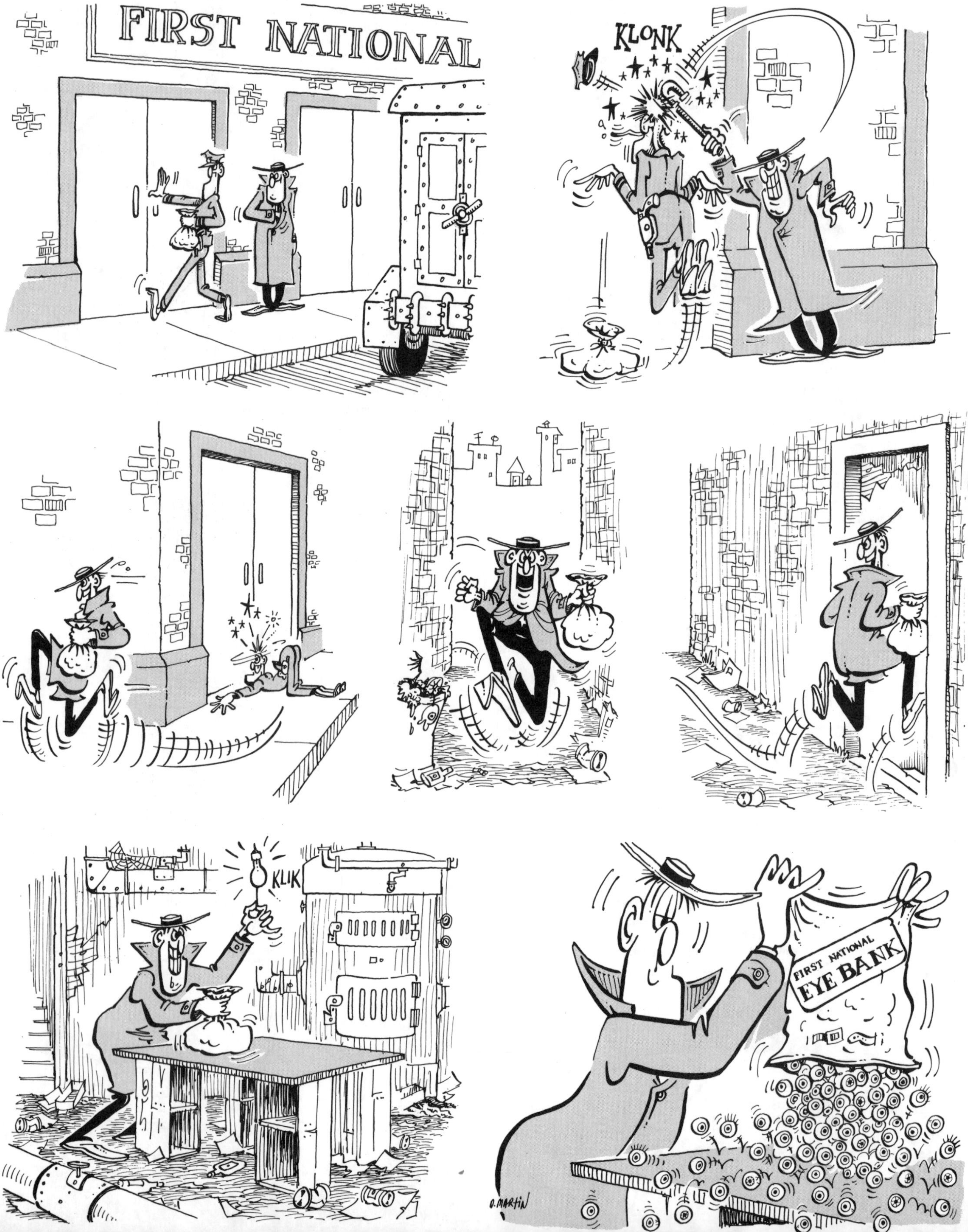
FIRST NATIONAL
KLONK
KLIK
FIRST NATIONAL
EYE BANK
D. MARTIN

Today, in every field of commercial endeavor, the trend is toward "Bigness" . . . and Crime is no exception. Today, when a Racketeer refers to "those lousy Bulls", he isn't talking about the "Fuzz"—he's talking about the wheelers and dealers in the Stock Market. That's because Crime in America is "Big Business", and it's growing bigger every day. In fact, we can forsee a time when, just as U.S. STEEL and GENERAL MOTORS publish "Annual Reports", so will the big Underworld Operations, and we'll be seeing something like . . .

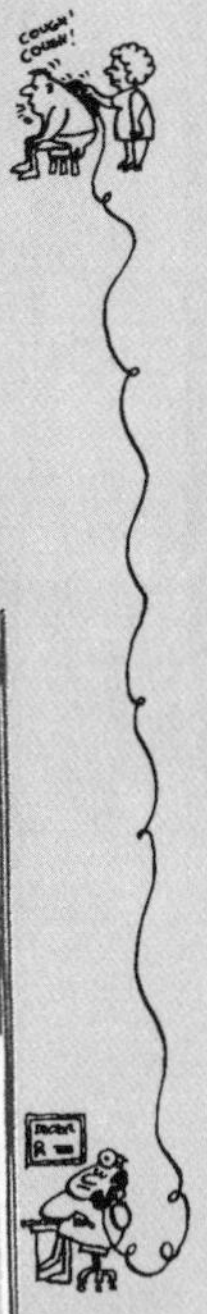

1968 ANNUAL REPORT

MAFIACO

INCORPORATED

PRODUCTS & SERVICES FOR A GROWING IMMORAL AMERICA

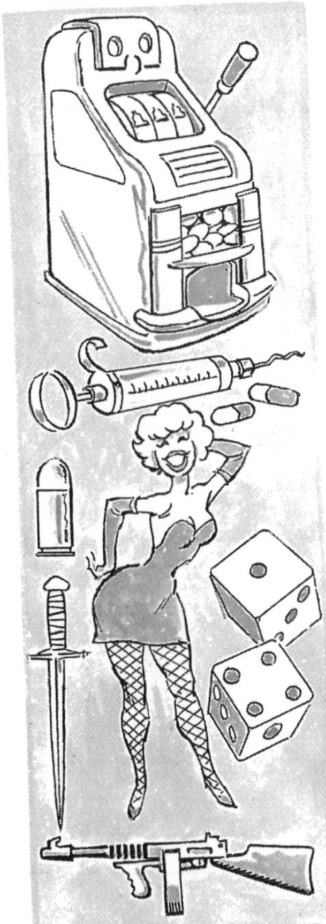

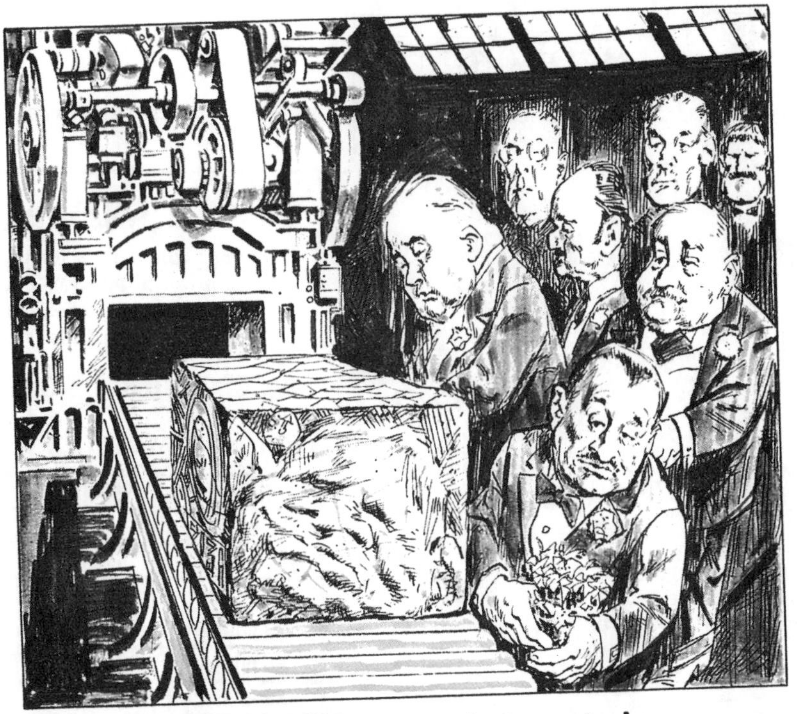

MafiaCo Goes Automated

Advanced technology has provided the means for making our operations more efficient and productive. This newly-acquired hydraulic Scrap Metal Crusher compresses an automobile into a 3-foot cube of solid steel in a matter of seconds, thereby disposing of any corpus delicti occupant without a trace; just one facet of MafiaCo's progress in the field of Automation. Above photo shows members of MafiaCo's research Staff testing the new device with the late Louis "Fink" Finstermacher.

ARTIST: JACK RICKARD WRITE: LOU SILVERSTONE

MAFIACO's BOARD OF DIRECTORS

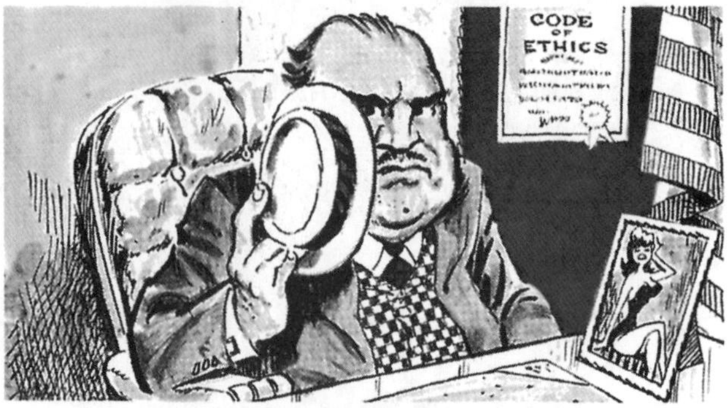
CODE OF ETHICS

ALFONSO "BIG FISH" BACCALA
alias "The Man"
PRESIDENT
("Commissioner")

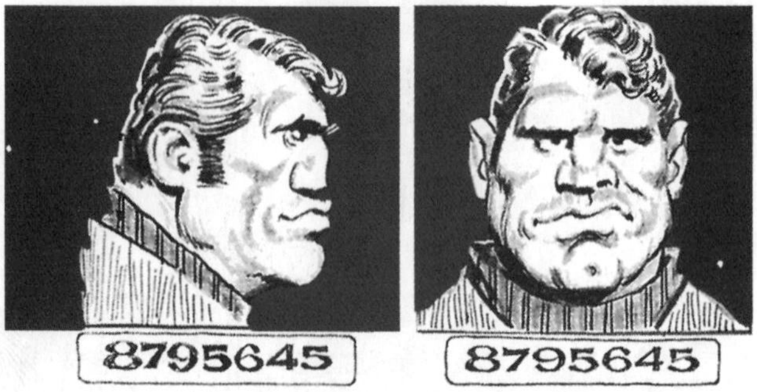
8795645
8795645

ANTHONY "LITTLE FISH" BACCALA
alias "Tony Flounder", alias "Andy Gefillte"
VICE-PRESIDENT
("Capa")

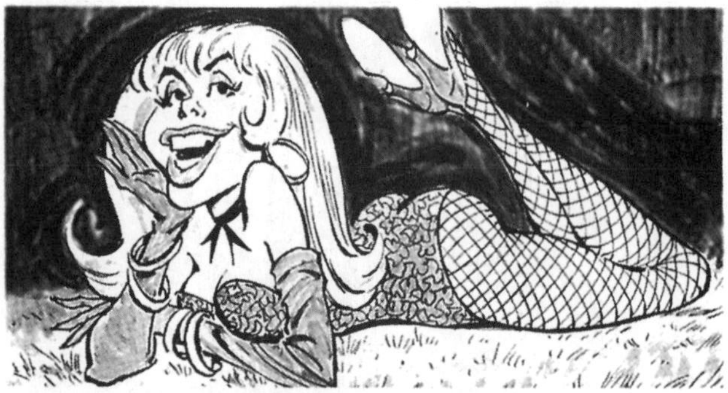

MRS. ALFONSO BACCALA
formerly "Laverne Lamour"
SECRETARY & TREASURER
("Hands Off")

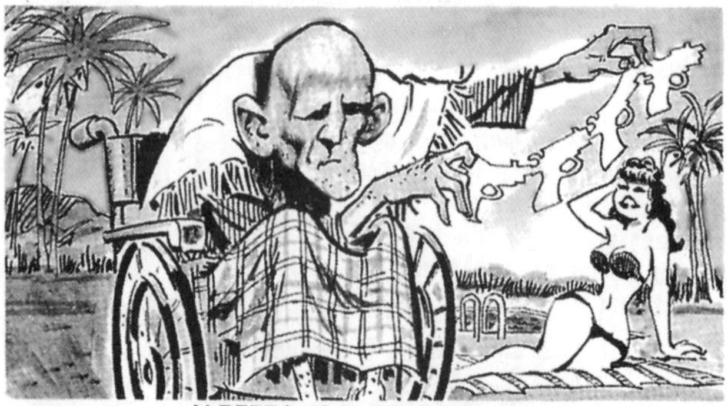

ALBERTO "SCARFACE" BACCALA
alias "The Old Man"
CHAIRMAN OF THE BOARD
("Retired Commissioner")

A MESSAGE TO STOCKHOLDERS

During the fiscal year just completed, **MAFIACO** continued to progress significantly toward its ultimate goal—the complete take-over of the United States. To this end, your Board of Directors is pleased to announce that several new cities and two entire States have recently joined the ever-growing family of **MAFIACO**-controlled communities. Also, our program of expansion reached an important milestone in 1968 when we acquired a controlling interest in **THE WATERPROOF CEMENT COMPANY**, thereby permanently eliminating the costly middleman (who also happened to be the majority stockholder) from our "Marine Disposal" operation.

As a stockholder, you will be pleased to learn that **MAFIACO** enjoyed its most successful year. The principal factors that contributed to this record profit-making period included the following*:

A 10% increase in crimes of violence across the nation.
A 150% increase in all types of gambling (including legal State Lotteries, Pari-Mutuels and Bingo Games—which are considered to be excellent training areas for future **MAFIACO** customers).
A 45% increase in interstate cigarette smuggling, and
A 25% increase in bootlegging and illegal whiskey-making (the growth-rate of which both coincide with increased Federal and State taxes).
A 57% increase in drug use.
A 68% increase in Gangster Movies.

We here at **MAFIACO** are justly proud of our accomplishments in 1968, but we are not yet completely satisfied. Unless certain Subsidiary Managers show an increase in Operating Efficiency and Return, the matter will be turned over to our Contract Department. And youse guys know who you are!

(Signed)
Alfonso "Big Fish" Baccala
President ("Commissioner")

*THESE FIGURES ARE BASED ON THE LATEST FBI REPORTS

MAFIACO's Growth Record

Your company is fortunate in having a strong financial position (due to certain tax advantages, like we don't pay them), and therefore it is growing at a faster rate than the general economy of the country. This is clearly demonstrated by the charts below:

GROWTH RATES OF SELECTED AMERICAN CORPORATIONS

UNITED STATES STEEL CORP.

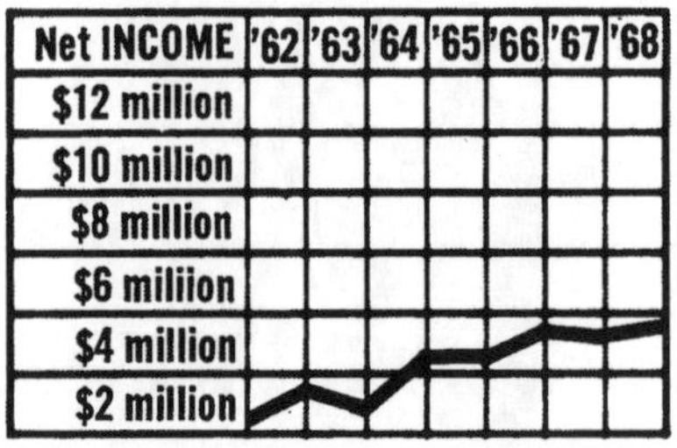
Net INCOME '62 '63 '64 '65 '66 '67 '68
$12 million
$10 million
$8 million
$6 million
$4 million
$2 million

MAFIACO INCORP.

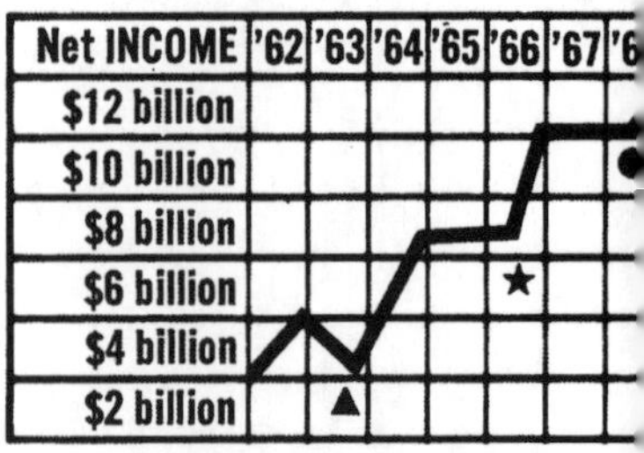
Net INCOME '62 '63 '64 '65 '66 '67
$12 billion
$10 billion
$8 billion
$6 billion
$4 billion
$2 billion

GENERAL MOTORS CORP.

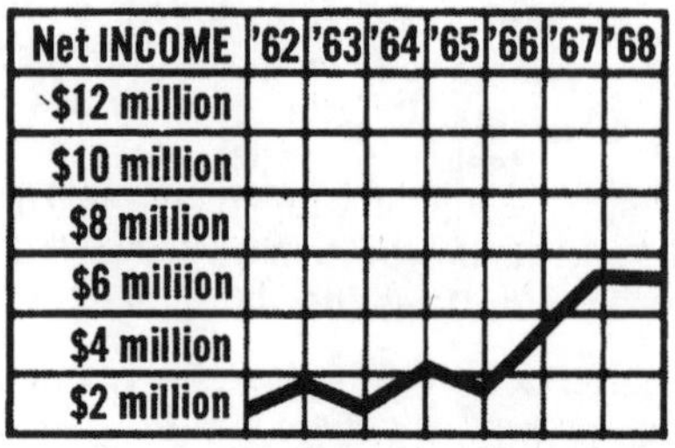
Net INCOME '62 '63 '64 '65 '66 '67 '68
$12 million
$10 million
$8 million
$6 million
$4 million
$2 million

MAD MAGAZINE, INC.

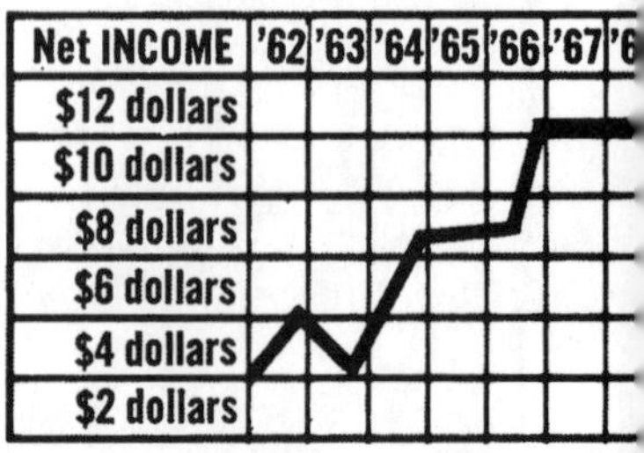
Net INCOME '62 '63 '64 '65 '66 '67
$12 dollars
$10 dollars
$8 dollars
$6 dollars
$4 dollars
$2 dollars

▲ "The Untouchables" cancelled
★ Courts outlaw evidence obtained by wiretapping
● Congress votes against strong "Gun Control" law

HIGHLIGHTS OF THE 1968 MafiaCo STOCKHOLDERS' MEETING

The Annual Meeting of the Stockholders of **MafiaCo** was held this year appropriately enough on February 14th (St. Valentine's Day) in Finky's Bar & Pizza Parlor, Apalachin, N. Y. A transcript of the meeting is included in this Annual Report for those Shareholders who were detained by the Government, out of the country, laying low, or otherwise unable to be present, so they will know what transpired.

SHAREHOLDERS PAY THEIR RESPECTS TO RECENTLY DEPARTED **MafiaCo** MEMBERS

OPENING REMARKS BY PRES. BACCALA (ALIAS "THE COMMISSIONER")

Welcome to the Annual Meeting of the Stockholders of **MafiaCo.** Everybody shaddup and listen. Since our last meeting, several members of our Organization have met with unfortunate accidents, and are no longer with us. Time does not permit me to mention all of these individuals by name, but I think it would be nice if we showed our respect to our departed Gumbas by observing a moment of silence... Okay, that's enough! All this quiet reminds me of stir!

The progress of our Company over the years from a small-time Bootlegging Outfit to one of the world's largest diverisified Industrial Concerns is due in no small part to the vision and leadership of your Board of Directors. Therefore, I am sure that you will happily join with me in voting a bonus of 600 Gs to each of your hard-workin Executives.

Before opening the meeting to general discussion, I want to say that your Company is making every effort to fulfill the promise of its great potential, and with the help of a gullible public, crooked policemen and corrupt politicians, we will continue to meet the challenges and opportunities that lie ahead, and reach our goal—Control of the Whole World! And then, we'll start working in other areas!

SHAREHOLDERS EXPRESS THEIR OPINIONS DURING THE GENERAL DISCUSSION PERIOD

SUMMARY OF MAFIACO BUSINESS CONDUCTED AT THE MEETING

PROPOSED MERGER WITH W.C.C.A. (White Collar Crooks Of America)

Statement by Vice-President Baccala (Alias "The Capa")

It is estimated that 462 million dollars in office supplies and equipment are stolen annually from Business and Industry by the W.C.C.A., operating independently. Your **MafiaCo** Board of Directors feels that a merger with the W.C.C.A. will afford our company an excellent opportunity to participate in this lucrative growing field, as well as creating an excellent base for further diversification into other fields, such as the re-selling of office supplies and equipment back to Business and Industry. Management urges an affirmative vote on this merger. Or else!

RESULTS OF VOTE ON PROPOSED MERGER WITH W.C.C.A.

For the Resolution 1189
Against the Resolution 0

ELECTION OF BOARD OF DIRECTORS

All members of the Board were re-elected by unanimous vote.

PROPOSED EXECUTIVE BONUS OF 600 Gs EACH

A motion was made to increase the proposed bonus of 600 Gs each to a bonus of 700 Gs each, plus a Stock Option plan amounting to an additional 300 Gs each.

RESULTS OF VOTE ON PROPOSED BONUS AND STOCK OPTION PLAN

For the Resolution 1188
Against the Resolution 1

SHAREHOLDERS VOTE ON THE EXECUTIVE BONUS AND STOCK OPTION RESOLUTION

HIGHLIGHTS OF THE GENERAL DISCUSSION AT THE MEETING

President Baccala, in answer to a question by shareholder Vincente Linguini, stated that there is no truth to the rumor that Lucky Luciano is alive and living in Argentina.

A proposal by shareholder John Smythe (formerly Luigi Marinara) to Americanize the names of all Executives and employees of **MafiaCo**, thereby helping the Italian Anti-Defamation League in its campaign, was soundly defeated.

Shareholder Mario "The Knife" Machetti complimented the President on the manner in which the meeting was conducted, and made a motion that it be adjourned. The motion was seconded and carried, and the 1968 Meeting of the Stockholders of **MafiaCo** came to an end.

EX-SHAREHOLDER LEAVES MEETING AFTER SUFFERING A SUDDEN UNTIMELY ILLNESS

MafiaCo
INCORPORATED
FINANCIAL STATEMENT — FISCAL YEAR 1968

INCOME BEFORE TAXES	$ 12,789,568,598.04
INCOME AFTER TAXES	12,789,568,598.04
ADJUSTED NET INCOME	12,789,568,598.04

ASSETS

Cash and Securities

Buried in cellars, etc.	$ 47,368,537,907.98
Deposited in Swiss Bank Accounts, etc.	8,638,209,448.11
Invested in Sicilian Savings Bonds	700.000,000.00
Stashed in Bus and Railroad Terminal Lockers	3,860,389,680.67

Accounts Receivable

Short Term Notes	126,578,790.50
Interest Due On Short Term Notes	29,589,477,202.29

Inventories

Contracts and Work In Progress	589,700,000.00

Equipment

Bullet-Proof Cadillacs and Lincolns	2,863,985.17
Tanks and Armored Cars, etc.	1,685,389.54
Guns and Ammunition	58,806,276.49
Brass Knuckles, Black Jacks and Other Weapons	388,974.39
	90,936,637,655.14

Less Depreciation for Obsolescence	
(238,589 Doubled-Breasted Striped Suits)	417,685.25
	90,936,219,969.89

Properties and Other Interests

Las Vegas	127,568,778,622.03
Miami Beach	70,433,889,457.86
Hoboken	1,687,742.59
Sands Point	980,066.23
Grosse Point	6,299,754.01
Salerno (122,689,500,000 lire)	1,022.00
TOTAL ASSETS	**$288,947,856,634.61**

LIABILITIES

Wages and Salaries

Executives..	150,000,000,000.00
Executives' Wives	81,000,000,000.00
Executives' Relatives	47,000,000,000.00
Executives' Relatives' Wives	9,000,000,000.00
Employees	890,000.00

Expenses

Payoffs To Law Enforcement Officers	927,908,567.00
Payoffs To Government Officials and Judges	69,865,427.00
Funeral Costs	12,680,287.21
Dental Bills For Show Biz Personalities We Own	72,684.00
Auditors Fee*	439,669.40
TOTAL LIABILITIES	**$288,947,856,634.61**

AUDITOR'S REPORT TO STOCKHOLDERS

* We have examined the books and financial statements of MAFIACO and in our opinion it represents fairly the results of its operations and the financial position of MAFIACO for the fiscal year of 1968, and anybody don't like it gets his.

(signed) Alfonso "Big Fish" Baccala
President, Baccala and Baccala
Certified Public Accountants

PUT YOUR FUNNY WHERE YOUR MOUTH IS! DEPT.

AN AL JAFFEE SNAPPY ANSWERS TO STUPID QUESTIONS

Gangland Episode

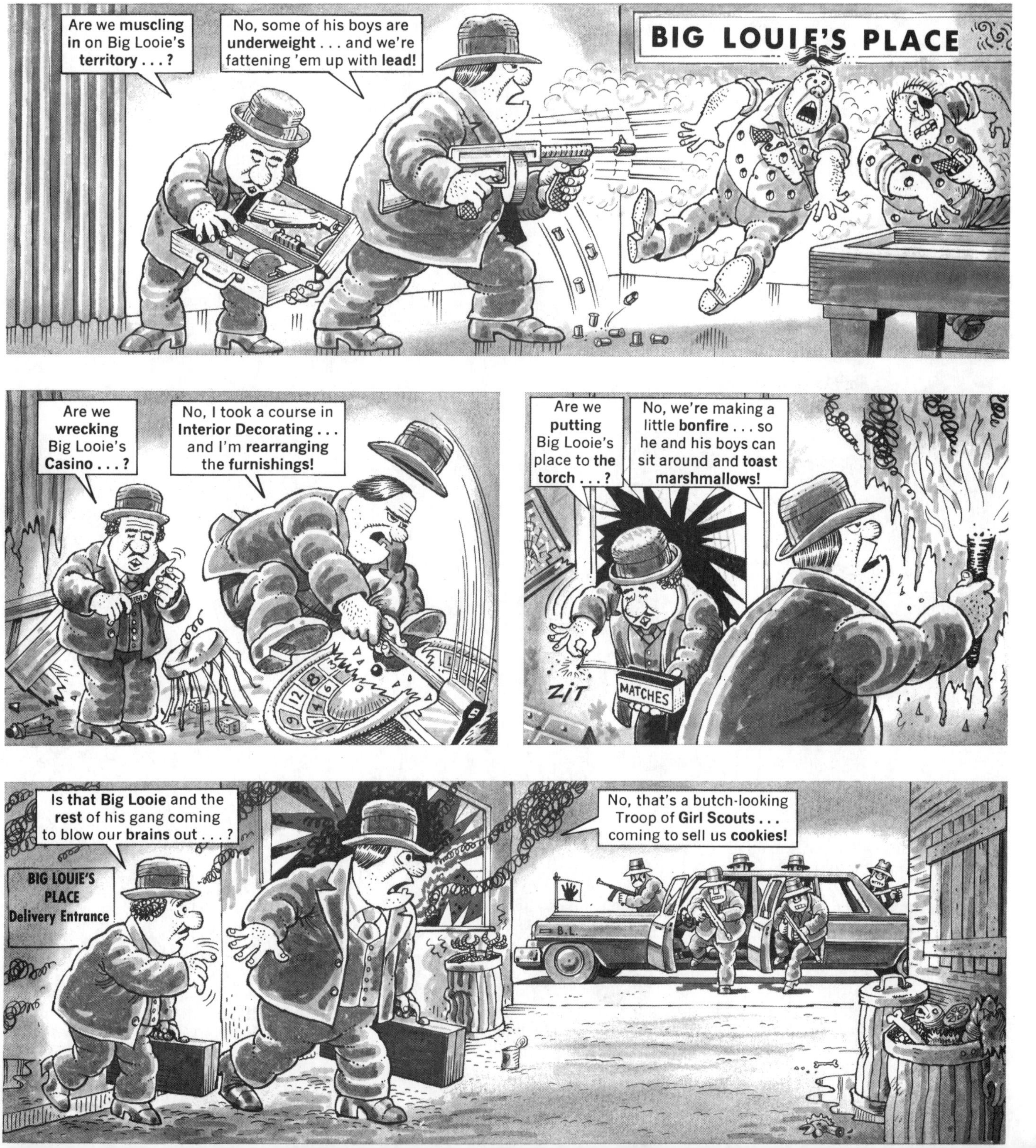
Are we **muscling in** on Big Looie's **territory . . . ?**
No, some of his boys are **underweight** . . . and we're fattening 'em up with **lead!**
BIG LOUIE'S PLACE
Are we **wrecking** Big Looie's **Casino . . . ?**
No, I took a course in **Interior Decorating . . .** and I'm **rearranging** the **furnishings!**
Are we **putting** Big Looie's place to **the torch . . . ?**
No, we're making a little **bonfire** . . . so he and his boys can sit around and **toast marshmallows!**
ZIT
MATCHES
Is **that Big Looie** and the **rest** of his gang coming to blow our **brains** out . . . ?
BIG LOUIE'S PLACE Delivery Entrance
No, that's a butch-looking Troop of **Girl Scouts . . .** coming to sell us **cookies!**
B.L

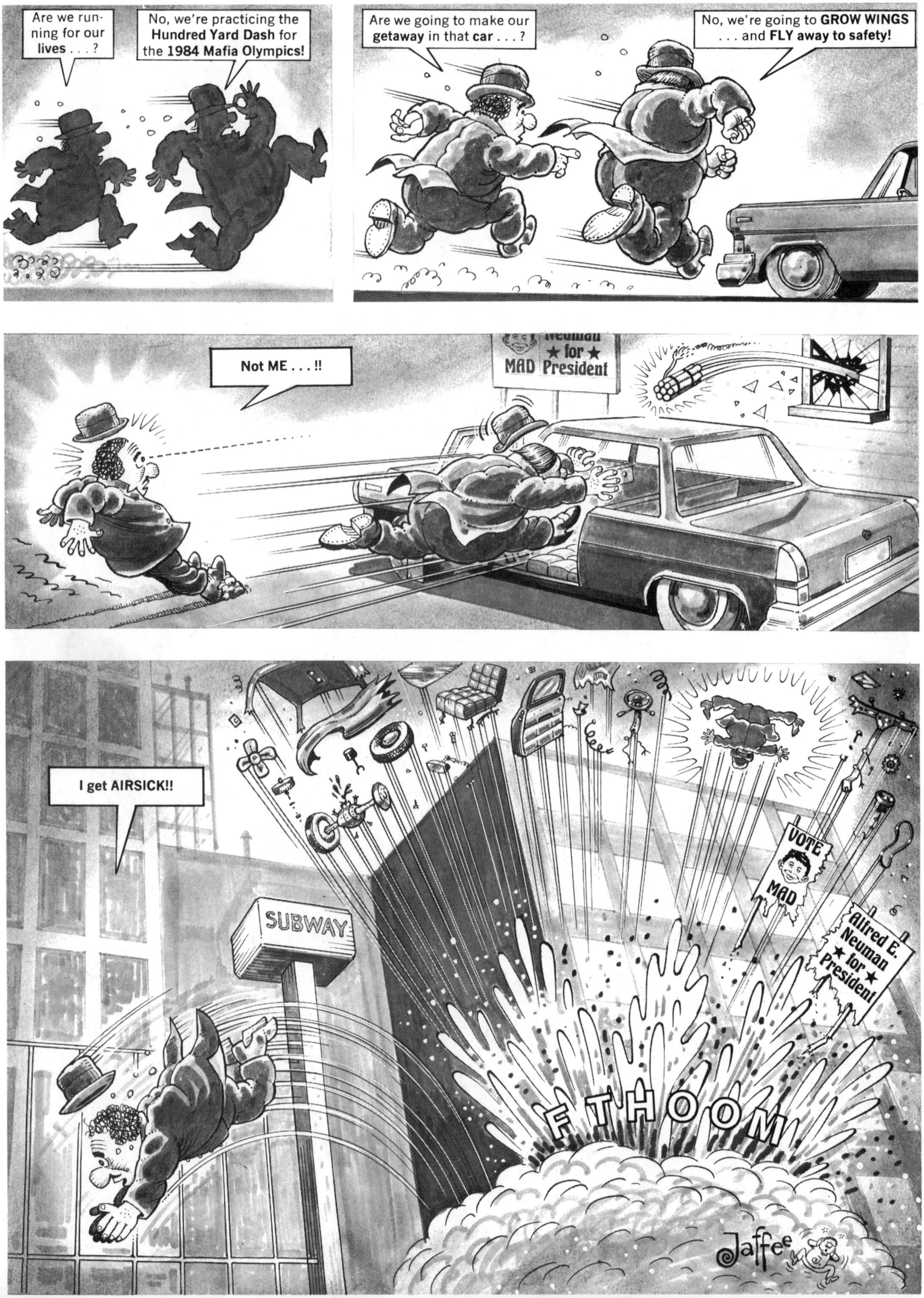

Are we running for our **lives** . . . ?
No, we're practicing the **Hundred Yard Dash** for the **1984 Mafia Olympics!**
Are we going to make our **getaway** in that **car** . . . ?
No, we're going to **GROW WINGS** . . . and **FLY away to safety!**
Not ME . . . !!
★ for ★
MAD President
I get AIRSICK!!
SUBWAY
VOTE
MAD
Alfred E. Neuman ★ for ★ President
FTHOOM
Jaffee

OFFERS YOU CAN'T REFUSE DEPT.

Rather than face the unruly crowds, uncaring sales persons and unbelievably slow-moving lines in department and discount stores today, many people are doing their shopping via mail from their own homes. Mail order shopping is especially helpful to those people who don't want to show themselves in public for other reasons... like members of "The Mob." Recently, we came across a mail order catalogue filled with items aimed directly at all these underworld consumers. So here we go with:

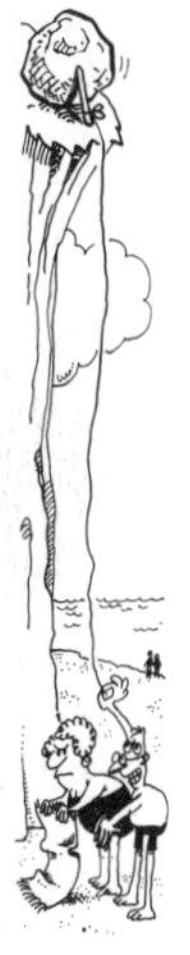

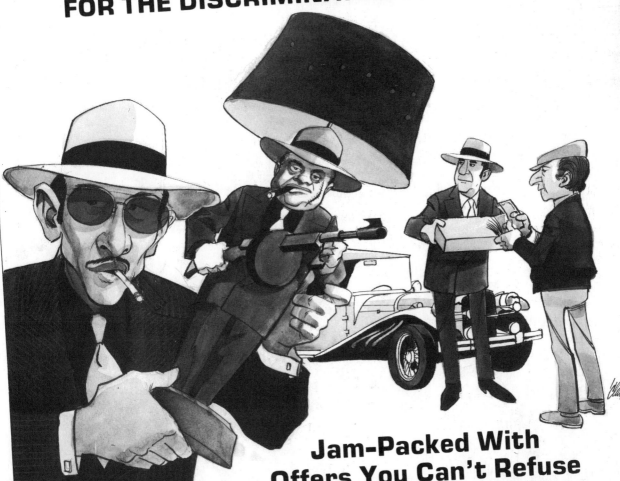

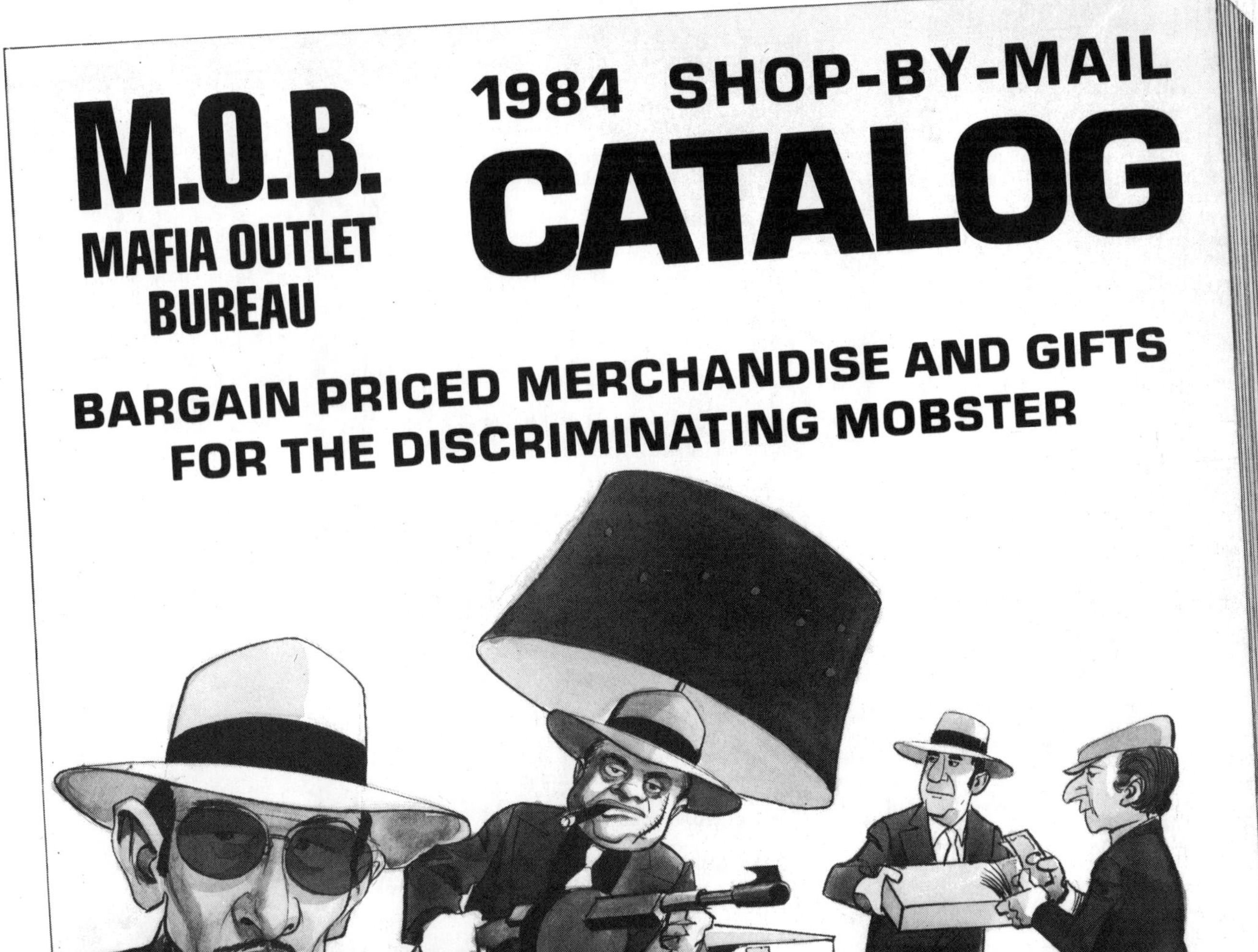
M.O.B.
MAFIA OUTLET BUREAU
1984 SHOP-BY-MAIL
CATALOG
BARGAIN PRICED MERCHANDISE AND GIFTS FOR THE DISCRIMINATING MOBSTER
Jam-Packed With Offers You Can't Refuse
SERVING THE UNDERWORLD SINCE 1927
The Al Capone Commemorative Lamp (see Page 49)
Clarke

WRITER: FRANK JACOBS ARTIST: BOB CLARKE

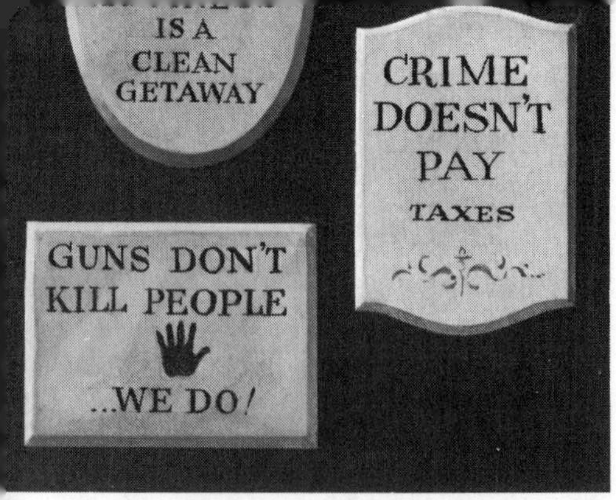
IS A CLEAN GETAWAY
CRIME DOESN'T PAY TAXES
GUNS DON'T KILL PEOPLE ..WE DO!

INSPIRATIONAL WALL PLAQUES

Wise sayings, witty epigrams that will dress up your hideout and impress your fellow thugs when they come to visit. Choose from (1) "I never met a man I couldn't bribe." (2) "If crime doesn't pay, how come I drive a Cadillac?" (3) "God hates squealers." (4) "Tomorrow is one more day you're not doing time."

 # 4407—Each plaque $3.95
All four $12.00

LUCKY LUCIANO'S THUMB-PRINT

The thumb-print of the Mob's most celebrated hero now becomes a dazzling piece of modern abstract art. This is a 16″ x 24″ blow-up of Lucky's thumb-print taken by the FBI just before he was deported to Sicily. A real conversation-piece that will add class to any mob-leader's office or clubroom. State whether you want right or left thumb.

 # 4115—LEGENDARY THUMB-PRINT $9.95
SAME, FRAMED IN RICH GOLD-LEAFED PLASTIC $19.95

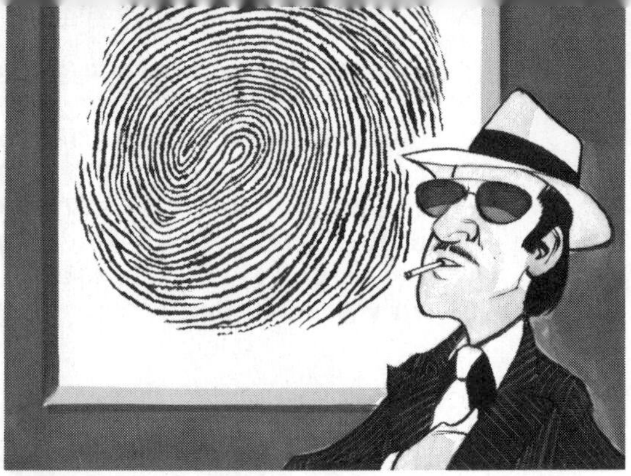

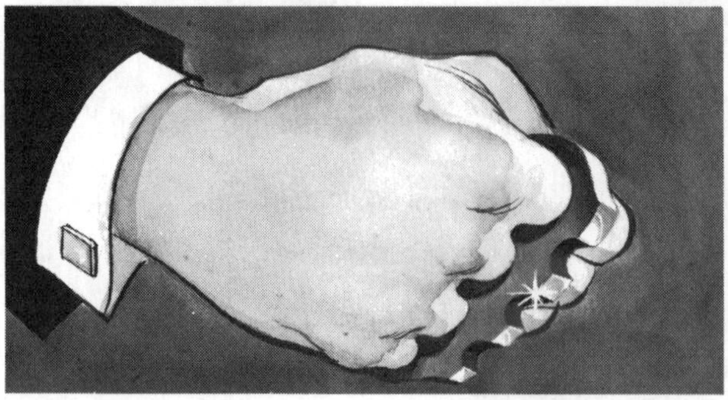

GENUINE BRASS KNUCKLES

You can't beat this rap—a rap, that is, right on the kisser using good old "brass knucks." Reliable, perfect for enforcement problems, they save wear and tear on the hands. One size fits all, unless fingers are disfigured from punching without them. A must for the up-and-coming hoodlum; a great sentimental gift for your capo.

 # 6512—BRASS KNUCKLES $19.95

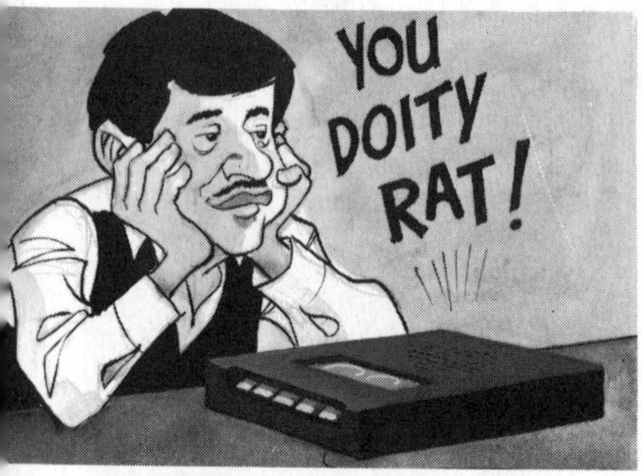
YOU DOITY RAT!

"TUFF-TALK" CASSETTES

You can't be a believable mobster unless you talk like one. And now you can, with "Tuff-Talk," the easy way to master underworld lingo. Just play the cassettes and you'll be taught all the "right" expressions by Sal "Shades" Tartini, ex-capo of the famed Palazzo Family in Cleveland. Soon you'll get the handle on phrases like "Lean on the creep," "Tailpipe the rat," "Deep-six the fink which fingered Little Izzy," and hundreds more.

 # 3459—"TUFF-TALK" CASSETTES. . $29.50 per set of six

LOAN-SHARK'S DATE BOOK

More than just a daily calendar or memo pad, this item is designed especially for the money-lender. Provides spaces for names of who owes you money, how late they are in payment, which limb you'll break if they don't come across. Special! Order now and get Free Bonus Book: "Torture Techniques For Fun & Profit."

 # 2167—LOAN-SHARK'S COMPANION $5.95

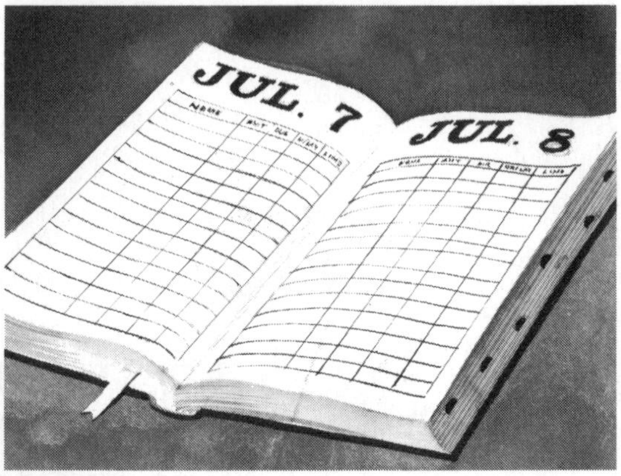
JUL. 7
JUL. 8

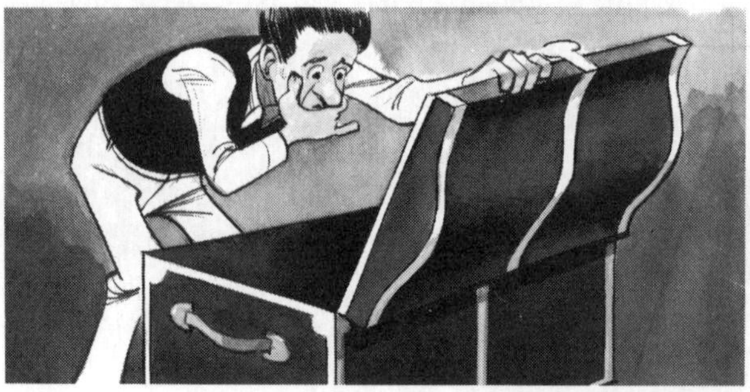

MYSTERY TRUNKS

What's in them? Hi-jacked appliances? Bank loot? A dead squealer? We've got dozens of them gathering dust in our warehouse—all left over from gang wars, heists, the estates of dead fences, etc. If you like the fun of opening surprise packages, then this item is for you!

 # 3345—SURPRISE STUFFED TRUNK. $14.95

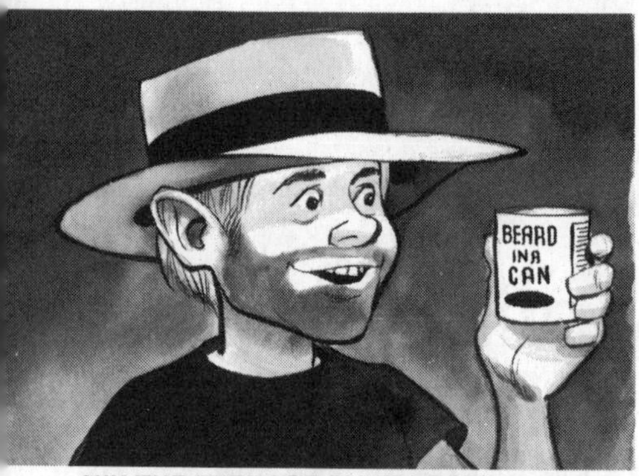
BEARD IN A CAN

NIX THE TEENAGE PUNK LOOK

Even if you are one! Now, with "Beard In A Can," you can instantly add years to your looks. Simply rub the ash-like flakes on your face and you'll come off as a veteran hitman with a two-day beard. They'll never know you only shave once a week and have to show I.D. in bars. Choose from three lifelike shades—macho black, bigshot brown, honcho red.

 # 2276—"BEARD IN A CAN". $4.95

"DIAMOND" PINKIE RING

Just because you're not a high-level Mafioso doesn't mean you can't look like one. Wear this glittering ring in your neighborhood. Only you will know the "rock" isn't real as local toadies kiss it and grovel at your feet while they thank you for letting them live. "Diamond" available in three sizes.

 # 2414—Impressive giant size. . $19.95
Extra-large Capo size . $29.95
Super-large Don size . . $39.95

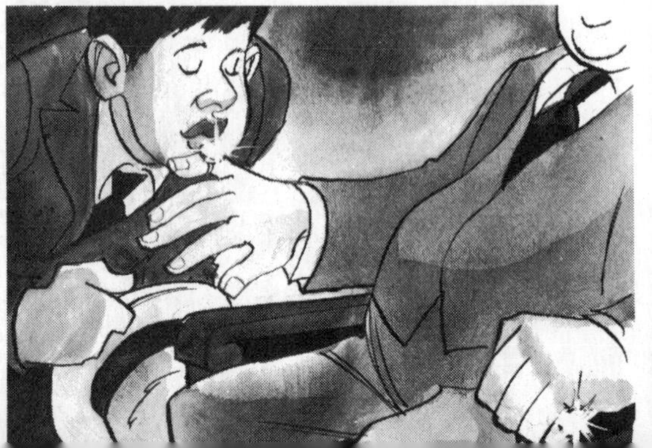

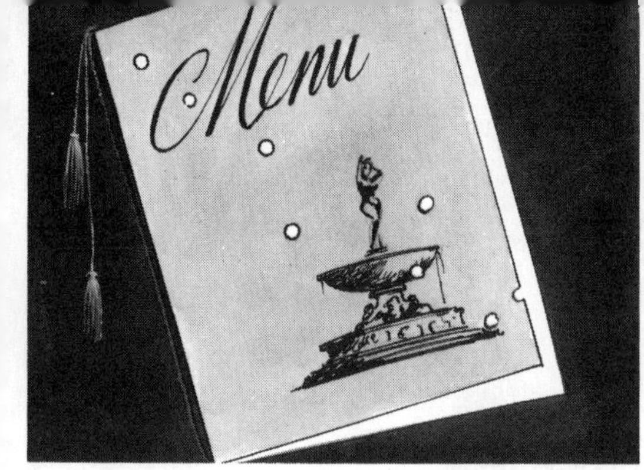
Menu

HISTORIC GANGLAND MENU
Now you can own a replica of the famed menu of the historic "Peace Parley Banquet," partaken by the Collazo and Bombagni Families in 1967 just after they agreed to split up Pittsburgh and only moments before Bombagni realized he was being set up to be rubbed out during the fifth course.

 # 8002—HISTORIC MENU $5.95
 # 8003—SAME, WITH SIMULATED BLOODSTAINS $7.95

BEGINNER'S COUNTERFEITING KIT
It's never too late to master this time-honored "money-making" craft. A few days practice, and you'll be turning out $10's and $20's that will fool a bank officer! Kit comes complete with dyes, paper, printing press and plates. A great "second income" for "nothing-to-do" days when you're between heists.

 # 2098—COUNTERFEITING KIT $298.95

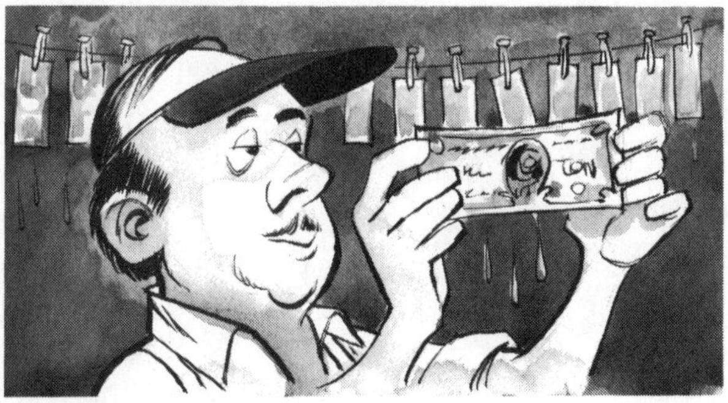

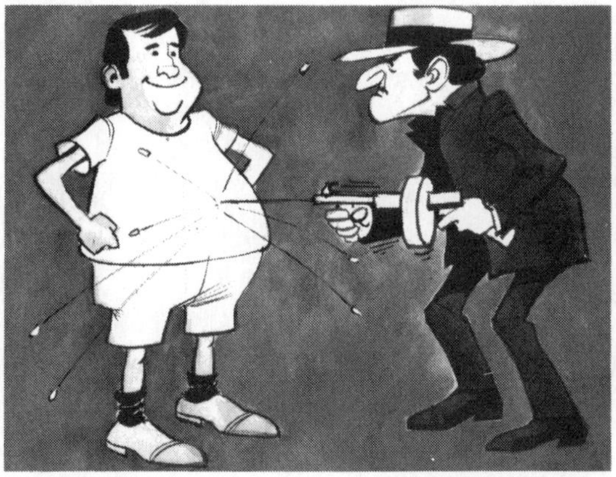

BULLET-PROOF UNDERWEAR
A flashy suit and tie mean nothing if you're not protected underneath. Our lead underwear will keep you alive when rival mobs try to gun you down. Let them plug away—you'll come through without a scratch. Choose from three fashion-plate colors—Marinara red; Zucchini green; Eggplant purple.

 # 4416—T-shirt $22.50
 # 4417—Shorts $19.95
Add $5.00 and have your monogram inscribed.

"HOW TO PICK UP BIMBOS"
Without a bleach-blonde floozie on his arm, a mobster counts for nothing. In this info-packed book, you'll learn where to find them, how to make a good first impression, when to slap them around, other valuable tips.

 # 3345—BIMBO BOOK . . $7.95

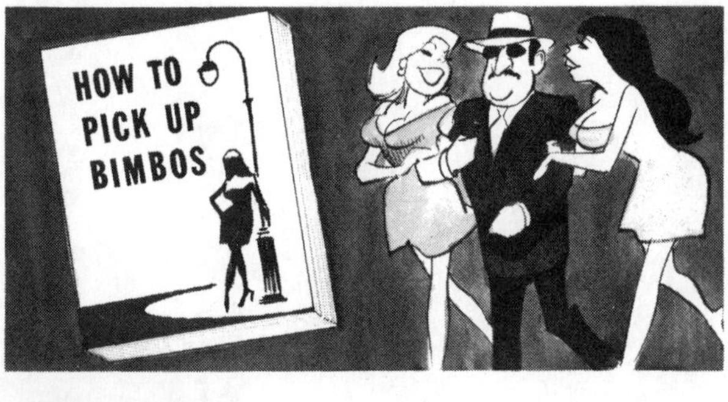
HOW TO
PICK UP
BIMBOS

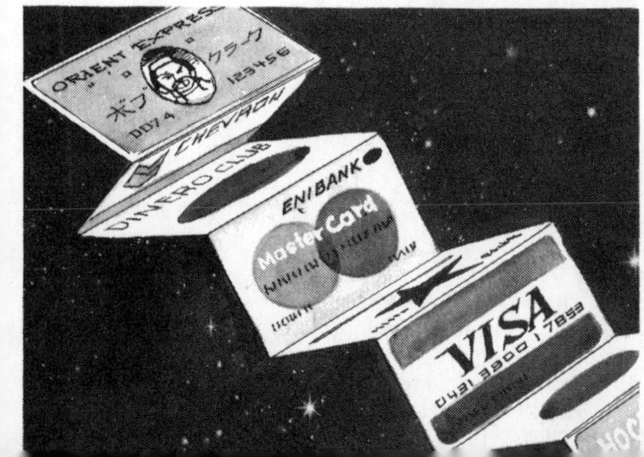
ORIENT EXPRESS
CHEVRON
DINERO CLUB
ENIBANK
Master Card
VISA

STOLEN CREDIT CARDS
The handy alternative to using cash, especially when they're in someone else's name. Visa, Mastercard, Diners Club, you name it—we've got thousands taken from burglaries, heists, other sources we'd be foolish to name. Use them in restaurants, shops, wherever you can get away with it.

 # 1891—CREDIT CARDS Per dozen $19.95

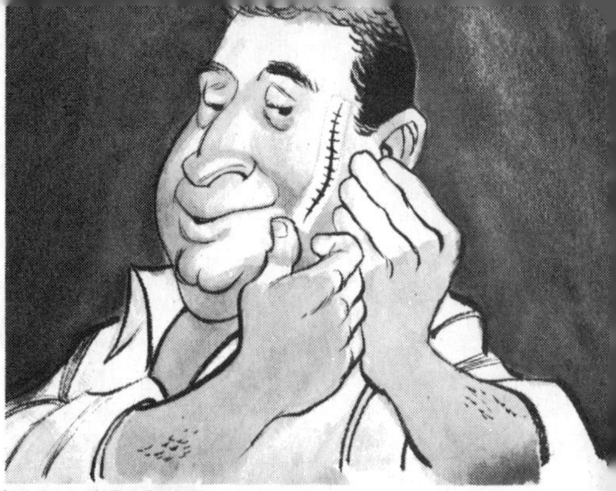

ADD-A-SCAR KIT
Top mobsters know that shakedowns are more successful when they look menacing. Now you can make your victims cower and cringe when you "touch up" your cheek with a life-like, chilling scar. Just follow the easy instructions and you're a cinch to frighten the life out of shop-keepers, news-dealers and others you prey upon.

 # 1113—SCARFACE KIT. $14.95

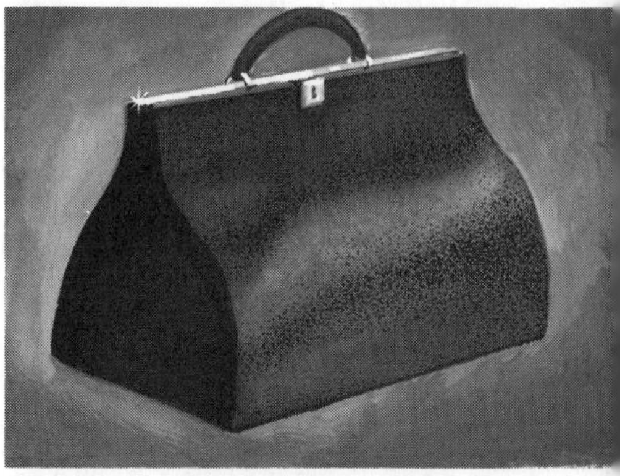

LEATHER PAY-OFF SATCHEL
Next time you visit a politician, drop off the cash in one of our plush leather Pay-Off Satchels. It's the class way of bribing, and separates you from mugs who use paper bags. Handy inside compartments can be used to separate small bills from $50's and $100's.

 # 27—LEATHER PAY-OFF SATCHEL. . $27.50
DELUXE VELVET-LINED VERSION FOR GOVERNORS AND U.S. SENATORS . . $37.50

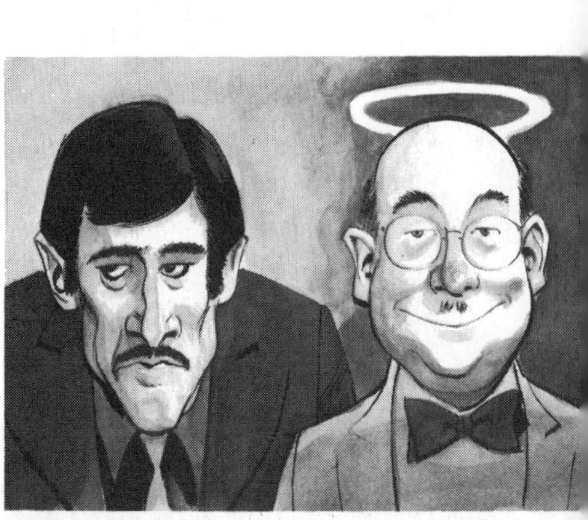

NEW IDENTITY KIT
The Feds are hot on your trail and you need to lay low or else face 10-to-20 years in the slammer. What to do? Just order one of our New Identity Kits, and in minutes you can turn yourself into, say, retired druggist Harold Pierson of Pueblo, Colorado. Each kit comes complete with new birth certificate, driver's license, social security number, the works.

 # 6167—NEW IDENTITY KIT $99.95

HEAR NO EVIL, SPEAK NO EVIL, PACINO EVIL DEPT.

In Odd Father I, Luca Broccoli "sleeps with the fishes." In Odd Father II, Freako Minestrone "sleeps with the fishes." In this long-awaited sequel, the "fishes sleep with the audience!" Here is our version of...

The Odd

ARTIST: MORT DRUCKER WRITER: ARNIE KOGEN

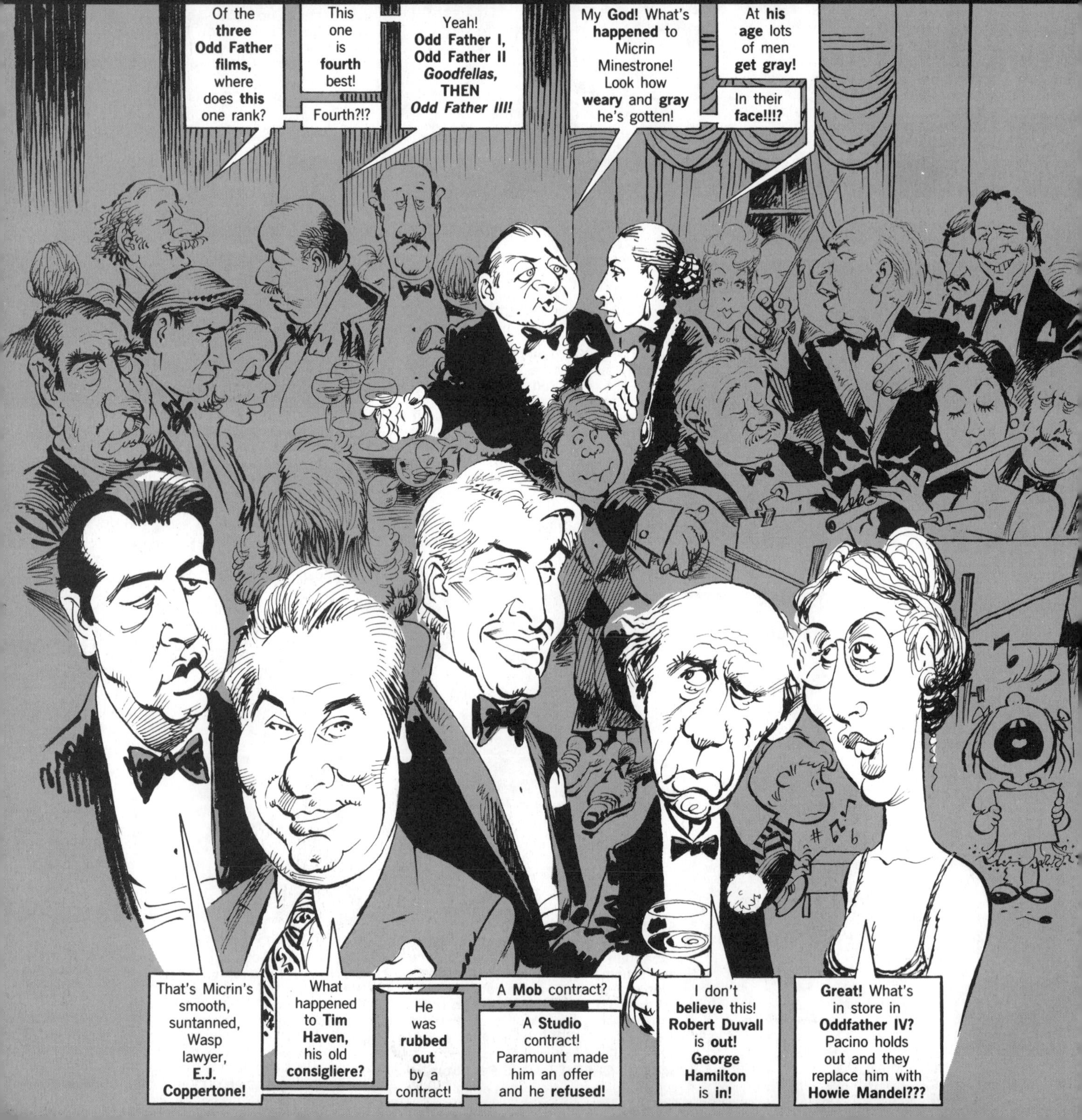

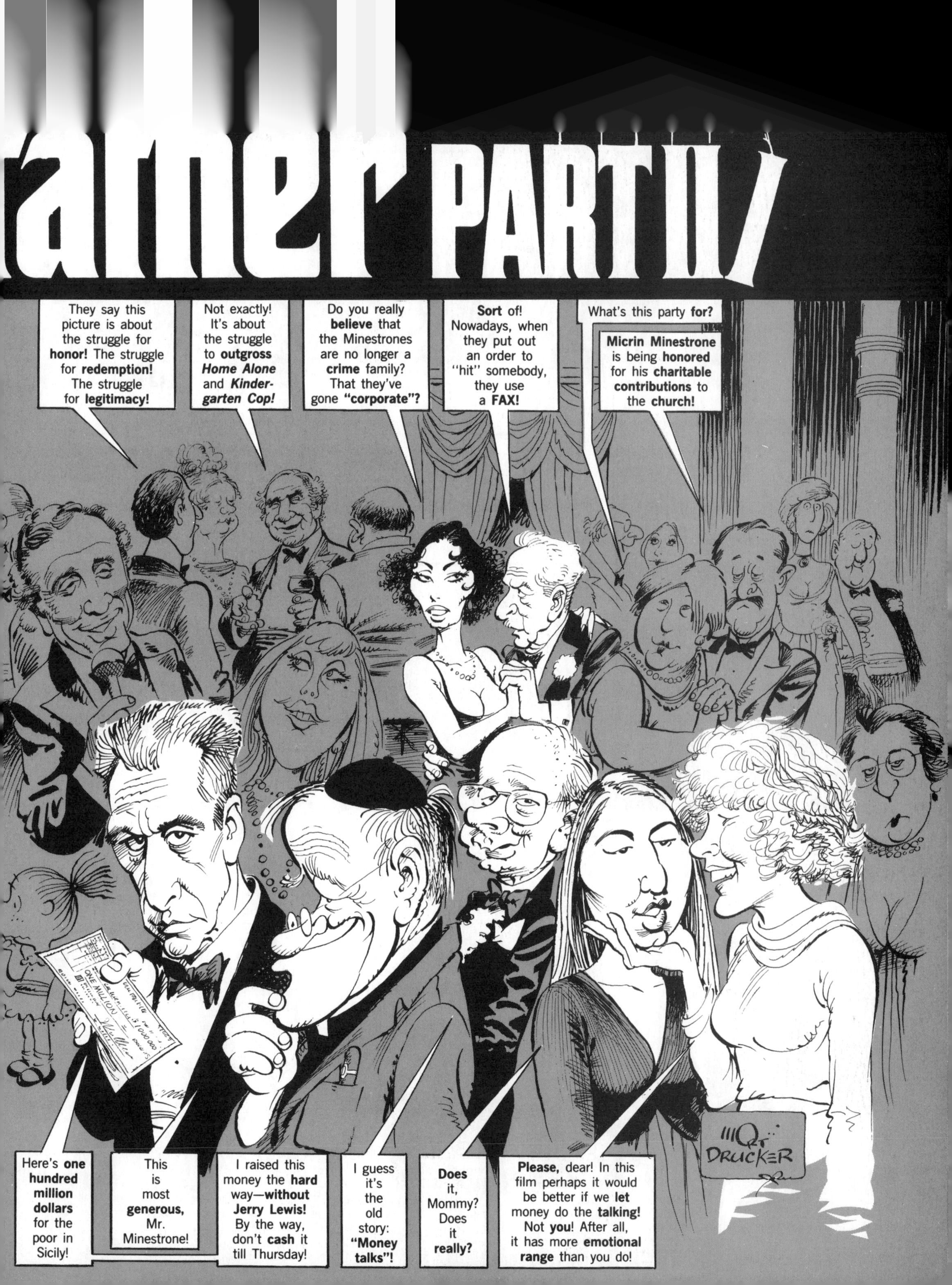

ather PART III
They say this picture is about the struggle for honor! The struggle for redemption! The struggle for legitimacy!
Not exactly! It's about the struggle to outgross Home Alone and Kindergarten Cop!
Do you really believe that the Minestrones are no longer a crime family? That they've gone "corporate"?
Sort of! Nowadays, when they put out an order to "hit" somebody, they use a FAX!
What's this party for?
Micrin Minestrone is being honored for his charitable contributions to the church!
ONE MILLION
Here's one hundred million dollars for the poor in Sicily!
This is most generous, Mr. Minestrone!
I raised this money the hard way—without Jerry Lewis! By the way, don't cash it till Thursday!
I guess it's the old story: "Money talks"!
Does it, Mommy? Does it really?
Please, dear! In this film perhaps it would be better if we let money do the talking! Not you! After all, it has more emotional range than you do!
DRUCKER

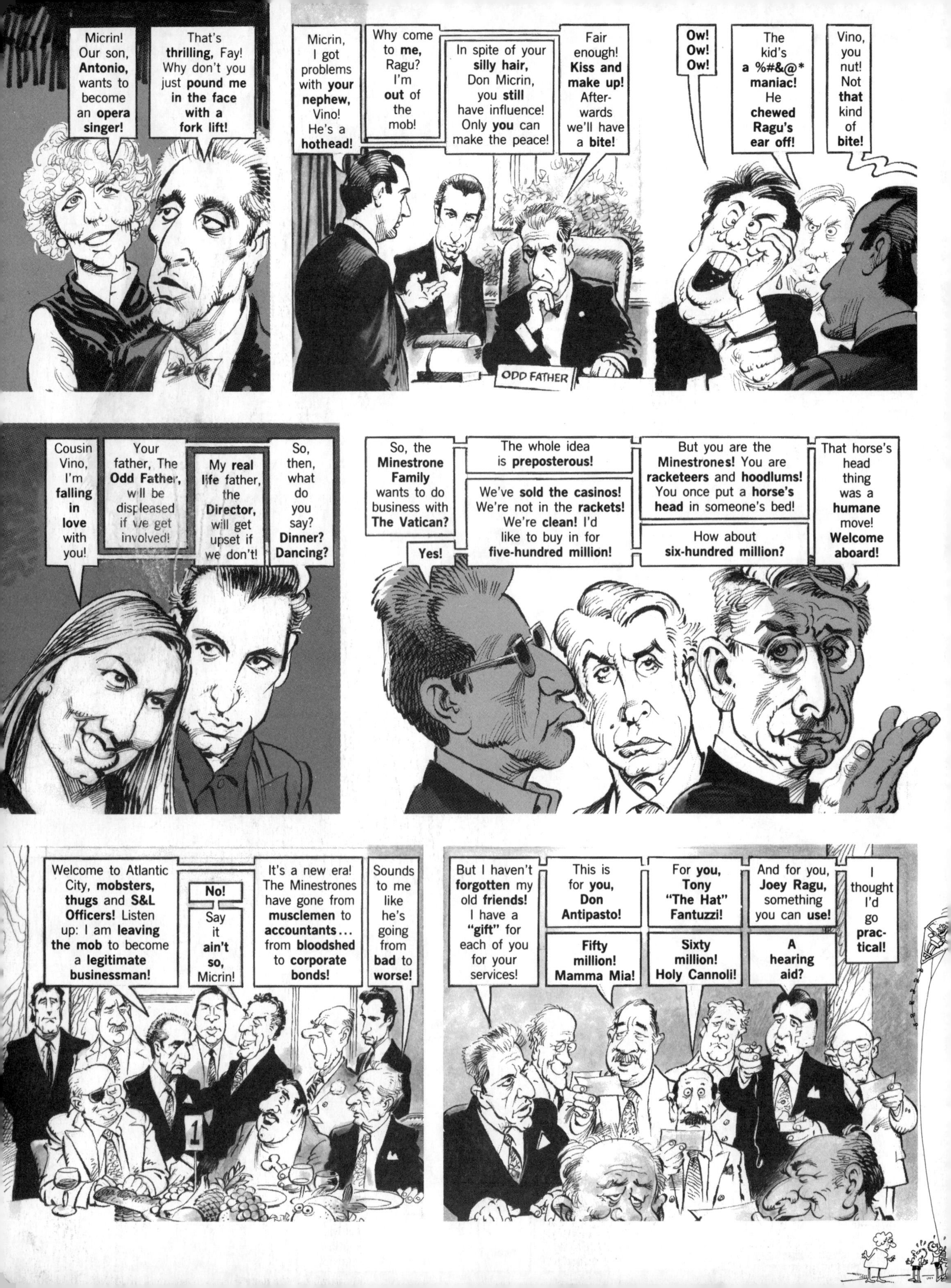

Micrin! Our son, Antonio, wants to become an opera singer!
That's thrilling, Fay! Why don't you just pound me in the face with a fork lift!
Micrin, I got problems with your nephew, Vino! He's a hothead!
Why come to me, Ragu? I'm out of the mob!
In spite of your silly hair, Don Micrin, you still have influence! Only you can make the peace!
Fair enough! Kiss and make up! Afterwards we'll have a bite!
ODD FATHER
Ow! Ow! Ow!
The kid's a %#&@* maniac! He chewed Ragu's ear off!
Vino, you nut! Not that kind of bite!
Cousin Vino, I'm falling in love with you!
Your father, The Odd Father, will be displeased if we get involved!
My real life father, the Director, will get upset if we don't!
So, then, what do you say? Dinner? Dancing?
So, the Minestrone Family wants to do business with The Vatican?
Yes!
The whole idea is preposterous!
We've sold the casinos! We're not in the rackets! We're clean! I'd like to buy in for five-hundred million!
But you are the Minestrones! You are racketeers and hoodlums! You once put a horse's head in someone's bed!
How about six-hundred million?
That horse's head thing was a humane move! Welcome aboard!
Welcome to Atlantic City, mobsters, thugs and S&L Officers! Listen up: I am leaving the mob to become a legitimate businessman!
No!
Say it ain't so, Micrin!
It's a new era! The Minestrones have gone from musclemen to accountants... from bloodshed to corporate bonds!
Sounds to me like he's going from bad to worse!
1
But I haven't forgotten my old friends! I have a "gift" for each of you for your services!
This is for you, Don Antipasto!
Fifty million! Mamma Mia!
For you, Tony "The Hat" Fantuzzi!
Sixty million! Holy Cannoli!
And for you, Joey Ragu, something you can use!
A hearing aid?
I thought I'd go prac-tical!

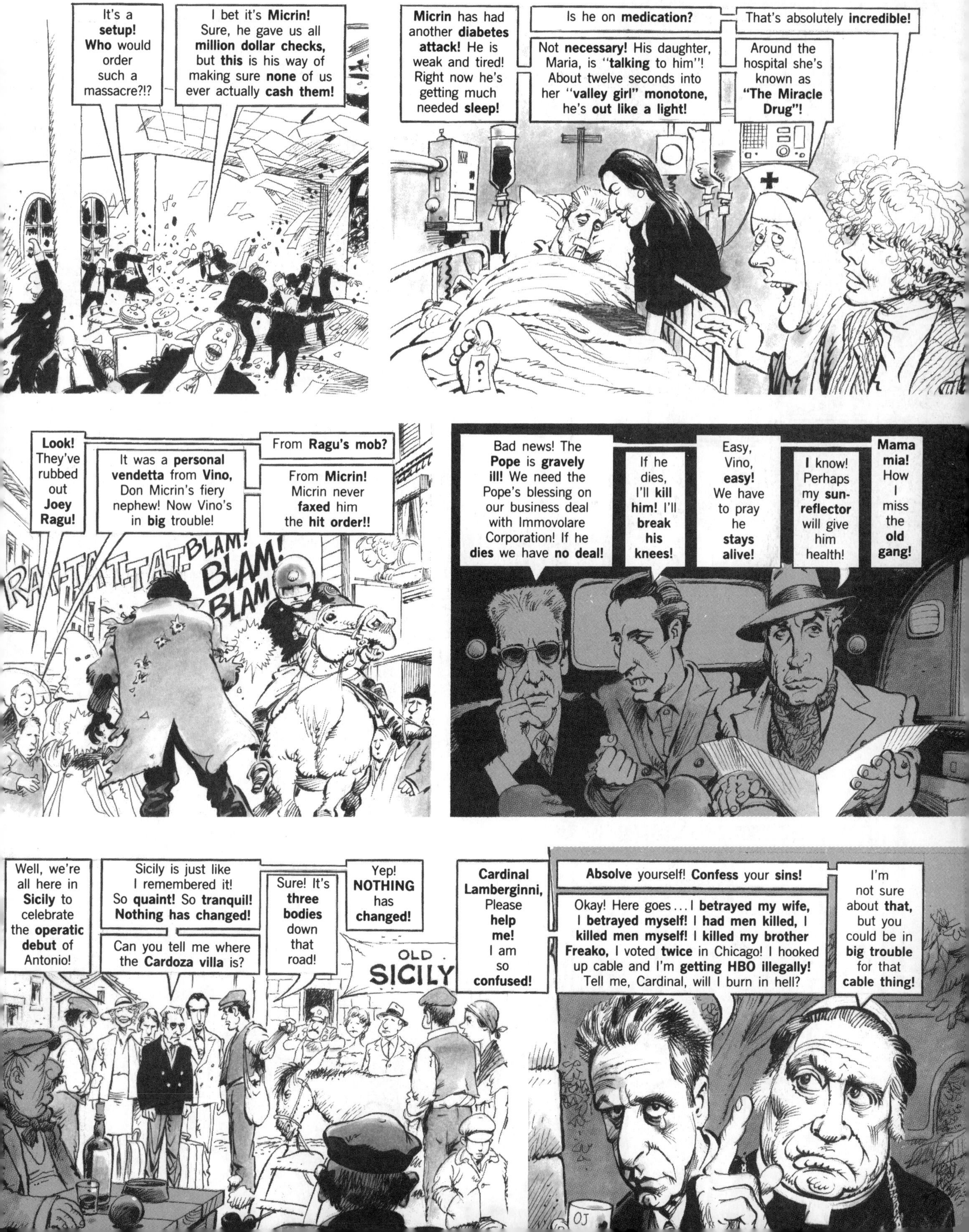
It's a **setup! Who** would order such a massacre?!?
I bet it's **Micrin!** Sure, he gave us all **million dollar checks,** but **this** is his way of making sure **none** of us ever actually **cash them!**
Micrin has had another **diabetes attack!** He is weak and tired! Right now he's getting much needed **sleep!**
Is he on **medication?**
Not **necessary!** His daughter, Maria, is "**talking** to him"! About twelve seconds into her "**valley girl" monotone,** he's **out like a light!**
That's absolutely **incredible!**
Around the hospital she's known as **"The Miracle Drug"!**
?
Look! They've rubbed out **Joey Ragu!**
It was a **personal vendetta** from **Vino,** Don Micrin's fiery nephew! Now Vino's in **big** trouble!
From **Ragu's mob?**
From **Micrin!** Micrin never **faxed** him the **hit order!!**
RAT-TAT-TAT-TAT BLAM! BLAM! BLAM
Bad news! The **Pope** is **gravely ill!** We need the Pope's blessing on our business deal with Immovolare Corporation! If he **dies** we have **no deal!**
If he dies, I'll **kill him!** I'll **break his knees!**
Easy, Vino, **easy!** We have to pray he **stays alive!**
I know! Perhaps my **sun-reflector** will give him health!
Mama mia! How I miss the **old gang!**
Well, we're all here in **Sicily** to celebrate the **operatic debut** of Antonio!
Sicily is just like I remembered it! So **quaint!** So **tranquil! Nothing has changed!**
Can you tell me where the **Cardoza villa** is?
Sure! It's **three bodies** down that road!
Yep! **NOTHING** has **changed!**
OLD SICILY
Cardinal Lamberginni, Please **help me!** I am so **confused!**
Absolve yourself! **Confess** your **sins!**
Okay! Here goes... I **betrayed my wife,** I **betrayed myself!** I **had men killed,** I **killed men myself!** I **killed my brother Freako,** I voted **twice** in Chicago! I hooked up cable and I'm **getting HBO illegally!** Tell me, Cardinal, will I burn in hell?
I'm not sure about **that,** but you could be in **big trouble** for that **cable thing!**
OJ

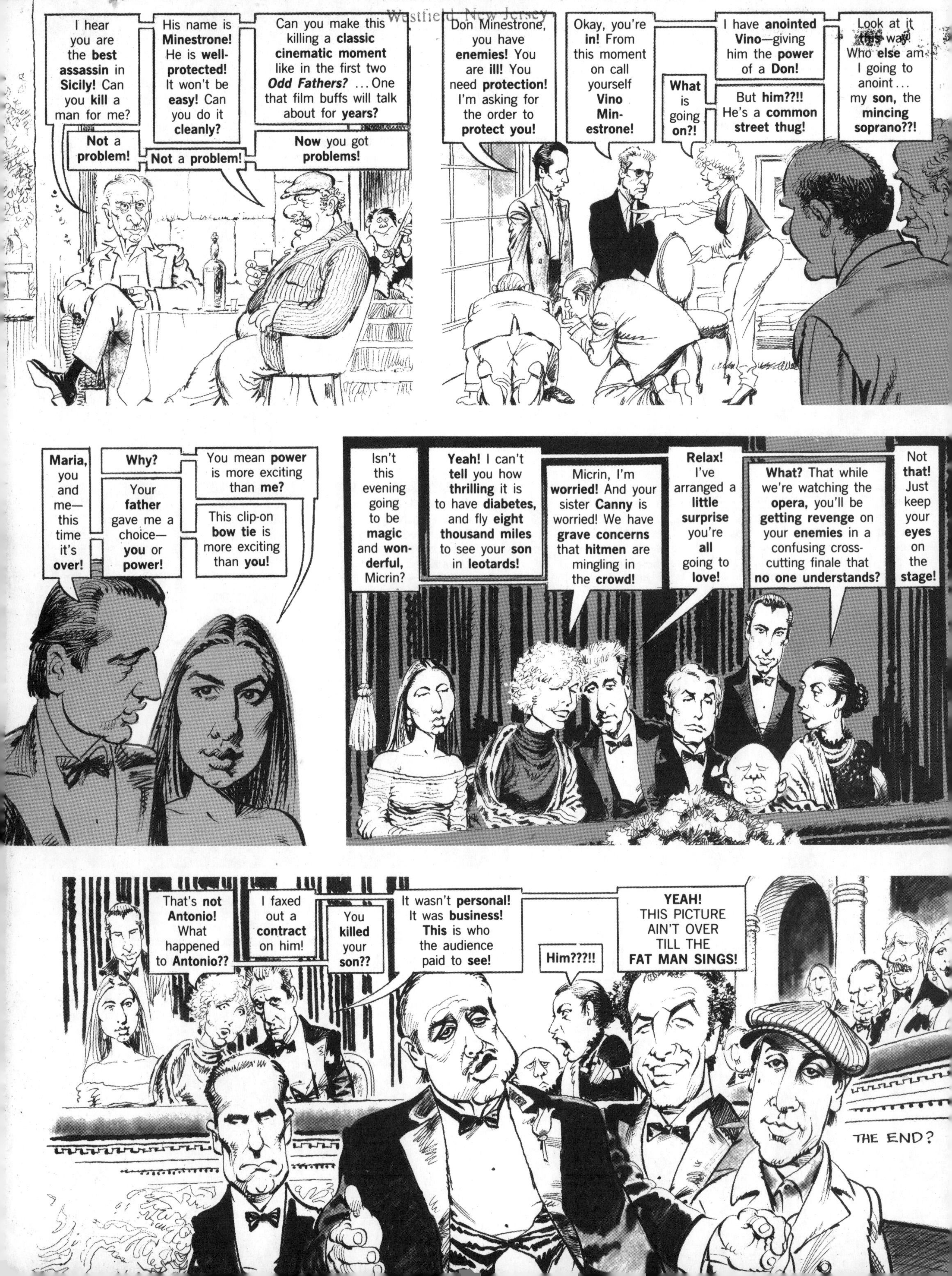
I hear you are the **best assassin** in **Sicily!** Can you **kill** a man for me?
Not a **problem!**
His name is **Minestrone!** He is **well-protected!** It won't be **easy!** Can you do it **cleanly?**
Not a **problem!**
Can you make this killing a **classic cinematic moment** like in the first two ***Odd Fathers?*** . . . One that film buffs will talk about for **years?**
Now you got **problems!**
Don Minestrone, you have **enemies!** You are **ill!** You need **protection!** I'm asking for the order to **protect you!**
Okay, you're **in!** From this moment on call yourself **Vino Minestrone!**
What is going **on?!**
I have **anointed Vino**—giving him the **power** of a **Don!**
But **him??!!** He's a **common street thug!**
Look at it **this** way! Who **else** am I going to anoint . . . my **son,** the **mincing soprano??!**
Maria, you and me—this time it's **over!**
Why?
Your **father** gave me a choice—**you** or **power!**
You mean **power** is more exciting than **me?**
This clip-on **bow tie** is more exciting than **you!**
Isn't this evening going to be **magic** and **wonderful,** Micrin?
Yeah! I can't **tell** you how **thrilling** it is to have **diabetes,** and fly **eight thousand miles** to see your **son** in **leotards!**
Micrin, I'm **worried!** And your sister **Canny** is worried! We have **grave concerns** that **hitmen** are mingling in the **crowd!**
Relax! I've arranged a **little surprise** you're **all** going to **love!**
What? That while we're watching the **opera,** you'll be **getting revenge** on your **enemies** in a confusing cross-cutting finale that **no one understands?**
Not **that!** Just keep your **eyes** on the **stage!**
That's **not Antonio!** What happened to **Antonio??**
I faxed out a **contract** on him!
You **killed** your **son??**
It wasn't **personal!** It was **business! This** is who the audience paid to **see!**
Him???!!
YEAH! THIS PICTURE AIN'T OVER TILL THE **FAT MAN SINGS!**
THE END?